College Voices

College Voices

The Story of Christ's College Aberdeen
Told Through Its People

Clare Davidson

SAINT ANDREW PRESS
Edinburgh

First published in 2018 by
SAINT ANDREW PRESS
121 George Street
Edinburgh EH2 4YN

ISBN 978-0-7152-0953-0

British Library Cataloguing in Publication Data

A catalogue record for this book is available from the British Library.

It is the publisher's policy to only use papers that are natural and
recyclable and that have been manufactured from timber grown
in renewable, properly managed forests. All of the manufacturing
processes of the papers are expected to conform to the environmental
regulations of the country of origin.

Typeset by Regent Typesetting Ltd
Printed and bound in the United Kingdom by
CPI Group (UK) Ltd

Contents

v

College Voices is dedicated to my husband, Steve, for his belief that I could do this and for his never-ending patience, encouragement and love.

The history of any institution is colourless indeed unless it takes into account the personalities of those who have built their lives into the structure.

(D. S. Cairns)

Preface

There will be names missing from this book that some will feel should have been included. So many wonderful people have formed the history of Christ's College but some voices clamoured louder than others for inclusion. Those who didn't get named still played their part in the story and I heard their voices. The decisions on what to include were mine alone, so for missing voices – I apologize. The privilege I feel working for Christ's College has increased massively during this research, and to see my name as only the tenth Secretary/Treasurer in its entire history and to see the footsteps in which I have followed is immensely humbling.

My own family background has helped me understand this story and, having met the last six Masters over the years and knowing of others through my parents' first-hand memories going back to D. S. Cairns, I now see that I was meant to write this book. Although Edinburgh is my alma mater, my parents Charles and Caroline Gimingham were Aberdeen University through and through so I do have a sense of belonging.

I would like to thank my mother for her memories and proof-reading, my father for sharing his love of church and academy and the many friends who have sustained me on this journey. My 'kids', Ross, Aileidh, Jack and Mark, just for being wonderful (and Mark for the book title and Jack for teaching me how to reference).

Clare Davidson
May 2018

Foreword

The history of any institution is colourless indeed unless it takes into account the personalities of those who have built their lives into the structure.

The above quotation by D. S. Cairns, one of the most important and influential of the College Principals, sets the tone for this book and offers some insight into the approach that will be taken as it unfolds. The aim is to tell the story of the Church College in Aberdeen – Christ's College – from its earliest days in the 1840s to the present day. The author writes not as a historian, but rather as an active *participant* in the history of the College. The assumption is that the history of the College is not simply a series of facts and figures. Rather, it comprises a series of persons and personalities, all of whom have contributed to the creation of the College today. The intention therefore is, following Cairns' statement, to present what we might describe as a narrative history of the College which tries to throw fresh light, not only on its historical development, but on the people that lived out that history over the years.

With just a few gaps, the story of the College over 175 years can be teased out of the minute books and documents stored in the Special Collections Department in the Sir Duncan Rice Library at Aberdeen University. For most of its existence the College had two governing bodies: the Financial Board and the Senatus. The careful manner of minute taking has gifted us a wealth of knowledge about the processes, the procedures and most importantly the personalities of the people who shaped the College. The characters of teachers and students alike shine through the formal language of the minutes and other correspondence. It is a rich and colourful history with vivid characters who travelled the world and left great legacies. Hundreds of young men (and later women) have passed through the doors seeking to meet the demands of the College and authorities to become ministers of religion for the Free Church, the United Free Church and, from 1929 to the present day, for the Church of Scotland. From the first benefactor in 1843 to the current Master in 2018 we have an abundance of stories and can see the College growing and evolving alongside the history not only of Scotland but of the world. We see the effects of two world wars, victories and defeats, we see the College struggling for existence and surviving scandal. From the very first graduates to those of today we see a College that existed for the benefit of the students who have taken the ethos and values of College life with them all around the world.

The Church College in Aberdeen has encountered a number of significant changes over the years. It has had three main phases:

- It began as the 'Free Church College' in 1843.
- In 1900 it became the 'United Free Church College'.
- Following the reunion with the Church of Scotland in 1929 it was renamed 'Christ's College' in 1936.

The intention of this book is to bring to life the story of these years.

Reverend Professor John Swinton
Master
Christ's College
May 2018

List of Photographs with Sources

Colour section

Black and white

Page

The College Established
1843–63

The story of the Church College in Aberdeen begins in 1843. 'In the very year of the Disruption the Free Churchmen of the North-East demanded a College in Aberdeen. Nor were they long in making a beginning. Dr Alexander Black was appointed Professor of Theology and in the winter of 1843–44 taught Hebrew and Theology in a room in South Silver Street.'[1]

In the meantime, Thomas Chalmers, the first Moderator of the Free Church Assembly, had founded New College in Edinburgh, and many felt that one great college in Edinburgh was the ideal situation. This was not acceptable to the churchmen in Aberdeen who began the fight for their own college. The quick departure of Dr Black to New College did not help, but the Aberdeen team showed a determination and tenacity which has had to be the hallmark of the College on a number of occasions in its history. Classes continued under the guidance of three local clergymen. The leading Aberdeen layman was a local advocate, Mr Francis Edmond, who at this stage was providing finance and encouraging the support of local businessmen with the aim of finding a site and building a college.

In 1845, the Assembly of the Free Church met in Inverness and agreed to the appointment of a Professor of Theology in Aberdeen. Dr James Maclagan took up the post, and the following year Mr Marcus Sachs joined him to teach Hebrew. At this stage there were twenty-one students. Despite this the future was still

---

1 R. A. Lendrum, 'The Founding', in *The Church College in Aberdeen* (Aberdeen: Aberdeen University Press, 1936), p. 7.

uncertain and following Assemblies did not appoint or provide the means to appoint any more staff to Aberdeen.

Thomas Chalmers died unexpectedly during the Assembly of 1847. His successor as Principal of New College was Dr William Cunningham who, together with Chalmers, had quickly made New College a distinguished centre of Reformed Theology. Their combined standpoints, Chalmers 'a liberal evangelical social theologian with strong roots in the Scottish Enlightenment, the other a conservative Calvinist historical theologian',[2] worked well in tandem, but Cunningham on his own was said to lack 'the broadminded vision of Chalmers'.[3] He vehemently insisted to the Assembly of 1848 that there was no necessity for any college other than New College, and he carried the debate. Aberdeen virtually ignored this. They had a college entity with students and staff, the only thing lacking was the building. Mr Francis Edmond rallied a group of elders to take on the financial responsibility and a site at the west end of Union Street was bought. Aberdeen Presbytery gave the go-ahead and building work started.

Edinburgh was not happy and declared Aberdeen Presbytery disloyal. 'For six months the controversy raged, by pamphlets, by letters and by leading articles in the press.'[4] When the Assembly met again in 1850, a compromise was reached and it was agreed students could start their training in a college in Aberdeen but were to complete it at New College. Throughout all this, the building work continued and the Free Church College in Aberdeen opened its doors in November of that year, as did New College on the Mound. It is said that the Aberdeen building was opened the day before New College, to much rejoicing.[5]

---

2 Stewart J. Brown, 'The Disruption and the Dream', in *Disruption to Diversity*, eds David F. Wright and Gary D. Badcock (Edinburgh: T&T Clark, 1996), p. 29.

3 Ibid., p. 43.

4 Lendrum, p. 8.

5 Henry Sefton, interview by author, Aberdeen, 2016.

Sadly, Dr Maclagan died two years later and Dr Cunningham, seeing this as an opportunity to renew the fight, proposed
to the Assembly that the chair should not be filled. The debate
is reported to have taken fourteen hours and the proposal was
eventually defeated by '222 votes to 147'.[6] Aberdeen College had
been saved again and not for the last time.

The College then entered a period of growth and success with
new staff and increasing student numbers. Prior to the opening
of the building seventy students had already received their theological training. The names are listed in the Roll of Alumni from
1843 to 1929 which appears in the small volume entitled *The
Church College in Aberdeen*, printed by Aberdeen University
Press in 1936. It contains three essays under the title 'The History
of the College':

1 The Founding. By the late Rev. R. A. Lendrum D.D.
2 Chapters From Its History: 1855 to 1900. By the Rev. R. G.
   Philip, M.A.
3 From Union to Union: 1900 to 1929. By the Very Rev. Principal
   D. S. Cairns, O.B.E., D.D.[7]

---

6 Lendrum, p. 8.

7 *The Church College in Aberdeen* (Aberdeen: Aberdeen University
Press, 1936), Contents page.

It also contains a list of the Professors, the Thomson Lecturers and the Roll of Alumni 1843–1929, including non-regular and foreign students. It is illustrated with thumbnail photos of many of the Professors of which few of the originals have been found.

This unique volume enriches the minute books and correspondence held in the Special Collections at Aberdeen University and adds a new dimension to the story of the College.

Its 'Roll of Alumni'[8] carries information on the destinations of most of the students but many were reported to have 'died as student' or 'died as probationer'.[9]

An impressively large number of students went overseas on mission work. Many weeks must have been spent at sea and one student, David Masson of Fetteresso, is reported to have lost his life overboard, drowning in the sea off China a few days before he was due to reach his field of service. Many went to Australia and New Zealand, others to America and Canada. South Africa, India and China also saw eager young men arriving from the Church College in Aberdeen.

Roll of Alumni

The first listing for Australia is Alexander Forbes who was ordained in Methlick but on arrival in Australia became a school teacher and later Inspector of Schools. 'Alexander Forbes was conservative in theology, a strong-minded and honest man, fearless and straightforward and outspoken to friends and foes alike, but he was not a "people person" which may explain why he did not persist in the ordained ministry.'[10]

It was his daughter Elizabeth Mary Forbes, born in Singleton, New South Wales, whose name figures more significantly in church history. Her interest in missions was said to be 'motivated

---

8 Ibid., pp. 27–52.
9 Ibid.
10 *Australian Dictionary of Evangelical Biography*, www.webjournals. ac.edu.au (accessed 03/03/2018).

by a clear and unclouded evangelical understanding of the gospel and the responsibility of the believer to their Lord'.[11]

Elizabeth became the secretary of the Women's Missionary Association and was its central figure for the next thirty-five years. She travelled widely including a trip in 1894 to Cairo where she saw American mission work at first hand. From there she travelled to Aberdeen where she reported 'having had much kindness shown her during her visit to Scotland by members of the Aberdeen Auxiliary of the Church of Scotland's Women's Missionary Association among her father's people'.[12] In 1904 she married a widower, John Hay Goodlet, and together they continued in mission work. She attended the famous World Missionary Conference in Edinburgh in 1910, which figured hugely in the lives of future Aberdeen College staff and students.

Charles Fraser, a contemporary of Alexander Forbes, went the following year to New Zealand. He was sent by the Colonial Committee of the Free Church to Canterbury where he was ordained and ministered to three hundred Scottish emigrants. His first services were held in a Wesleyan church while the new St Andrew's Free Church in Christchurch was being built. Fraser inducted himself there in 1857 and went on to establish many new churches in the area.

Fraser was an independent thinker with a 'wide ranging understanding of ministry to the whole community'.[13] It seems he did not always play by the rules and at times the Assembly had to intervene.

He was a keen naturalist with views on theistic evolution which did not sit well with many of his congregations. He was a founding member of both the Philosophical Institute of Canterbury and the Canterbury Museum and Library, and was elected a fellow of the Geological Society of London. He later resigned from

---

11 *The Presbyterian and Australian Witness* (Sydney, NSW), 4 November 1895, https://catalogue.nla.gov.au/Record/1491476 (accessed 16/01/2018).

12 *Australian Dictionary of Evangelical Biography*, www.webjournals.ac.edu.au (accessed 03/03/2018).

13 Ian Breward, *Dictionary of New Zealand Biography*, Vol. 1, 1990, www.teara.govt.nz (accessed 05/03/2018).

these Boards because of their decision to open on Sundays. He opened the first public cemetery in Christchurch which, although controlled by trustees from St Andrew's, was to be open to all denominations. He was vocal in the debates in church and community over a national system of education, 'advocating secular education in order to overcome sectarian bickering and to free the churches for their proper work of religious education'.[14]

Despite having achieved much, Fraser's last years were not happy. He disputed a claim of sexual misconduct brought by the Presbytery but the claim was upheld by the Assembly. He retired to his farm and unsuccessfully stood for Parliament and the North Canterbury Education Board in 1884. A supporter built him a small church where he ministered until his death on 25 August 1886.

Another notable name in the Roll of Alumni in the early years will be remembered, like Alexander Forbes, not for his own achievements, but for those of one of his children. After leaving Aberdeen, Daniel Gordon went into the mission field in Quebec and then in Ontario. He married a well-educated lady from a well-known Quebec family. Daniel was said to be 'an eloquent and passionate preacher of the Free Church of Scotland'.[15] All their children were high achievers.

One of the seven was Charles Gordon who, following a Bachelor of Arts degree from Toronto, travelled to study at New College in Edinburgh. He was interested in overseas mission but was persuaded to stay in Canada and work for the Home Mission. To help raise funds and public awareness he wrote a fictional account of life in the northwest. As a writer, he was an instant success and launched his new career under the pen name of Ralph Connor. He continued his work as a Free Church minister while writing many bestselling novels. The outbreak of the First World War altered his path. He enlisted and went overseas as a chaplain of the 43rd Cameron Highlanders, soon becoming Senior Chaplain to the Canadian armed forces in England and France. His

---

14 Ibid.
15 http://umanitoba.ca/libraries/archives/collections/complete_holdings/ead/html/gordon.shtml (accessed 05/03/2018).

views were profoundly changed by war and he became a pacifist. He continued writing until his death in 1937.

Like Charles Fraser, many students at Aberdeen University and the Free Church College in the early days were naturalists, and the study of natural science had a prominent position in the syllabus. Robert Hunter studied in the Aberdeen College and was ordained in the Free Church of Scotland in 1847. He went to Nagpur in India as a missionary accompanying the Reverend Stephen Hislop. Both men were keen geologists and wrote papers about their discoveries while travelling on their mission work. The mineral Hislopite is named after Hislop. Hunter lasted in India for eight years before ill health forced him home where he continued with his Free Church mission work in England. His life's work was his *Encyclopaedic Dictionary* which took seventeen years to complete.

From the Disruption of 1843 to the erection of a permanent home in 1850, the Free Church College in Aberdeen sent students all over the world. In this period the most famous was perhaps Dr George Wisely of Malta (see Chapter 7). While these students of Aberdeen were spreading the word throughout the world, work at home on the building of the College was completed. Mr Francis Edmond continued to be a great benefactor to the College and new staff were appointed, Patrick Fairbairn in Divinity and George Smeaton in New Testament. Marcus Sachs was promoted to a Chair in Old Testament.

Marcus Sachs was born in 1812 in the Grand Duchy of Posen, Prussia. He attended Berlin University where he studied French literature. 'Voltaire became his idol but the idolatry resulted in an eclipse of faith in the religion of his fathers and in the scriptures of the Old Testament. The infidel views which he adopted were entirely unfavourable to his advancement in his own country.'[16]

He travelled to England in 1842 and after a short time in London he moved to Edinburgh. '[H]ere it was that, through the instrumentality of the late Dr John Brown, this Jewish free thinker was brought to Christ. When he had made his public

---

16 W. D. Geddes, *Marcus Sachs: In Memoriam* (Aberdeen: King and Company, 1872), p. 7.

profession, he betook himself to the study of the ministry and attended the lectures of Dr Chalmers.'[17] He arrived at the Free Church College, Aberdeen in 1846 to tutor Hebrew. 'In his mode of teaching he was very patient and laborious in laying the foundations. While full of encouragement to, and rejoicing over, humble earnest aspiring after more light and more knowledge on the part of even the slowest student, he administered in the case of ignorant presuming pseudo students, rebukes little to be envied. The fire of the old Hebrew race for truth and uprightness flashed out, on such occasions, in a manner to be remembered.'[18]

Sachs married Mary Shier whose father was the manager of the Leith and Clyde Shipping Company. The couple became well-known figures in Aberdeen intellectual and artistic circles and they travelled widely on the continent. 'He was a man of extraordinary learning, yet humble, and although a caustic critic, was kind to backwards students. He was a coadjutor of Dr John Duncan in the reviving of Hebrew learning in Scotland, and he trained quite a succession of Hebrew scholars at Aberdeen. It was indeed felt that he was a man raised up by God for the position he filled.'[19]

Sachs died in 1869 at the early age of 57, leaving his Chair vacant. It was filled the following year by Mr William Robertson Smith, a famous name who brought a heresy trial to the College

17 *McClintock and Strong Biblical Cyclopedia*, www.biblicalcyclopedia. com/S/sachs-marcus.html (accessed 27/01/17).

18 Geddes, p. 14.

19 R. G. Philip, 'Chapters From Its History: 1855 to 1900', in *The Church College in Aberdeen* (Aberdeen: Aberdeen University Press, 1936), p. 11.

(see Chapter 3). Marcus Sachs is buried in the Shier family plot, Nellfield Cemetery, Aberdeen. In his memorial to Sachs, William Geddes, Principal and Vice-Chancellor of Aberdeen University, wrote: 'Professor Sachs was or seemed to be a strong man physically and his friends would have thought he had many years of honour and usefulness before him. In the inscrutable providence of God it was not to be so. The robust constitution which he once possessed was seen to betray signs of weakness and three years ago in 1868 his friends were pained to observe the threatening signs of a paralytic affection. Against all remonstrations he persisted in discharging all his duties during the winter in hope of shaking it off but the fatigue he imposed on himself was great and after the session he was advised to visit his native country and try some of the spas with which it abounds. He spent a great part of the summer in one of the baths in Bohemia but with sad hearts his friends saw him return not stronger as they had fondly hoped but weaker. He did not survive the fall of that year and he died in the month of September passing away with the leaves of autumn a ripe sheaf into the garner of God.'[20]

Sachs' widow Mary remarried in 1877, her new husband being Mr Francis Edmond who had been widowed the previous year, and so she continued her association with the Free Church College in Aberdeen.

Francis Edmond was a year older than Mary. His father had been a wood merchant and his uncle was Professor of Natural Science at King's College. He graduated in 1823 and became a member of the Aberdeen Bar in 1829. He became advocate and legal advisor to King's College and a staunch adherent of the view that the Right of Patronage was not acceptable to the spiritual independence of the Church. He was ready with his financial support as soon as the Disruption took place. In the same year as the Free Church College building opened its doors he founded his firm Edmonds and McQueen, and the connection of the College with this legal firm lasted into the twenty-first century. The Free Church College was not Edmond's only beneficiary. He was generous to local hospitals and to the village of Kingswells. He

---

20 Geddes, p. 19.

bought Kingswells House in 1855 and set up the Kingswells Trust which ran the house for benevolent purposes after his death. He gifted the land for the church; its rafters and wood-lined ceiling, which are still in place and very unusual, were also gifted by him. Kingswells House is now owned and run by the Summerland Trust for the investigation, promotion and enhancement of spiritual learning. It can only be guessed if this is an approach to religion of which Francis Edmond would have approved.

Edmond became the first official Secretary and Treasurer to the Financial Board of the Free Church College in Aberdeen which was set up in 1869.

He died in 1892 and is also buried in Nellfield Cemetery. His widow Mary moved to Cambridge with her niece and husband, Dr and Mrs Griffiths, and then followed them to Wales where Dr Griffiths was appointed Principal of the University College of South Wales.

She remained in Wales until her death in 1915 at the grand age of 105. It is partly thanks to her longevity that there is so much of her history. Her life was featured under the headline, 'Oldest Welsh Woman is Dead' in the *Pittsburgh Post Gazette* on Sunday, 16 May 1915.[21]

Just after Marcus Sachs was made a Professor, another member of staff was appointed. The Reverend James Lumsden arrived from the parish of Barry to be Professor of Systematic Theology in 1856. He was later to become the first Principal of the Free Church College in Aberdeen and this begins the second chapter in the history of the College.

---

21 www.newspapers.com/newspage/85758312/ (accessed 05/03/2018).

2

The First Principal and the Banchory Bequest 1864–76

'In 1864 when the sum of £1000 was given by a member of the Church to endow the office of Principal to the College he [James Lumsden] was selected for that position by the General Assembly.'[1] It is widely documented that James Lumsden was appointed Principal as the result of an endowment but who the member of the Church was is never revealed. It could well have been a further donation by Mr Francis Edmond, the greatest of benefactors. This endowment ensured the status of Principal to the College, an appointment still made by the General Assembly although since 1936 known as Master of the College.

James Lumsden

The Reverend James Dryburgh Lumsden was born in Dysart, Fife in January 1810. He studied at St Andrews and then Edinburgh University. His first charge was Inverbrothock Church in Arbroath. 'In 1838 he was presented to the Parish of Barry near Dundee, the Crown having acceded to the wish of the people in the making of this presentation.'[2] Lumsden was an ardent follower of Thomas Chalmers and took part in the campaign which ultimately led to the Disruption and the forming of the Free Church.

---

1 John Rae, *Principal Lumsden: A Memorial and Estimate* (Aberdeen: Milne, 1876), p. 32.
2 Ibid.

During his nineteen years in the parish, Lumsden took a great interest in the religious life of Sweden and made frequent trips to that country. In 1855 he published *Sweden: Its religious state and prospects: with some notices of the revivals and persecutions which are at present taking place in that country.*[3] A well-preserved copy of this is in the Special Collections in Aberdeen University, having belonged first, according to the fly leaf, to Andrew A. Bonnar at Collace and subsequently ex libris John Bently Philip MA. The seventy-four-page book is a collection of essays including chapter titles such as 'Compulsory Baptism', 'No Religious Tolerance' and 'Prayer Meetings Illegal'. His interest in Sweden and his assistance given to Swedes visiting Scotland led to his being decorated by the King of Sweden with the honour of Knight of the North Star in 1871.

In 1856, he was appointed by the General Assembly to be Professor of Systematic and Pastoral Theology and Early Church History in Aberdeen Free Church College. The College was still in its infancy and one of the first things Lumsden did was to set up, with the assistance of Professor George Smeaton, who had been promoted to the second College Chair, a Students' Association which met fortnightly in the College building, often referred to as 'the Divinity Hall'. After tea and music, papers on a variety of subjects were read and discussed. This initiative was well supported by staff and students alike and has remained a mainstay of College life to the present day.

The Missionary Society in Lumsden's early days laid the foundation of what was to become the Shuttle Lane Mission, which played a huge part in the practical training of generations of Church College students. Lumsden 'was a man born to rule and a prominent churchman. A lover of Calvinism, he was at the same time deeply interested in Home Missions and several Church Extension charges in the North East owed their origin to him'.[4] He brought his old friend and contemporary from New

---

3 James Lumsden, *Sweden: Its religious state and prospects* (London, 1855).

4 R. G. Philip, 'Chapters From Its History: 1855 to 1900', in *The Church College in Aberdeen* (Aberdeen: Aberdeen University Press, 1936), p. 10.

College, Dr Alexander Duff, to the College in Aberdeen and it seems it was his visit that 'awakened great interest in the foreign missions'[5] among the students. Dr Duff founded the Scottish Church College in Calcutta, the first mission to India from the Church of Scotland (known post Disruption as Duff College and from 1929 as the Calcutta Christian College).

The New Financial Board

On 10 June 1869, the Financial Board of the College was constituted in terms of a Resolution of the General Assembly of the Free Church of Scotland. It stated inter alia that 'Local Boards be appointed in connection with each of the three Colleges at Edinburgh, Glasgow and Aberdeen for the management of their financial affairs; that such Boards shall be empowered to receive and disburse the funds accruing to the Colleges in conformity with the appointments of the General Assembly and with the specific destination of particular endowments; that it shall belong to such Boards with the concurrence of the General Trustees of the Church to advise and determine respecting investments of money for College purposes and to see that the same be properly executed; also, with consent of the College Committee to make such alterations and repairs as may be required from time to time on the College Buildings; that the Financial Board shall be subject to the College Committee to which it shall present annually a Statement of Accounts to be laid before the General Assembly.'[6] And so the Financial Board of the Free Church College was formed and continues to this day. The minutes of the meetings from that time on are accessible in the Special Collections at Aberdeen University and although some are hardly legible a wonderfully colourful picture of the day-to-day running of the College emerges. A governing body for the College had been set up in 1856 as a Senatus but the first minute book is missing. So until January 1897 when the second one begins the only available

---

5 Ibid., p. 14.
6 Financial Board Minute Books, Vol. 3, p. 2.

information on the day-to-day running of the College is the Financial Board minutes.

No precise rules were laid down as to the number of Members of the Financial Board or their qualifications, if any. The first Members of the Aberdeen Financial Board were Principal Lumsden, Dr Davidson, Dr Alexander Spence (Ministers), Messrs Francis Edmond, William Henderson of Devanah House, W. Rose, William Henderson, J. B. McCombie, Dr R. J. Brown and Dr G. G. Brown (Elders). The Board was to have a Secretary and Treasurer and keep a record of its proceedings to be sent up to the Assembly annually.

At that first meeting, Principal Lumsden was appointed to be Chairman and Mr Francis Edmond to be Secretary and Treasurer. The first task assigned by the Board to Mr Edmond was to 'submit to the next meeting a report relating to the state of the property and the funds that belonged to the Aberdeen College'.[7]

Only four days later the Board met again to look at Mr Edmond's report. This is the first evidence of the financial state of the College. It also shows us that there had already been several very valuable bequests. Miss Barbara Innes had not only left money for all the Professors, but she had also left £550 for the Library and £550 to set up the long-continuing 'Sick Fund' for 'assisting deserving students who were sick or weakly'.[8] The Foote Scholarship, which is still in existence today, had also been in operation for 'the best Hebrew student'.[9]

The Banchory Bequest

At the end of the report almost as an afterthought comes, 'In addition to the above, Mr Thomson of Banchory who died 1868 by his deeds of settlement made certain valuable provisions for this College, but no official intimation has been made to the Principal or Professors on this subject.'[10] This, as we now know, was to have a considerable impact on the College.

---

7 Ibid., p. 4.
8 Ibid., p. 6.
9 Ibid., p. 7.
10 Ibid., p. 6.

George Smeaton, who was now Professor of Exegetical Theology at New College, wrote a lengthy memorial to Alexander Thomson in 1869. It begins: 'Christianity is destined not only to save the individual, but to fill and ennoble all art, all science, and all literature. Vessels to contain the heavenly treasure, they receive their highest consecration by being made subservient to the end. This is happily illustrated by the life of these men of science who, with an insatiable desire for all knowledge, yet find in Christianity a religion for their whole nature. The study of God's works does not with them supersede the study of His word, nor conversely. They have a keen desire to know all that can be known. They think no study more pleasant than tracing the greatness and goodness of the Creator in HIS works except the still more elevated study of the wonders of redeeming love. Such a man was Mr Thomson of Banchory'.[11]

Alexander Thomson had been one of the early benefactors of the College in Aberdeen and had supported Francis Edmond in the speedy erection of the building in Alford Place while the debate was raging in Edinburgh concerning local colleges. 'Mr Thomson, who had seen much of colleges, held that instead of being limited to one central institute, colleges should rather be established in as many places as possible; that it required an effort but was by no means impracticable, and a number of students would be lost to the Free Church without it. Nor was this out of keeping with the great principle which he always advocated – a high standard of education ... Nor did he or his friends slacken their exertions till a full Divinity Hall was established in Aberdeen ... To the end of Mr Thomson's life the success of this Theological College was an object dear to him; its professors and students receiving from him every mark of kindness. How deep an interest he had taken in it appeared after his death, when it was found that he had left what would amply endow it and secure its future permanence against all hazards.'[12]

Mrs Alexander Thomson of Banchory died soon after her husband and on her death the extent of the 'valuable provisions'

11 George Smeaton, *Memoir of Alexander Thomson of Banchory* (Edinburgh: Edmonston and Douglas, 1869), p. 1.
12 Ibid., p. 313.

became known. While it financially secured the future of the College, the Financial Board must at times have wondered if it was worth it for the enormous amount of work it created.

On 16 August 1870, the Clerk to the Board read the deed of settlement which is recorded in the minutes covering seven pages. It was found that Alexander Thomson 'had made arrangements, after present life interests were served, to dispose of his estates and had set apart so many twenty-fourths of the whole for the permanent endowment of the Free Church Divinity Hall at Aberdeen. His valuable museum and notable library were also bequeathed to the Free Church College.'[13]

It is also stated in the deed of settlement: 'The following articles to be delivered along with my museum and to form part of it hereafter viz the amethyst bracelet given to Mrs Thomson by the late Prince Consort and all the Roman and Italian models in the drawing rooms, library and dining room, the pictures of John Knox, Queen Mary and the Marquis of Montrose and Thomson of Portlethen by Jamieson. The lithograph of the Queen and Prince Consort in the large drawing room to be delivered to and form part of my museum and to be preserved therewith in the Free Church College, Aberdeen.'[14]

The Financial Board were of the opinion that their first duty was to provide accommodation for the library and museum along with Mr Thomson's collection of microscopes. They accordingly instructed the Principal and Mr Edmond to form a committee and talk with an architect about extending the College building. An amazing legacy indeed – but the conditions of the legacy and subsequent controversy were to prove arduous for the College administration for the next 100 years.

By the time the Financial Board met again on 27 September 1870 there had been considerable correspondence with the Misses Fraser at Banchory House.

Banchory House is situated in Banchory Devenick, among Tollohill Woods where Alexander Thomson erected a monument,

---

13 Financial Board Minute Books, Vol. 3, p. 23.
14 Ibid., p. 29.

still standing, to commemorate the visit in 1859 by the Prince Consort.

Alexander Thomson's wife, Jessy Fraser, was a daughter of a previous Lord Provost of Aberdeen, Alexander Fraser, so it is assumed that the Misses Fraser who also resided at Banchory House were her spinster sisters. One of the Misses Fraser, Angelica, was later to achieve fame and the title 'The Tailor's Friend'. As such she was recognized by King Edward VII who 'presented her with an article of jewellery in token appreciation of the work she had done for a portion of his subjects ... She read in tailors' shops, using books of all kinds but always ending with a portion of the Bible. Then this service led to other ministrations in the families of the men; and the work grew on her hands spreading from city to city, many other ladies being enlisted in the cause till at last she spent her time in a kind of episcopal supervision of the whole.'[15]

Legal Questions

The Misses Fraser had found an initialled but not dated memorandum from Alexander Thomson regarding removing his library and museum, 'in which he explained that in bequeathing his museum and his library he included the book cases and cabinets with the specimens as far as they could be of use'.[16] The committee (Lumsden and Edmond) 'arranged for the removal of the book cases to the College Hall and had all the books taken out of them and laid on the floor of the dining room in the hope that in a few days the book cases would be put up in the Hall and be ready for having the books removed and set up in them in their former order'.[17]

It transpires that the tradesmen employed for this task were prevented by the Misses Fraser from removing some of the

---

15 James Stalker, 'The Advocate's Sermon', in *Sub Corona*, ed. Henry Cowan and James Hastings (Edinburgh, T&T Clarke, 1915), p. 282.

16 Financial Board Minute Books, Vol. 3, p. 31.

17 Ibid.

bookcases 'as the removal of them would disfigure the room'.[18] Further, the Misses Fraser insisted that the lithographs of the Queen and Prince Consort, identified separately in Thomson's deed of settlement, had already been bequeathed to Mr Arthur Fraser and the Misses Fraser had claimed them on his behalf.

Another letter then detailed the books which the Misses Fraser intended to retain, and also queried whether the Lobby Library was indeed intended for the Free Church College as well. After much deliberation, the Board agreed that the 'whole book cases, cabinets, books and specimens and curiosities in the Museum belonged to the College and that if it was so the Board were not entitled to give up any part of them but they resolved to join with the Trustees in referring the whole question to an arbiter. They also agreed that in the event of the whole bookcases being removed, to bearing their share of the expense of lathing and plastering such parts as may be thought necessary of the walls at present covered by the bookcases.'[19]

There followed two months of legal comings and goings and, at the Financial Board meeting of 18 November, Francis Edmond reported that relations between his firm and the firm representing the Trustees for Thomson of Banchory, Yeats and Flockhart, had deteriorated. Edmond had written that 'time was of immense importance for the removal of the library and museum in "fine weather" as expressed by Mr Thomson'.[20] The Board were concerned that further delay 'would carry us into the winter months [and] expose the books in the meantime to serious damage from Dust, Damp and Mice, lying as they are on the dining room floor'.[21] This drew a sharp response from Yeats and Flockhart which started another chapter in the controversy. They replied, 'The books have not been placed on the dining room floor by the Trustees and they will accordingly regret if any injury arises from their having been placed there.'[22] They went on to say that they were now questioning if they could 'deliver any part of the

18 Ibid., p. 32.
19 Ibid., p. 36.
20 Ibid., p. 38.
21 Ibid.
22 Ibid., p. 39.

Library or Museums until the bequest has been accepted by the Church under the conditions and qualifications annexed to it by Mr Thomson'.[23] There was a curt response from Edmond and Macqueen to this new issue. The response on 12 November must have been hard for Francis Edmond to read to the Board. It said that the Banchory Trustees had 'ascertained that acceptance of the bequests to the Aberdeen College is not within the province of the College Board at Aberdeen and have made intimation of them to the proper quarter'.[24]

One can only imagine the feelings with which the Board received the news that this was now in the hands of the General Trustees of the Free Church. The Free Church decided that the College Committee having oversight of all the Colleges should be consulted. '[T]he Committee was satisfied that it was right that they should be informed ... and they resolved to send a deputation to Aberdeen to ascertain the present position of matters connected with Mr Thomson's Trust as far as relating to the bequests to the Free Church.'[25]

The deputation met with the Board on 22 November and the meeting is minuted as follows: 'The Deputation informed the Board that they had had a meeting with two of Mr Thomson Trustees and after a lengthened conversation relative to Mr Thomson's bequest, the meeting was closed with prayer.'[26] The minute is signed as ever by James Lumsden and Francis Edmond. It is frustrating in its brevity but the situation seems to have moved on, as the following meeting in December 1870 deals with other items but finishes with: 'The Board requested the treasurer to advance the necessary funds for repayment of the expenses connected with the additions which had been made to the College buildings at the request and with the concurrence of the Thomson Trustees with the view of receiving the Library and Museum bequeathed to the College by Mr Thomson and offered and partly delivered by the trustees of this board.'[27]

---

23 Ibid.
24 Ibid., p. 40.
25 Ibid., p. 41.
26 Ibid., p. 45.
27 Ibid., p. 47.

The Thomson Trust is not mentioned by name again until the Board meeting of 4 September 1871 when Principal Lumsden reported that the General Assembly had addressed the question of the Thomson Legacy and set up a special committee. Interestingly this was the same General Assembly that extended the powers of College Boards.

'The General Assembly extend the powers and functions of the local College Boards in Glasgow and Aberdeen and appoint the Board Trustees for holding property and funds belonging to or connected with the College; empowering them to employ a Law Agent for the transaction of their business and instructing them annually to lay before the General Assembly an account of their intro-missions and state of their property, funds and investments.'[28]

The Special Committee appointed by the General Assembly wasted no time and wrote to the Financial Board concerning the design of the new bookshelves and other alterations and modifications. On 15 January 1872 the Board retaliated: '[H]aving taken into consideration the said minute of the Assembly Committee and report and considering that The Banchory Trustees at first acknowledged this Board's right to receive and deal with the bequest, but after the differences arose as to the extent of it, denied the Board's right or authority and as the Colleges Committee on the application of the Banchory Trustees interfered in the matter and as the Assembly on their suggestion appointed a Special Committee who have taken the matter into their own hands and virtually superseded the Board, the Board resolved that they will not do anything in reference to the Bequest without special instructions, nor take any responsibility in the matter and further that in acting upon any instructions which have been or may be given they shall not be understood as acquiescing in the resolutions of the Committee or giving up their own opinion as to the duty of the church to see Mr Thomson's recorded wishes carried out.'[29]

---

28 Ibid., p. 56.
29 Ibid., p. 61.

However, later that year the Board purchased No. 2 Alford Place, immediately opposite the College, using funds from the Thomson Trust. They did this in order to properly accommodate the 'purpose' of the Banchory Bequest. It did this by converting it to hold the museum and microscopes, a reading room for students and an additional library room. The upstairs rooms became an apartment for the janitor who was also to become the curator of the museum. It is possible that the Misses Fraser were successful in their bid to keep the royal lithographs as they do not appear in the collection. However, the beautiful bracelet gifted by the Prince Consort to Mrs Thomson is in the collection along with many other valuable pieces now housed in the Special Collection at Aberdeen University.

The missing volume of Senatus minutes might have given us more insight and colour to add to these years, but for the Financial Board things seem to have settled down and they were the recipients of many more legacies and bequests which luckily did not cause the same level of distress. It has to be noted that troubles caused by Mr Alexander Thomson's great generosity and love for the Free Church continued into the 1980s.

It is minuted at the meeting on 13 May 1874 that the Board was aware that the General Assembly held that the bequest should have been made over directly to itself and not to the College Board. That would indeed have altered the history of the Church College in Aberdeen.

Resignation of first Secretary/Treasurer

At the following meeting a letter was read from Mr Edmond intimating his resignation. 'The Board having considered this communication unanimously resolved to record their deep regret that Mr Edmond should have felt it necessary to tender his resignation of these offices, the duties of which he had so ably, zealously and so disinterestedly performed from the beginning and their grateful appreciation of his laborious, generous and unintermitted services to which in so great a measure the foundation and the prosperity of the College are due and at the same time the Board cherish the hope that he will continue to take the same warm and friendly interest as heretofore in all that concerns its usefulness.'[30]

Francis Edmond's son Alexander Edmond was to take on the duties of Secretary and Treasurer from that point.

Throughout all this time the teaching at the College continued and student numbers increased – as did their demands on improving the facilities, which included lighting, heating and the request that one of the classrooms be turned into a gymnasium.

Opening Lecture

In the Opening Lecture of 1871, Principal Lumsden delivered a paper entitled 'The Unity of the Church'. There is a small, bound, eclectic collection of writings which carries the full text of this lecture. It sits among two sermons preached by the Reverend James Iverach at Ferryhill Church in 1875 and 'Preacher in the wrong box', a letter addressed to 'Dr Forbes, Minister of Old Machar and Professor of Humanity and Classics in the Kings College Aberdeen' in 1836 with the subtitle:

It's bad enough when bears play on the fiddle
But worse, far worse, if you with Popery meddle!

Lumsden's lecture is finely constructed and clearly shows that in spite of his ardent support of Thomas Chalmers and the Disruption he was none the less saddened by the split. 'Therefore Gentlemen, in your studies it is well that on the one hand you give more than ordinary heed to the mutual interdependence and relative importance of the several doctrines of faith and on the other hand that you listen to the many warnings which the history of the church affords, both against compromising any portion of the truth, and also against attaching an exaggerated importance to particular phases of doctrines or to mere influences from them.

---

30 Ibid., p. 100.

'One cannot help thinking that but for misunderstanding of one another's meaning and the unfortunate influence of human passions, the schism between the Lutherans and the reformed might have been averted and thus the protestant cause throughout the world saved from great scandal and great injury. A more thorough study of the word of God and a more plentiful outpouring of the Spirit both for the enlightenment of the minds and the sanctifying of the hearts of the children of God, may, let us hope, bring about a new era in which the dissolutions of many generations shall be repaired and the church of God united in truth and love shall more than ever heretofore vindicate for herself a free and commanding position amongst the nations of the earth.'[31]

A Student's Memorial

In his first year as a member of the staff at the Aberdeen College, James Lumsden had John Rae in his class. This student was a great admirer of his new teacher and it is through his writing of *Principal Lumsden: A Memorial and Estimate* that we learn a lot about him.

John Rae is interesting. He served in Gamrie after graduation and was then sent out to Syria by the Board of Mission to the Suk El Gharb boys' school which had been built under the auspices of the 'Scotch Lebanon Schools'. The school was 'dedicated in 1870 by the celebrated Dr Alexander Duff and his co-commissioner, Principal J. Lumsden whose names were carved in the massive limestone blocks near the entrance on the west wall of the building'.[32]

Unfortunately, due to the refusal of the existing Syrian Superintendent to hand over the keys, John Rae had to move on to Shweir in Lebanon where he remained until 1879, when he returned home and took the charge of Causewayend back in Aberdeen.

---

31 James Lumsden, *The unity of the Church: A lecture delivered in the Free Church College Aberdeen, at the opening of session 1871–72* (Aberdeen: A&R Milne etc., 1871).
32 *A Handbook of Foreign Missions*, www.forgottenbooks.com (accessed 05/03/2018).

Rae's book was printed in 1876 with a preface by G. M. Rae, who enrolled in the College seven years after John and may have been related. He says: 'The author of the following "A memorial and Estimate" was a member of Principal Lumsden's first class in the Aberdeen College and he desires this expression of his views and feelings on hearing of the Principal's death to go forth as "the tear of an old student's gratitude and sorrow shed over the grave of a much loved, much revered Professor".'[33]

John Rae's writing is gushing and effusive and worth quoting.

'The interest which Dr Lumsden took in young men and in the Young Men's Christian Associations, was well known, not only in Aberdeen but far beyond it also. Many came from distant places, friendless and un-introduced to Minister or Christian friend or anyone who could take a friendly interest in them. Young men left alone, friendless and companionless in such circumstances with permanent life principles not yet formed are sometimes drawn aside from the right way of the Lord ... It was with spirit worthy of that Greater Friend that the Professor thought of these students away from their homes and far from the guides of their youth and was mainly instrumental in forming and guiding the Free Church Students' Association.'[34]

'How approachable Dr Lumsden was to students [pressed with questions or anxieties and subtle intellectual doubts] struggling with difficulties; how willing he was to hear their story; with what patience he could enter into it; with what gentleness he could speak of it and feel and weigh and consider it; with what light he was able to surround the matter of difficulty, and to exhibit the various points of it and to find for his young friends a way out of it.'[35]

'He was firmly rooted and unshaken in the great doctrines of the reformation, and in the general scheme of Calvinistic teaching. You might call him dogmatist; but on these matters he was ready to confess always that he had made up his mind, and he had already studied so fully the word of God, and he had already

33 Rae, Preface.
34 Rae, p. 20.
35 Rae, p. 8.

so distinctly heard the voice of the Lord, through his teachings of His word that he had taken up his position.'[36]

'The Principal was very careful and earnest in his instructions to the students of the Pastoral Theology Department with special reference to the matter of public prayer ... The subjects of public prayer he held should be carefully considered before hand in a humble and prayerful spirit and one's own spirit should be diligently looked to and prepared and the exercise of leading the prayers of the congregation not rushed into thoughtlessly and at random.'[37]

However, another side of Principal Lumsden is shown: 'He had a terrible power of impatience with trifling and his potentiality of slumbering wrath, sometimes awakening and kindling also, was a proof – when important interests were at stake, or moral considerations had to be weighed – that he at least was thoroughly sincere; a proof that is to say in his case when we take him all in all for he had an intense love of justice.'[38]

'He had no patience with any so-called preaching of the gospel which mystified or obscured it. On all this ['Justification by Faith alone'] Dr Lumsden was quite intolerant, intolerant absolutely, without any compromise or surrender.'[39]

Principal James Lumsden died just before 7pm on 17 October 1875 in his residence in Bon-Accord Terrace. A full obituary from the *Dundee Advertiser* of 18 October 1875 is printed at the end of Rae's memorial and gives the Principal's cause of death as a 'paralytic attack'. It is unlikely that John Rae was present at the death but he writes: 'He [Lumsden] had spoken in the evening of the claims of the sustentation fund [at a meeting of the Provincial Synod of Aberdeen] when he felt too ill to remain any longer. He withdrew and went home never to leave his house again. He went through his plans for the coming session on one of his last days with a brother professor ... When it became apparent that death was near he was calm as usual and ready for the will of the Lord. Nor thought he of himself alone – it was in his heart to live and

---

36 Rae, p. 11.
37 Rae, p. 6.
38 Rae, p. 10.
39 Rae, p. 13.

die with and for his students. To them he caused a last message to be written for him in his Master's behalf, committed himself to his Lord, and died.

'Oh! How we could have wished to have him among us a little longer! Yet we do not grudge him his rest and his reward. He rests from his labours and his works follow him ... "But go, O man greatly beloved – go thou thy way till the end be; for thou shalt rest and stand in thy lot at the end of the days.'[40]

---

40 Rae, p. 25.

3

Principal David Brown and the Heresy Scandal 1876–98

David Brown chaired his first meeting of the Financial Board as Principal on 21 September 1876. He had arrived nearly twenty years earlier as Professor of New Testament. When he died, William Garden Blaikie, a former Professor at New College and well-known author of *The Personal Life of David Livingston*, wrote his biography, commenting in the preface, 'David Brown kept no diary and preserved but a very few letters. This has rendered the task of his biographer difficult.'[1] However, an article in *The Spectator* in August 1898 comments, 'Dr. Blaikie occupies too much space, perhaps, in telling the story of the late Principal Brown, of the Free Church College, Aberdeen, whose life extended from 1803 to 1897; but that story was worth telling.'[2] It is a closely typeset volume with 364 pages and is a comprehensive biography which together with the Financial Board minutes gives a good picture of the second, and longest-serving, Principal of the Aberdeen Free College.

David Brown was born in Aberdeen in 1803 and died there in 1897 having witnessed nearly a century of remarkable events and achievements, as noted by his biographer. 'It embraced the period of Waterloo, the Crimean War, the Indian Mutiny and the Civil War in the United States; of Catholic emancipation, the Reform

---

1 W. G. Blaikie, *David Brown D.D., LL.D.: Professor and Principal of the Free Church College, Aberdeen: A Memoir* (London: Hodder and Stoughton, 1898), Preface.

2 *The Spectator*, http://archive.spectator.co.uk (accessed 05/03/2018).

Bill, Free Trade, the adoption of India into the Empire, and the great expansion of our Colonies; of the Evangelical revival, the Tractarian Movement, the Voluntary Controversy, the Disruption of the Church of Scotland, and the disestablishment of that of Ireland. Further it included the era of rationalism, of "the higher criticism", and the development of the sensational philosophy; of the Anti-Slavery struggle, the rise of social reform and philanthropy, the conflict of Labour and Capital, the era of great cities, of rapid travelling and of extended intercourse between country and country.'[3] The list goes on and much of what is mentioned can be seen reflected in the history and stories of the Free Church College in Aberdeen.

Brought up in Aberdeen, Brown lived for much of his childhood in Broad Street as close as was possible to Marischal College. His father was a bookseller with entrepreneurial instincts. He started a circulating library with his stock, and by regularly auctioning surplus created a good business. He was Lord Provost of Aberdeen on two occasions. Brown's mother was the daughter of James Chalmers, editor and proprietor of the *Aberdeen Journal*. He was one of eight children and enjoyed the bookish circles his parents moved in. His early education was at Aberdeen Grammar School, then Marischal College for his four-year MA before entering the Aberdeen Free Church College Divinity Hall. Following that he became Assistant Minister of Regent Square Church in London for two years before returning to Scotland. Coming home he was met with a degree of distrust due to his time in London, but eventually found a position in Dumbarton. This was followed soon after by a move to Banffshire where he became the first minister of a new church called 'The Ord'. Here, he finally achieved ordination in 1836 and settled with his new wife, who was his cousin Catherine Dyce, sister of the now famous painter William Dyce.

Then came the Disruption. 'On the memorable 18 of May 1843 Mr Brown was in Edinburgh and, as one of the 474, cordially attached his name to the Deed of Demission. Returning to the Ord, he had a very bleak prospect to face. Lord Seafield sent, though reluctantly, for the key of the church and the manse – a

3 Blaikie, p. 1.

plain proof that Mr Brown's connection to both was to cease.'[4] The family moved to Glasgow where Brown became the minister of St James' Free Church, where he stayed for fourteen years until he was appointed to the Free Church College in Aberdeen.

David Brown's Arrival at the College

David Brown's appointment to the Professorship in Aberdeen was not without controversy. He had hoped to attain the newly endowed Chair of Exegetical Theology of the New Testament in New College, Edinburgh but the General Assembly had favoured George Smeaton by 181 votes to 163. The General Assembly gave Brown the now vacant chair in Aberdeen which was seen as something of a consolation prize. Aberdeen Free Church College was not an ideal place for him as he had sided with Dr Cunningham and those who felt that there should not be a College in Aberdeen. It is reported that 'at first he was received rather coldly by some',[5] but it appears that his inaugural lecture, 'Christ the ultimate refuge for the doubter', showed that his appointment was sound and he was fit for office. Although he arrived in Aberdeen a disappointed man, his biographer claims: 'In after years he came to see that this arrangement had been carried out under God's guiding hand, and to rejoice in the manifold sphere of usefulness which he had in Aberdeen.'[6]

His teaching commitments in Aberdeen covered not only his speciality of Exegetics of the New Testament but also Apologetics and Church History. In a letter to his brother-in-law, William Dyce, at the end of his first teaching session, he wrote: 'I have got through much better than I ventured to expect. I think the plan I took to economise my labour was wise. Believing that of the two classes of students I had to teach (1st years and 4th years), it was of much more importance to throw my strength into the work of beginners whose good or bad start would affect their whole future course than to spend my labour in perfecting those

---

4 Ibid., p. 6.
5 Ibid., p. 118.
6 Ibid., p. 117.

whose studies were already far advanced.'[7] William Dyce is then given a long account of the content of all Brown's courses, but the letter finishes with news of one of his children: 'Poor Alexander, I much fear that I can hardly hold him on in Oxford till he gets a fellowship, and I *think* he would rather not go in for an Indian appointment if he could do the other. I am greatly at a loss at present what is proper. His mother is much averse to his going to India.'[8]

Poor Alexander indeed. The family could not afford his further education for the Bar and his parents expressed their disappointment at his 'apparent want of decision and heartiness in religious profession'.[9] They had wanted him to become a minister in the Free Church but he felt strongly that he did not have the right personality for this, so in the end he did choose the Civil Service in India. He arrived in Calcutta at the beginning of 1859 and did very well, but his health deteriorated quickly and less than a year later he was ordered home. His parents received news that he was due in Weymouth in the spring but Alexander did not survive the voyage, dying at sea on 3 January 1860. The ship arrived in Weymouth at the end of March and David Brown had already set off to meet his son when the telegram bearing the news reached his house. 'Dr Brown and his wife went immediately to London, in order to obtain details of his death and if possible learn the state of mind in which he died. For this last was their great anxiety. They had never heard from him any such explicit declaration of his trust in Christ as satisfied them.'[10] They were greatly cheered when they met with a Reverend Joseph Scudder who had been on the voyage; he had been in the company of Alexander during his last days and was able to confirm that 'his trust in Christ was unclouded'.[11] David Brown chose to tell his son's story in a memorial volume called *Crushed Hopes Crowned in Death.*

---

7 Ibid., p. 122.
8 Ibid., p. 124.
9 Ibid., p. 172.
10 Ibid., p. 173.
11 Ibid., p. 175.

Appointment to Principal

Twenty years after he arrived at the Aberdeen Free Church College, Brown's colleague, James Lumsden, Principal of the College, died. David Brown was the obvious choice of successor and his name was put forward to the General Assembly, who duly appointed him in 1876 although not without opposition: some considered him, at the age of 73, to be too old and that 'he had been somewhat discursive as a Professor and much occupied with outside matters'.[12]

His biographer describes his duties as Principal as 'mainly limited to presiding at meetings of the Senatus and delivering the closing address at the end of the session'.[13] He also chaired the Financial Board and from these minutes we can see that he had rather more to attend to as Principal than Blaikie described. On 25 April 1877 he read a letter to the Board from Mr Francis Edmond who, although no longer Secretary and Treasurer, was still taking a keen interest in the business of the College. 'An attempt was made several years ago after the death of Professor Sachs to raise sufficient funds for a fellowship in the Aberdeen Free Church College as a memorial of him and more recently following the death of Principal Lumsden a similar attempt was made but both attempts having failed, certain parties who take an interest in the college and treasure the memory of these men are desirious to see instituted two fellowships in the names of "The Lumsden and Sachs" memorial fellowships to be then competed for by students of the fourth class at the end of the session ... £80 every six months until £2000 is provided and invested for a permanent endowment.'[14]

'The Board desired to record their satisfaction on the receipt of Mr Edmond's communication and their thanks for the benefit he intends to be the means of conferring on the College in addition to many benefits for which the College is already indebted to him.'[15]

---

12 Ibid., p. 288.
13 Ibid.
14 Financial Board Minute Books, Vol. 3, p. 135.
15 Ibid.

One hundred and forty years later the Lumsden and Sachs prize is still awarded at the end of the academic year. The prize is now £100 of book tokens and is greatly enjoyed by those who receive it.

The *Expository Times*

In 1877 a new student arrived at the Divinity Hall having graduated MA at Aberdeen University. James Hastings came from Huntly and after his ordination in 1884 he ministered in Kinneff, Dundee and, up to his retirement, in St Cyrus. He found life in the city parish of Willison, Dundee, difficult but during this time he founded the *Expository Times*. It quickly became a popular periodical and is still published today. 'James Hastings had a lively Christian faith, which was coupled with a love of learning. He was a notable preacher, simple and direct, and an eager supporter of social welfare. But over and above all these concerns, his real achievement lies in his commitment to promoting knowledge of the Christian faith, but especially of the Bible. He is particularly remembered for his works of reference. These include his two-volume *Dictionary of Christ and the Gospels* (1906–07), his *Dictionary of the Bible* (1898–1902), and his *Dictionary of the Apostolic Church* (1915–18); but these pale into insignificance when compared to his thirteen-volume work, the *Encyclopaedia of Religion and Ethics* (1908–21). These works bore witness to Hastings's conviction that modern biblical criticism, far from undermining Christian belief, would serve to reinforce the fundamental tenets of his faith. A plaque in memory of him is still displayed in the corridors at King's where the Divinity staff have their rooms.'[16]

16 Michael D. McMullen in *The Oxford Dictionary of National Biography*, https://doi.org/10.1093/ref:odnb/33755 (accessed 05/03/2018).

William Robertson Smith

Arguably the biggest scandal in the history of the Church College in Aberdeen was the William Robertson Smith heresy case which came soon after Brown became Principal.

Smith was brought up in the manse of Keig and Tough in Donside. His father, the Reverend W. Pirie Smith, attended to his early education, very successfully it would seem as William came to Aberdeen University at the age of 15. On his graduation in 1865 he was awarded the town council's medal for the best student. He went on study at New College in Edinburgh intending to follow his calling (and his father) into Free Church ministry. However, such was the reputation he made as a student, he was called by the General Assembly of the Free Church in Scotland to succeed Marcus Sachs in Aberdeen. Smith had been described by a New College Professor as 'the most distinguished student I have ever had in my department', who showed 'maturity as well as the striking independence of mind'.[17] Another praised his 'power of clear and strong original thinking, his comprehensiveness of view, his penetrative keenness of insight, his masculine sobriety of mind and his extraordinary capacity for work', adding that he was the 'most gifted young man I have ever known'.[18]

Aged only 24 and still a probationer, William Robertson Smith took on the Professor's position in a College where some of his students were older than him. He was destined to provide plenty of colour in the College history. Smith's inaugural lecture was entitled 'What history teaches us to look for in the Bible', which perhaps gave a foretaste of what was to come. 'Brilliant alike in range of knowledge, linguistics acquirements, and dialectical skill, he profoundly impressed his students.'[19]

---

17 Bernhard Maier, *William Robertson Smith: His life, his work and his times* (Tübingen: Mohr Siebeck, 2009), p. 124.

18 Ibid.

19 R. G. Philip, 'Chapters From Its History: 1855 to 1900', in *The Church College in Aberdeen* (Aberdeen: Aberdeen University Press, 1936), p. 11.

He thrived under the Principalship of James Lumsden to whom he became very close. Lumsden's death in 1875 not only affected him personally but was also to have an impact professionally.

William Robertson Smith travelled often in Europe and in the summer of 1872 he spent some months at the University of Göttingen where he mastered Arabic with the Professor of Oriental Languages. This study was to prove extremely useful and a lifeline for his future academic career. While in Göttingen he visited Leipzig and met with a Dr Biesenthal.

Biesenthal, born Raphael Hirsch in Lobzenica, was well educated with the intention of becoming a rabbi. As a postgraduate he went to Berlin University, where he studied theology and philosophy. It seems that he had already had some doubts about the Talmud, and soon after gaining his doctorate he was baptised into the Christian faith and changed his name to Johann Heinrich Biesenthal. Known as Henry Biesenthal, he worked for the London Society for Promoting Christianity amongst the Jews in Berlin. He moved to Leipzig where he was visited in 1872 by William Robertson Smith, who wrote, 'I paid a visit to Dr Biesenthal, a noted Rabbinist who is anxious to sell his collection of Hebrew books. If we could get hold of them for Aberdeen we should have one of the finest Rabbinical Collections in Great Britain.'[20]

The collection duly arrived at the Free Church College in Aberdeen and it is assumed that the funding came from the Thomson of Banchory Bequest, although curiously this is not mentioned in the Financial Board minutes. The first time the figures in the Banchory Bequest are clarified is in May 1874 when it appears that £1592/18/9 is available for books. The following meeting requested the Banchory Trustees to extend the time period for purchasing books, as the Professors had been obliged to defer the purchase of books due to the debate regarding the legacy and the lack of clarity regarding the amount available.

The Biesenthal collection comprised over 2,000 volumes and was seldom used after Smith left Aberdeen. It was a highly specialised collection and at that time Aberdeen was seen as relatively

---

20 Henry Sefton, typewritten sheet: Papers of Professor William Robertson Smith, MS 3674/2/1.

inaccessible so it never took its place in the world of rabbinical scholarship. In 1968 the collection was deposited in King's College Library on permanent loan.

Heresy

In 1875 Professor Smith was appointed to the Old Testament section of the committee that was producing the Revised Version of the Bible. He was also working on some articles he had been commissioned to write for the ninth edition of the *Encyclopaedia Britannica*. It was these articles that formed the basis of 'the most outstanding case in the whole history of the free church of Scotland which shook it to its foundations',[21] and which led to Smith being accused of heresy. The first of these appeared in 1875, 'Angel' in Volume 2 and 'Bible' in Volume 3. These articles marked a turning point in his career. Had Lumsden still been alive there might have been a different outcome to the debate. 'Although conservative in theology, he had a mind open for new ideas. There is no reason to believe that he ever saw the article "Bible" before it went to press, but he might well have proved a mediating force in the controversy which soon followed.' [22]

It took six years after the publication of the articles for the case to reach its conclusion and in 1881 Smith found himself removed from his Chair. He had not taught since 1877 when he was in effect suspended while meetings and discussion through Presbytery, Synod and General Assemblies debated the controversy.

Throughout the debate, Smith insisted that 'he accepted that the Bible was the one sufficient and authoritative record of divine revelation, and that his critical views were the fruit of studies carried out under the guidance of his teachers at New College, Edinburgh. He therefore demanded that he be given a formal trial by libel (indictment) for his alleged heresies and errors.'[23]

---

21 Philip, p. 15.
22 Ibid.
23 Henry Sefton in *The Oxford Dictionary of National Biography*, www.oxforddnb.com/search?q=william+robertson+smith&searchBtn=Search&isQuickSearch=true (accessed 05/03/2018).

At the General Assembly of 1880 he secured a majority of seven in a vote of nearly 600, but there was a further article about to be published entitled, 'Hebrew Language and Literature' which raised questions again. In the Assembly of 1881 Principal Rainy carried the majority to decree that it was 'no longer safe or advantageous that Professor Smith should continue to teach in one of the Church Colleges'.[24]

The Reverend R. G. Philip, writing in 1936, suggests that the case did lead to greater freedom and describes Smith as 'a true pioneer in liberty of inquiry and the search for truth and one of the most brilliant scholars of his age and the loss of such a teacher to the church is greatly to be regretted. It must be added, however, that he did not introduce the "Higher Criticism" into his preaching: he was a really devout man and warmly attached to his evangelical faith.' He finishes by adding that 'we need not follow his subsequent career: he died at an early age in 1894'.[25] And so one of the greatest scholars is dealt with. Had the writer followed his subsequent career he would have discovered that Smith moved to London and became Editor in Chief of the work that had caused his downfall, the *Encyclopaedia Britannica* which was published in 1888. Thereafter he was Professor of Arabic at Cambridge University, supposedly on twice the salary he had been earning in Aberdeen. Having experienced bouts of ill health throughout his life he succumbed to tuberculosis in 1894 at a young age and is buried in the Aberdeenshire village of Keig where he was born.

Just seventy years after William Robertson Smith was suspended from teaching, the centenary of his birth in 1946 was seen as an occasion to celebrate by the Aberdeen College and the University, and his portrait by Sir George Reid was hung in the College Hall alongside the portraits of the Principals and Masters. More recently he was commemorated in a circular plaque on the wall of the College building as Aberdeen Art Gallery sought to bring Aberdeen's eminent citizens of the past to the public eye; and in 1994 Professor William Johnstone, Professor of Hebrew

---

24 Philip, p. 16.
25 Ibid.

and Semitic Languages, organised a Congress to mark the centenary of William Robertson Smith's death (see Chapter 10).

Throughout the William Robertson Smith case, Principal Brown was very much on the side of the opposition. Blaikie argues that having to take this standpoint was painful to Brown who liked Smith and admired his work. In his obituary of Brown in the *Expository Times*, the Rev. Stewart D. F. Salmond writes: 'The one occasion in which he departed from his usual position was that over the controversy of the writings of his brilliant colleague Professor Robertson Smith. His anxieties regarding the effect which the critical reconstruction of the Old Testament books might have on the authority of the Divine Word led him in this case to take up an attitude of strenuous opposition to those who stood for liberty of opinion. It was a painful and unexpected incident in his career.'[26]

During this time Principal Brown lost his wife after a long and debilitating illness which is documented in great detail by Blaikie. 'The affection between him and his wife had been uniformly of the warmest kind. Often did he speak of his forty-three years of cloudless sunshine. When she died his heart was stirred to its utmost depth. Many a visit he paid to the chamber of death, most tenderly he stroked the cold hand and cold face'.[27] However, it appears that his 'bravery of spirit was never shown by him more remarkably than now ... People who knew what he had lost wondered to find him so like his old self. Certainly this was not due to want of feeling, but to that remarkable self-control that checked the excess to which grief might naturally have run because there was still work for him to do in the world; there were still friends whose life he was called to brighten; there was a sphere for faith to show her power to transform trouble and darkness into light and joy; and there was the sure and certain hope of reunion in a better world, where light would fall on the mysteries of life, and God would wipe the tears from every eye.'[28] Wonderful prose!

---

26 S. D. F. Salmond, 'Obituary Part 2', *Expository Times*, Vol. 9/4 (1898), p. 169.

27 Blaikie, p. 330.

28 Ibid., p. 331.

The Colleges Committee

Over the following few years the Principal and the Financial Board were much exercised by dealings with the Colleges Committee in Edinburgh and relations between the two were not good. Much work of maintenance and repair was being carried out on the College building and it was reported in April 1878 that payment had been withheld for the Treasurer's outlay on building repairs. The Secretary was requested to point out to Mr Macdonald of the College's Committee 'that the college buildings being invested in the Free Church the church must bear the burdens of proprietors'.[29]

The works included the construction of an access from the tower to the roof to enable snow clearing and the upgrading of the gas lighting of the college which was defective due to lack of pressure. There was also substantial work to be carried out on the 'Sewerage arrangements'.

Minutes in the early 1880s are full of discussion on the contentious issue of the Professors' salaries. The Board heard that the Edinburgh Professors had received increased salaries and sent a strong letter to the Colleges Committee urging that the agreement reached in the General Assembly of 1876 be strictly adhered to. This agreement stated that the salaries in Edinburgh, Glasgow and Aberdeen Colleges should be the same. There was no reply to this letter and the situation was soon to be made worse: 'The Financial Board of the Aberdeen College have heard with concern and regret from the Principal that a proposal has been made which will have a serious effect on the Professors' salaries in the Aberdeen College.'[30]

It seems that not only were the Edinburgh salaries higher but Aberdeen and Glasgow Professors were to have a pay cut to make up the deficit! 'The Board desires further again to point out that the salaries in Aberdeen are in themselves greatly inadequate and would be made disproportionately so in relation to those in Edinburgh unless the arrangement of 1876 is strictly adhered to' – and so it goes on for pages. It took until October 1886 for the Board

29 Financial Board Minute Books, Vol. 3, p. 138.
30 Ibid., p. 173.

to hear that an agreement had been reached with the Colleges Committee.

Foreign Mission

Principal Brown took a great interest in foreign mission and in his closing address, at the age of 80, he said to the students: 'Some of the best students in our divinity halls are offering themselves as missionaries, and are willing to go where, in the judgment of the church, they are most needed. I want you gentlemen to watch this light in the religious life of the country. The spiritual life of the church has to be maintained, else it will decline, for nothing can stand still. Your part, gentlemen, is to throw yourselves into it and take your own share of your Master's work. For this purpose you must cherish your own spiritual life. For you cannot impart that which you have not yourselves. Suffer not your theological studies to deaden your spirituality. Walk closely with God in the midst of your studies.'[31] In proportion to its numbers the Aberdeen Free Church College contributed more missionaries than any other.

Moderator of the General Assembly

In 1884 David Brown's name was put forward by William Garden Blaikie for consideration for the role of Moderator. Blaikie felt strongly that Brown was not being given the recognition or status he warranted. 'It is not easy to account satisfactorily for the fact that such a man as Principal Brown should have passed his eightieth year before being called to the chair of the General Assembly of his church.'[32] He was put up in opposition to a candidate supported by Principal Rainy of New College so it was no surprise that he came second (yet again) in the vote. However, he received such a number of votes that he could not be overlooked the following year, and in May 1885 he delivered his opening address, 'Watchman, what of the night?' Blaikie writes:

---

31 Blaikie, p. 292.
32 Ibid., p. 313.

'It was a survey on the condition of the whole of the church and in relation to the great purpose for which the church had been instituted. That purpose was twofold, missionary and pastoral. As to the missionary purpose the church had been woefully remiss and though the spirit of the missions had been revived during the century, the mass of mankind was yet in darkness. Why was this?'[33] Eight pages follow with the majority of the address narrated by Blaikie.

The end of Blaikie's chapter on Brown's Moderatorial year lists the Moderator's duties: 'Opening all the diets of the Assembly with prayer, maintaining order, addressing deputations and representatives of other churches, presiding at breakfast entertainments, delivering a closing address and throughout the following year, opening churches, halls and bazaars, preaching anniversary sermons and acting generally as the representative of the church in public occasions.'[34] Today, 130 years on, the list is much the same although without the breakfast entertainments!

During the year, Brown was presented with a marble bust of himself given by Sir William Henderson, Lord Provost of Aberdeen and a great supporter of the College, who with friends presented it 'as a mark of their appreciation of the services he has rendered to the Christian Church and their affection and esteem for him as a friend and citizen'.[35] The bust was said to occupy a conspicuous place in the Divinity Hall. Unfortunately its whereabouts are now unknown.

David Brown retired from his Professorship the following year but continued as Principal of the Aberdeen Free Church College. His retiral led to two chairs being vacant at the same time, 'and the cry, "close the Aberdeen College" echoed through the Assembly Hall and its corridors'.[36] However, again the College survived and the General Assembly of 1887 divided up Brown's teaching between Professor Salmond and the newly appointed Professor James Iverach. The Reverend James Robertson, formerly Principal of Duff College, Calcutta, was appointed to succeed Dr Binnie,

33 Ibid., p. 321.
34 Ibid., p. 322.
35 Ibid., p. 332.
36 Philip, p. 16.

who had died the previous year, in Church History and Pastoral Theology.

Brown's regular attendance in the chair of the Financial Board continued until 1892 when he suffered an accident again described in great detail by his biographer. 'On his way to post some letters, he did not observe that the lid of a coal cellar under the pavement had been removed and tripping over the opening with all his force, he sustained a very great shock, and had one of his legs severely injured.'[37]

After three months in bed he made a good recovery although he wrote to a friend about the strange symptoms he was experiencing: 'The nerves of the extremities (feet and fingers) have lost nearly all sensation. In walking, I don't feel the ground; it is as if walking on ice. And the tips of my fingers can scarcely fix my buttons in dressing. And although I wrote fairly well before, I am now scarcely legible.'[38] Anyone reading the minute books of the time and seeing his notes and signatures would disagree that he ever wrote well; certainly in comparison with his predecessor, he wrote very poorly. One can however see the decline.

Janitor and Curator

Brown returned to the chair of the Financial Board in 1893 when the business was concerned with the appointment of a new janitor and curator.

The following Statement of duties to be discharged by the janitor and curator was ordered to be placed on the record.

1 To see to the safety of the entire premises, to keeping them tidy, to the cleanliness of lavatories and closets and the washing of windows where practicable.
2 To have classrooms and other apartments tidy, heated and ready for ordinary use or for special meetings and to attend to the bell.

---

37 Blaikie, p. 339.
38 Ibid.

3 To attend to the heating of the premises whether by open fire or heating apparatus, to see that all is in good working order; and to give special attention in times of frost.

4 To communicate with the Financial Board as to the ordering of fuel, and to see to its delivery and economical use.

5 To attend to the Museum and microscopes, to keep the keys of the museum and acquaint himself of the contents, to keep all clean and do generally what is necessary for the preservation and exhibition of the collections all under supervision of the Senatus.

6 To carry out in general the requirements of the Senatus and the Financial Board, and to make himself generally useful in helping the librarian in the cleaning of books or otherwise.

7 To keep a petty cash book and a record of notabilia in matters of repairs to the buildings and other things requiring notice or record. These books to be submitted from time to time to the Secretary of the Senatus and the member of the Financial Board charged with oversight of the building.

8 To give his whole time to the discharge of the duties of his office except by the consent of the Senatus and the Financial Board.[39]

For this a weekly wage of £1 was offered with free accommodation, light and fuel in the attic of the Library and Museum building at 2 Alford Place. The newly appointed Mr William Beveridge died soon after taking up the post and there then followed numerous short appointments. The conditions of employment for this position were constantly documented through the meeting minutes and the Principals of the College were very much involved in decision-making regarding all aspects of the role, even down to choosing the fabric for the uniform.

39 Financial Board Minute Books, Vol. 3, p. 265.

Secretary/Treasurer

Throughout his time as Principal, David Brown had relied heavily on the organisational skills and support of the Secretary/Treasurer, Mr Alexander Edmond, son of Francis Edmond.

On 22 July 1891 the minute read, 'The Financial Board of the college meeting as they do for the first time this day without a Secretary cannot proceed with business without putting on record their deep sense of the irreparable loss which they have sustained by the death of their late Secretary/Treasurer Mr Alexander Edmond, who took the liveliest interest in the prosperity of the College and for so many years threw his eminent business abilities into its affairs sparing neither time nor pains in furthering its financial prosperity. The Board take this opportunity in expressing their deep sympathy with Mrs Edmond and Dr Francis Edmond under their heavy loss.'[40]

They then proceeded to appoint Mr John Edmond, a younger brother of the late Alexander, who thanked the Board for the honour they had done him. In 1895 he resigned having retired from business, and despite a deputation from the Board could not be persuaded to continue. Mr David Edwards was then appointed to the position, so for the first time since its inception the Aberdeen Free Church College Financial Board did not have an Edmond family member in this position. Edwards was however a partner in the Edmonds and McQueen legal practice so in that way it continued in the family firm.

'A Zest for Souls'

The last meeting David Brown presided over was on 24 April 1896 and Blaikie documents his decline over fourteen pages, until on 3 July 1897 he was nearing death: 'he then fell asleep but awoke an hour later and asked his daughter to repeat to him some lines of the well known hymn:

---

40 Ibid., p. 249.

Happy day ...
When Jesus washed my sins away.

'Soon after he fell into unconsciousness and remained in that state until the end came quietly, a little before six o'clock that evening.'[41]

And thus ended the 21-year reign of the longest-serving Principal of the College to this day.

The remainder of Blaikie's book is filled with tributes from colleagues and former students. Due to Brown's missionary zeal many were from far afield including Lovedale, South Africa; Princeton, America; Duff College, Calcutta and Wu-King-Fu, China. One of his students, who rose to fame as editor of the *British Weekly* and the *Expositor*, was Dr (later Sir) William Robertson Nicoll, who wrote: 'When I attended the Free Church College in Aberdeen 1870–1874 Dr David Brown was professor of Apologetics, the Exegesis of the New Testament, and Church History. There were about thirty students and the classes were necessarily very small. Although other colleges of the Free Church were better equipped, I question whether any of the Aberdeen students of the period have in after life regretted their choice, for the Professors were men of extraordinary mark, vigour and personality ...

'Dr Brown was a man whose eagerness and variety of interest, zest and tenacity of life and varied experience, made him always stimulating to those with whom he was brought into contact ...

'In private life Dr Brown was exceedingly accessible to his students. He had them at his home, drew them out and was quick to mark any signs of promise ...

'As I look back it seems that the truest thing said about Dr Brown after his death was that he had a "zest for souls". He was anxious to turn out good scholars and had a keen sense of literary form. But he was far more anxious that his students should be winners of souls.'[42]

Blaikie had started his book by suggesting that his job as biographer was difficult as Brown had not kept a diary, but in spite

41 Blaikie, p. 350.
42 Ibid., p. 135.

of this he manages a very full biography which continues beyond the death with information about the funeral.

'It was a graceful act on the part of the Lord Provost and Magistrates to offer the distinction of a public funeral for Dr Brown. The offer having been accepted, the Lord Provost and other members of the town council attended in their official robes; also the University Court and Senatus; the Free Church Presbytery and Synod of Aberdeen; his own colleagues and the students of the college; the office bearers of the Free South Church; Principal Rainy of Edinburgh; Mr Ross of Cowcaddens; a large number of ministers of various denominations, and in addition to the family and relations, very many friends and others desirous of showing respect for the deceased. The Hall of the Free Church College was crowded to overflowing. The streets were lined with spectators and on the way to the grave all the shop windows were closed.'[43]

Order of Funeral Service 8th July 1897[44]

Invocation: Rev. W M Clow

Hymn: 'Jesus these eyes have never seen'

Psalm XC 1 –12: Rev. Jas Sutherland DD Senior Clerk of the Synod

Prayer: Rev. Principal Rainy

1Cor XV 50–58, Rev XXI 1–4: Rev. Charles H Todd MA Moderator of the Presbytery

Prayer: Rev. Professor Salmond DD

Hymn: 'When the day of toil is done'

Benediction: Rev. Professor Cameron DD

Prayer at the grave: Rev. Professor Iverach

---

43 Ibid., p. 350.
44 'David Brown, Order of funeral service, 8th July, 1897' (Aberdeen, 1897).

Order of procession from the Free Church College, after the service at two o'clock, to St Nicolas Churchyard.

The Town Council

University Court and Senatus

Free Church Presbytery and Synod of Aberdeen

Other Clergy

Office bearers of the Free South Church

Students

Professors of the Free Church College

The Body

The Family

Relatives

Friends

At this point in the College history, Volume 2 of the Senatus Minutes comes into play. The account of the second meeting in that volume on 7 July 1897 reads: 'The Senatus being met for the first time since the lamentable death of Dr Brown the venerable head of the College which took place on Saturday last, the 3 July, resolve to put on record their deep sense of the loss sustained by the removal of one who occupied the post of Professor for thirty years and that of Principal for twenty one years in this college who in these positions did much for the advancement of New Testament studies and for the training of students for the Christian Ministry; and who was held in the highest esteem for the services he rendered to the community of Aberdeen and to the churches of which he was a devoted and honoured member. The Clerk was instructed to send a copy of this minute together with the sympathy of the Senatus to Miss Brown.'[45] This was the only piece of business.

'No man had died richer in all that constitutes real wealth and is entitled to real honour. Yet no man would have said more humbly or cordially, Non nobis, Domine!'[46]

---

45 Senatus Minute Books, Vol. 2, p. 2.
46 Blaikie, p. 364.

4

The Third Principal and the First Union
1898–1905

The third Principal, Professor Stewart Salmond, was at the helm of the College for a relatively short time but served as Principal of both the Free Church College and what was subsequently called the United Free Church College following the union in 1900.

A native of Aberdeen, Stewart Dingwall Fordyce Salmond's early education followed the pattern of Aberdeen Grammar School, then an Arts degree at Aberdeen University. He then went on to train for the ministry at the Free Church College but at the same time was also Assistant Professor of Greek at the University. He went to Germany to the University of Erlangen where he studied under, and was much influenced by, the great theologians of the day: Franz Delitzsch, Johannes Christian Konrad von Hofmann, and Gottfried Thomasius.

He returned to Scotland and became minister of the Free Church in Barry, near Forfar, only nine years after the first College Principal, James Lumsden, left that same charge. Salmond was known to be a diligent pastor but he was keen to move to an academic life, and following the death of Marcus Sachs he put himself forward for the Chair of Hebrew at the Aberdeen College. He was up against the young William Robertson Smith, who won the vote the following May at the General Assembly by 139 votes. 'While Salmond could boast a wider educational and ministerial experience, Smith managed to score an important success when the *British Quarterly Review* published his article *Prophecy in the*

Critical Schools of the Continent.[1] Immediately afterwards Smith was pleased to report to his mother, 'Candlish [Principal of New College] is much delighted with my paper and snaps his fingers at Salmond.'[2] Ultimately Smith's outstanding qualities as a Hebrew scholar carried the day.

It was six years later that Salmond fulfilled his professional ambition and was appointed Chair of Systematic Theology at the Aberdeen Free Church College. For just a year he taught alongside his rival William Robertson Smith, before the latter was suspended from teaching. It was Salmond who took up the teaching of Hebrew until Smith's successor George Cameron was appointed in 1882.

From time to time in the 1880s Professor Salmond's name appears 'in attendance' at the Financial Board meetings, but he was generally more involved with the students and his own church life rather than College proceedings.

The Rev. R. G. Philip, writing as a former student, says: 'Of the professors of the time the one who left the most marked impression as a teacher was Professor Salmond, very precise but very just. Although cold in manner, he took a warm personal interest in his students. He inspired them with the necessity of hard work, and earned their deep respect by his great learning, tireless industry, and lucid exposition.'[3]

The Christian Doctrine of Immortality

During this period Professor Salmond delivered the Cunningham Lectures and published them under the title *The Christian Doctrine of Immortality*. This became his most notable book. Alexander Balmain Bruce, formerly a Free Church minister and at the time of Salmond's publication, in the chair of Apologetics

---

1 Bernhard Maier, *William Robertson Smith. His life, his work and his times* (Tübingen: Mohr Siebeck, 2009), p. 124.

2 Ibid.

3 R. G. Philip, 'Chapters From Its History: 1855 to 1900', in *The Church College in Aberdeen* (Aberdeen: Aberdeen University Press, 1936), p. 12.

and New Testament Exegesis in the Free Church Hall in Glasgow, commented on it in an article in *The Biblical World*. 'Though forbiddingly large it is by no means a heavy book to read. The style is simple, direct, to the point, and the matter invariably interesting. Besides being interesting it is weighty, because it is obviously the ripe result of much patient research and hard thinking carried on from the time of the preparation of the Cunningham Lectures till the date of publication.'[4]

Salmond states in the introduction, 'The present inquiry limits itself to the question, what is the witness of Scripture on the subject? The words of Christ are to me the highest authority, beyond which I seek no other.'[5]

Bruce continues, 'In his theological attitude Dr. Salmond is on the whole more conservative than many of his Scottish contemporaries and comrades, but he knows nothing of the bigotry and intolerance of conservatism, or of the *odium theologicum*. His temper is calm and passionless, and his habit of mind scientific rather than dogmatic. Men of all schools, new and old, may read his work on immortality without fear of offense, and with good hope of theological instruction and spiritual benefit.'[6]

Reviewing it in the *Presbyterian and Reformed Review*, E. D. Morris claims, 'As it now stands, the volume is by far the most elaborate and valuable treatise that has yet appeared on the vital doctrine which it so fully and convincingly presents. The Christian Church owes Prof. Salmond an incalculable debt for such a discussion of such a theme.'[7]

Salmond also wrote primers which were much appreciated by his students, including *The Life of the Apostle Peter*, *The Life of Christ*, *The Shorter Catechism*, *The Sabbath* and *The Parables of Our Lord*.

---

4 Alexander Balmain Bruce, 'The Rev. Professor Stewart DF Salmond DD Free Church College Aberdeen', *The Biblical World*, Vol. 8/5 (1896), p. 348.

5 S. D. F. Salmond, *The Christian Doctrine of Immortality* (Edinburgh: T&T Clark, 1895), p. viii.

6 Bruce, p. 350.

7 E. D. Morris, in *Presbyterian and Reformed Review*, Vol. 7 (1896), p. 558.

Bruce is less complimentary about Salmond's church work. 'Dr. Salmond is a man of affairs as well as a man of letters. It would be difficult to say which is the stronger, the passion for business or the passion for study. School boards or presbyterial meetings have taken up much of his time and attention during the years of his professoriate, time which some might be inclined to think might easily have been better spent. The combination exhibited in his character and career is neither common nor easy. The ecclesiastic often kills the scholar, and the scholar the ecclesiastic. Many of our best-known students are hardly ever seen in church courts, and some of our most conspicuous ecclesiastics have belied the promise of fruitful authorship given in their early years. Salmond is an exception. I would not for anything be a presbytery clerk, though some good men I know occupy the dismal post. But it is quite a different affair if you use your presbytery as you use a novel, simply as the means of unbending the mental bow. I owe an apology to my ecclesiastical superior for so disrespectful a suggestion, but I mean no disrespect. I acknowledge that presbyteries have higher, nobler uses than to serve as an amusement to an overworked brain. I am sure Dr. Salmond does not look on them in any such low light. He regards them as opportunities of usefulness, and with commendable public spirit takes advantage of them as such. And that he has done good service in an ecclesiastical capacity all who know him will readily own.'[8]

In 1896 the General Assembly of the Free Church of Scotland ordained that one Professor besides the Principal would be appointed to a seat on the Financial Board of each College. This was put into place in September; Professor Stewart Salmond was duly appointed and could now attend in an official capacity as a Board member. This became very useful from then on, as if the Principal was absent the Board would always have a Professor's input to discussions.

8 Bruce, p. 352.

Sir William Henderson and Professors' Salaries

At the last Financial Board meeting Principal Brown had attended, a letter was read from Professor Salmond. It regarded the house at Number 8 Alford Place, immediately to the west of the College buildings, noting that it had been sold and that it was the intention of the purchasers to 'put up a large building which will occupy the whole of the ground and be brought out to the street'.[9] Professor Salmond told the Board that this would have a serious effect on the light of the College. Discussion ranged from considering asking the purchasers to sell the whole building to the College, or to selling eight feet, to whether they could be prevented from building for the said eight feet. This occupied the Board for several meetings. The eventual outcome was that the Financial Board purchased the building at a price less than was first intimated but more than the Board wanted to pay, and this debt was to prove a real encumbrance in the future. It wasn't long before they discovered that the drains and pipes were found by the Sanitary Inspector to be defective and that a substantial sum would be required to improve the building and the plumbing.

The Financial Board continued to be vexed with the matter of the Professors' salaries, which was further complicated by the Union. The salaries for the Professors in Aberdeen had fallen from £586 in 1892 to £493 in 1899, a reduction of £93 which is approximately 15 per cent.

One of the Trustees, Sir William Henderson, became a champion of the College at this time. He had been on the Board since its inception. He travelled widely as Senior Partner in the Aberdeen White Star Line shipping company and served as Lord Provost of the city from 1886 to 1889. He was knighted in Queen Victoria's birthday honours in 1893. In 1898, '[a]t a representative meeting of citizens presided over by Lord Provost Mearns, on the 19th ulto., it was unanimously resolved to make fitting recognition of Sir William Henderson's distinguished services to the city, and the

---

9 Daniel Mearns and S. D. F. Salmond, *Testimonial to Sir William Henderson LLD* (Aberdeen, 1898).

particular form approved of was that of a portrait, to be painted by an artist of eminence'.[10]

The testimonial continued: 'Sir William is one of the most energetic and most honoured of the members of the Free Church, in which he has been an office bearer for over fifty years. He has also been foremost in giving of his time, his talents and his means to the service of the city and the community. While Lord Provost he originated and carried to successful issue several projects of importance, the chief of which, it is almost superfluous to say, was the erection of the new block of buildings in connection with the Royal Infirmary. In all that he has done, whether for the furtherance of Christian and philanthropic work generally, or for the good of the people of Aberdeen, he has acted with singular disinterestedness and conscientiousness and has set a high idea of civic duty before the community.'[11]

Midway through 1899 Sir William addressed the Board. The minutes read: 'He thought something should be done in bringing the matter [Professors' salaries] prominently before the Church generally and to appeal for support in increasing the funds held for the purpose. He thought however that the friends of the College locally must in the first place show their willingness to give their support.'[12] At the first meeting of the new century Sir William Henderson was able to tell the Board that he had obtained substantial support for the fund locally prior to issuing the appeal. Lord Overtoun had donated £1,000, as had Sir William himself and an anonymous donor. 'The appeal was issued on June 26th along with a private letter to about 300 members of the Church generally.'[13] A total of £5,611 had been intimated or received. The names of donors are beautifully handwritten in the minute book and among those listed is a Mrs C. R. Barbour of Fincastle. She would have been delighted to know that seventy-one years later her grandson, Robert Alexander Stewart – 'Robin' – would be a College Professor and subsequent Master.

---

10 Ibid.
11 Ibid.
12 Financial Board Minute Books, Vol. 3, p. 338.
13 Ibid., p. 353.

The money continued to come in on what was the first and, sadly, not the last occasion that the College had to actively fundraise for staff salaries so that the teaching of future ministers could continue. Just a few months later there was concern at the Board meeting about a report from the 'Committee on the Union' which made recommendations concerning Professors' salaries: 'The Committee finding that the salaries of the United Presbyterian Professors are fixed at £600 per annum, and that the salaries of the Free Church Professors have averaged over the last three years in Edinburgh £608; in Glasgow £578; and in Aberdeen £519 recommend that these amounts be meanwhile fixed salaries of said Professors.'[14]

The Committee on the Union further decided that if a United Presbyterian Professor was to hold office in a Free Church College, then that College must make up his salary to the previous figure. So the Aberdeen College was faced with the possibility that it might have to pay a new Professor £608 while paying the other Professors £519. The Financial Board argued that the money raised by Sir William Henderson's appeal could only be used to make up the shortfall in the *existing* Professors' salaries.

Scandals

The concurrent minutes of the Senatus meetings give a welcome relief from the rather dry and lengthy discussions of the Financial Board. The Senatus meetings were concerned with the sacking of a janitor, the failed appeal by the students to reinstate him and the eventual appointment of Mr and Mrs Lewis Cruikshank out of forty applications. This was another short-term appointment, as following the death of his wife Mr Cruikshank resigned under a cloud of some sort. He was succeeded the following month by another Mr and Mrs Cruikshank and peace in the janitor-ship was finally restored. Peter Cruikshank had been coachman to the late Dr Francis Edmond and came well recommended by the Edmond family.

---

14 Ibid., p. 358.

Also documented was the case of the Librarian, a Mr R. S. Duncan, which was somewhat of a scandal but by no means the worst Principal Salmond was to have to deal with in the coming years. This event was documented in the Senatus minutes as '[c]ertain irregularities ... in the discharge of his duties as Librarian and his conduct as a student. They resolved to give him an opportunity of explanation at a meeting to be held on Friday.'[15]

He did not turn up at that meeting but submitted a letter in which he tendered his resignation as Librarian and acknowledged that he had been 'remiss in his duties and had not worthily performed the functions that we required of him'. The Secretary was instructed to write to him requesting him to give over without delay books, keys and all property belonging to the Senatus and asking him to appear at a further meeting. Duncan arrived at that meeting with his father and 'offered certain explanations and undertook to furnish full supplement of his intromissions'.[16]

Next mention of the case is on 16 April 1898. It was reported that 'Mr R. S. Duncan had left the country without giving the supplement he had under taken to give.'[17] We never hear of him again and his name does not appear in the Complete Roll of Alumni 1843 to 1929.

Further Senatus minutes deal with appointing the Thomson Lecturers and awarding bursaries and prizes. No mention is made of the looming union of the Free Church with the United Presbyterian Church. Following two blank pages in the minute book the meeting dated 9 November 1900 comes under the heading 'United Free Church College' and continues with little of note until the scandal of 1904.

Intoxicated and dishevelled

Dear Dr Salmond,
I have been requested by my Kirk Session to communicate to you, as Principal of the Aberdeen College the following facts

---

15 Senatus Minute Books, Vol. 2, p. 8.
16 Ibid., p. 10.
17 Ibid., p. 11.

concerning a man by the name of Mr McLean, native of Mull who is I believe a student in Aberdeen. He was sent by Mr Milne, Bookseller, to preach here on the 14th February in response to a request from me for pulpit supply. I sent full instructions to Mr Milne as to how he was to get to Forres in time to catch the post gig to Dallas on Saturday. These instructions Mr Milne impresses were handed to him. Instead of following these instructions and arriving here at two o'clock on Saturday afternoon he arrived at the Manse at half past twelve on Sabbath Morning in a dishevelled and incoherent state and smelling strongly of drink. On being questioned on Sabbath he had no explanation to give of how he had arrived at such an extraordinary hour. It has since transpired that the man was seen in an intoxicated condition on Saturday evening by various people at different parts of the road between Forres and Dallas. I understand that he was also guilty of a very grave offence against ecclesiastical order in the Parish of Rafford on his way home on Monday morning but concerning that, Mr Layton of Rafford will communicate with you on behalf of his Kirk Session. The conduct of this man, which of course has been known and talked about in every house in this parish and all the surrounding parishes, has created a great public scandal. This being so, my Kirk Session have requested me to request that whatever measures of discipline the Senatus of Aberdeen College may see fit to take in the case may be communicated to me in order that the public scandal may be removed by a public intimation from the pulpit.

I am

Yours truly

John H. Balfour

'The Senatus agreed to defer consideration of this case until they receive the communication from Mr Layton referred to in the letter from Mr Balfour.'[18]

The meeting was, as always, closed with prayer which must have been quite fervent on that occasion.

18 Ibid., pp. 37–9.

Only two days later they met again and the Principal read the following minute from a Kirk Session meeting in Rafford: 'The Moderator brought before the session a matter which has been much talked about in the parish and beyond during the past three weeks viz the conduct of a student from Aberdeen. He came to supply Mr Balfour's pulpit at Dallas on Sabbath the 14 February last and on Monday morning about 8 o'clock a.m. went into the house of James McIntosh, labourer at Rede, Rafford and went through the form of baptism for the illegitimate child of his daughter Mary. The Moderator reported that he asked Mr John Moore, a bona-fide acting elder to go with him to the house of James McIntosh to ascertain if the reports were true. They did so on Wednesday last and saw Mrs McIntosh who stated that the said John McLean went through the form of Baptism to her husband on his way from Dallas on Monday morning the 15 February but that it was done contrary to her wish and desire.'[19]

On 23 March, the Secretary reported that he had written to Mr McLean intimating to him the meeting of the Senatus on that date and requesting him to be present. 'The Senatus having waited some time and Mr Mclean not having appeared the Senatus resolved to ask Mr McLean to appear at a later meeting at 2.30 p.m. on Thursday and the Secretary was authorised to ask the janitor to deliver the intimation personally to Mr McLean.'[20]

At a meeting on 25 March Mr John McLean appeared and was asked for an explanation of the circumstances reported. 'Mr McLean explained that he had left Aberdeen on the 10.30 a.m. train and on arrival at Forres had found that the mail gig had left. He said that he waited in Forres for some time and had some food and also something to drink. He explained that he had for some time suffered greatly from toothache and neuralgia and was accustomed to take some whisky for the relief of the pain. He admitted also that meeting with James McIntosh on his way to Dallas, he travelled with him and on reaching the house of Mr McIntosh he went in and had some tea and also some whisky.

---

19 Ibid., pp. 39–40.
20 Ibid., p. 42.

'Being questioned on the statement that he had "arrived in a dishevelled and incoherent state and smelling strongly of drink" Mr McLean emphatically denied the statement and affirmed that his appearance was only such as was natural after a long walk. He said he called at the house of one of the congregation to ask his way and had tea there. The house was within a mile of the church. The farmer's son, a servant accompanied him to the Manse and Mr McLean said he distinctly remembered the conversation.

'His attention being called to the statement that he gave no explanation of the reason why he had arrived at the manse at such a late hour, he said that he had explained to Mrs Balfour that he had lost his way.

'In being questioned he admitted that he had had one glass of whisky at the refreshment room at Aberdeen Railway station, two glasses at Forres and one glass with James McIntosh about three miles from Forres.

'Questioned as to the statement that he had been seen in a state of intoxication by various people in different parts of the walk between Forres and Dallas and had asked the way from them but they were strangers to him. He did not admit there was any reasonable ground for their suspicion.

'Questioned as to the administration of the ordinance of Baptism, he explained that being asked of James McIntosh as they walked together to baptise the child and of being pressed of him the next day at Dallas where he said James had come to worship, he consented. He confessed that he had not realised the gravity of the circumstances and the grave breach of ecclesiastical order he had committed. Mr McLean having withdrawn the Senatus considered the whole circumstances of the case and resolved to deal with him further. On his return, The Principal then addressed Mr McLean regarding the gravity of the offence which on his own confession he had committed against the moral law and the ecclesiastical order.

'Mr McLean professed his deep penitence and sorrow for the sin he had done and the scandal he had caused. He promised to abstain completely from the use of strong drink and signed a written pledge to that effect.

'It was intimated to him that the Senatus ... withdraw all privileges until they are satisfied of his penitence and reformation. The Senatus engaged in prayer with him and commended him to the grace of God.'[21]

We don't know what happened to McLean. He appears in the Roll of Alumni as entering the Divinity Hall in 1902 but unlike all the others listed there is no further information.

An almost indecipherable minute appears on 19 October 1905 as follows: 'The Senate agreed to refund to Professor Stalker the sum of 10 Guineas which he had supended [expended] last summer with the consent of the Senatus on the necessities of Mr John McLean.'[22]

Was he paid to go quietly? Poor John McLean!

Death of Sir William Henderson of Devanah House

'The Senatus having in view the death of Sir William Henderson LLD of Devanah House which took place unexpectedly on 9th June last, take up the business of the day in sadness and with a deep sense of what that event means for themselves and for the College. They mourn the loss of a personal friend the memory of whose unfailing kindness can never die out of their minds. They mourn also the loss of one of the most constant and large hearted supporters of the College, one to whom they owe more than they can express. The interest of the departed in their College was not a thing of a few years but went back to the beginning of his public career in Aberdeen. Through his long and busy life he continued to watch over the college with thoughtful and generous care. In every way he sought to promote its usefulness, maintaining for many years the lectureship in Elocution contributing to its support, helping its students and encouraging its purposes. It was largely in his thoughts during the latter years and it was to him above all others that we are endebted for the origination

---

21 Ibid., pp. 43–7.
22 Ibid., p. 65.

and prosecution of the movement for the better endowment of its chairs.'[23]

Both the Senatus and the Financial Board mourn his loss. Principal Salmond chaired both committees but it is not clear who wrote the laments, which differ in style. The Financial Board Minutes read:

'Since it last met this board has suffered a very heavy loss by the death of one of its oldest and most valued members, Sir William Henderson LLD. In placing this mournful event on record, the board desires to give its expression to its grateful sense of the magnitude of the service rendered by the departed. From the first, Sir William Henderson identified himself in a remarkable way with the work of the board. Assiduous in his attention to its affairs and ever ready to help he was in most things its moving spirit giving counsel in terms of difficulty, devising measures conducive to the prosperity and usefulness of the College under its charge and watching over its financial position with sedulous and beneficial care.

'Conscious of what it has itself lost with this decease and thankful to God for all that has been done in the discharge of its responsibilities by the departed, the Board also wishes to convey its profound sympathy to his family and the wide circle of friends who mourn his removal.'[24]

Legal Issues with the Union

The Union of the two Churches had become a messy affair, with those from the Free Church who had refused to unite with the Presbyterian Church questioning the legality of the Union and attempting to retain all the assets. They were ruled against by a Court of Session but they appealed to the House of Lords, who in 1904 overturned that decision. Principal Salmond served on the advisory committee in Edinburgh in charge of the ensuing litigation. His colleague, Professor Stalker, who wrote an obituary for him, mentioned that he was not a great orator but added: 'The

---

23 Ibid., p. 48.
24 Financial Board Minute Books, Vol. 3, p. 400.

last time I heard him, when he was addressing a great audience on the troubles through which the United Free Church is passing in consequence of the judgment delivered, last August, against her by the House of Lords, he spoke not only with an extraordinary grasp of the subject, but with a depth of passion in which the tones of his voice acquired surprising compass and force.'[25] The consequences were that the Free Church congregations of the now United Free Presbyterian Church were to be deprived of 'churches, manses, colleges, missions, and even provision for elderly clergy. It handed large amounts of property to the remnant; more than it could make effective use of. A conference, held in September 1904, between representatives of the UF and the (now distinct) Free Church, to come to some working arrangement, found that no basis for agreement could be found. A convocation of the UF Church, held on December 15, decided that the union should proceed, and resolved to pursue every lawful means to restore their assets. As a result, the intervention of Parliament was sought.'[26] A resolution of sorts was reached in the Churches (Scotland) Act in April 1905 but by this time Principal Salmond was ill. We read in the Financial Board Minutes of the Aberdeen College on 7 March that 'the Financial Board views with much concern the continued illness of the Chairman Reverend Principal Salmond and instructs the Secretary to communicate with Mrs Salmond its great sympathy with her and her family'.[27]

Professor Stalker later wrote, 'He was in his sixty-seventh year, and, till quite recently, he seemed to have the prospect of a long life before him; but suspicious symptoms which had been noticed occasioned an operation at the New Year, when it became known that he was in the grasp of a fatal disease.'[28]

He died on 20 April so was unlikely to have known anything of the compromise reached regarding the assets of the Free Church.

---

25 James Stalker in *The Biblical World*, Vol. 26/3 (1905), p. 189.

26 N. Cameron et al., eds, *Dictionary of Scottish Church History and Theology* (Edinburgh: T&T Clark, 1993), https://en.wikipedia.org (accessed 05/03/2018).

27 Financial Board Minute Books, Vol. 3, p. 411.

28 Stalker, p. 188.

Funeral of Stewart D. F. Salmond

The Principal's funeral took place on Monday, 24 April 1905 in the Divinity Hall. The order of service is more ornate than that of Principal Brown just eight years previously and the order of the procession completely different.

Order of Funeral Service[29]

Prayer of Invocation: Rev. Professor Iverach DD

Psalm 103

Prayer: Rev. Professor G A Smith

Isaiah XXV 1–4, 8,9: Rev. Professor Cameron DD

Paraphrase 66

Revelation XXII, 1–5: Rev. Professor Stalker

Prayer: The Very Reverend Principal Lang

Hymn 305: 'Present with the Lord'

Benediction: Professor Johnstone DD

The order of Procession from the College to Allanvale Cemetery will be as follows:

The coffin
The relatives
The Senatus of the Aberdeen College
Students
Principals and Professors of other colleges
The Kirk session of Queens Cross
Members of Presbytery
Other ministers and office bearers
The General Public.

The following day the Senatus met and 'expressed their deep sense of the great loss sustained by the College in the sad event of the death of Stewart D. F. Salmond, Professor of Systematic

---

29 Steward D. F. Salmond, Order of Funeral Service, 24 July, 1905 (Aberdeen 1905).

Theology and Principal of the College. The members of Senatus mourn the loss of a personal friend whom they loved and trusted and their feeling of sadness at being bereft of the head of the college is intensified by the feeling of personal bereavement. The loss to the College the Senatus feel to be unspeakably great. Identified with the College through the great part of its history, caring for its interest as undergraduate student, Professor and Principal. Principal Salmond gave the strength of his manhood and the wisdom of his mature years to the service of the institution which had helped him train for the work of his life.

'The Senatus bears testimony to the fact that numerous as were the objects which attracted his care and thought and varied as were his services to the cause of religion, to Theological Science, to Education, the Principal ever recognised that the college and the students had the first claim on him. What his services to the college were none can know as well as his colleagues and students do and the Senatus gratefully send their thankfulness that for well nigh thirty years the college had the service of a man whose eminence was recognised in all the churches. As a man of affairs, as a theologian, as a scholar and as a Christian man the Principal shed lustre in the institution over which he presided and which he served ably and faithfully.'[30]

James Stalker wrote an obituary in *The Biblical World*. 'In him theological science has lost not only one of its most accomplished scholars and unwearied workers, but one of those rare natures which have the power of finding out the gifts of others and extracting from them labors which they would never have accomplished if left to themselves. Writes one of his best students: "It occurred to me this winter to re-read a large part of my notes of Dr Salmond's lectures on systematic theology. I recommend this excursion into old pastures to my fellow-students of Aberdeen. Their impression of the thoroughness and suggestiveness of these illuminating lectures will be deepened. They will understand, in re-reading, the exactness of the biblical theology which lies behind the dogmatic; and I am not sure if they will yet have found anywhere a clearer analysis of the results of

---

30 Senatus Minute Books, Vol. 2, p. 59.

theological thinking." And he adds, "I must not close this slight effort of appreciation without recording Dr. Salmond's loyalty to his old students, his unceasing interest in them, his willing-ness to help them, his unselfish sacrifice of leisure, if he could in any way advance their work.""[31]

Stalker ends his piece, 'This brief and imperfect notice cannot be better closed than with the opening words of this book [*The Christian Doctrine of Immortality*], which breathe the spirit of the writer:

'The eye of man looks wistfully to the end. Life, like love, believes in its own immortality. Heart, and mind too, cry for light upon what is beyond the grave. Nor do they cry in vain. They have their answer in themselves. They have it in the highest measure in those words of the Lord Jesus into whose depths men have never ceased to look since they were first spoken, and from which they have never turned unsatisfied.'[32]

---

31 Stalker, p. 194.
32 Salmond, p. vii.

5

Principal Iverach and the First World War
1905–23

Following the death of Professor Salmond in 1905, the General Assembly appointed James Iverach to be the fourth College Principal. He had been on the College staff since 1887 after the retirement from teaching of David Brown who had remained Principal. It had been a difficult time for the College as it was again facing the threat of closure. Brown's retiral meant there were two professorial vacancies following the death of William Binnie, Professor of Church History. 'The voice of suppressed criticism grew in volume and the cry, "Close the Aberdeen College" echoed through the Assembly Hall and its corridors.'[1] However, again after lengthy debate, the General Assembly was persuaded to appoint two new Professors, James Iverach to take on Apologetics and Exegesis of the Gospels, and James Robertson for Church History.

Prior to coming to the College James Iverach was the minister of the new Free Church at Ferryhill in Aberdeen where he had quickly made a name for himself. He was active in Presbytery business and established a busy and solid church which was to feature in College history again, over 100 years later. Born in Halkirk, Caithness, Iverach graduated MA at Edinburgh University where he achieved an honours degree in Mathematical

---

1 R. G. Philip, 'Chapters From Its History: 1855 to 1900', in *The Church College in Aberdeen* (Aberdeen: Aberdeen University Press, 1936), p. 15.

and Physical Sciences and then began his ministry training at New College.

Darwinism

During Iverach's first year in Edinburgh, Darwin's *Origin of Species* was published. This was of great interest to Iverach who, while building his flourishing congregation at Ferryhill, continued to study science and philosophy in an effort to relate his faith to modern thought. This led, first, to one of his earliest publications, *The Ethics of Evolution Examined* (1884) and then, in 1894, to *Evolution and Christianity*. In 1899 he was invited to be the first Charles F. Deems Lecturer in New York, where he travelled with his daughter and was greatly impressed by the city and its people.

'The subject of my lectures is Theism in the light of present science and philosophy. I shall endeavor to look at the world with the eyes of science, as science sets forth for us the story of the world in the ages of the past and unfolds for us the magnificence of the world as it now is. I desire to learn from the masters of science what kind of world I live in, what has been its past history and what is its probable outlook. Having learned from science all that I can grasp, I may have to ask questions which science cannot answer – ultimate questions which science leaves to philosophy and theology; and we shall ask what is the present attitude of philosophy toward these – questions which science has left unsettled ... Science, so far as it goes, is the record of man's understanding of the world in which he lives and his mastery over it. I say so far as it goes; for great as have been its achievements and vast as have been its consequences, it only stands on the threshold of the world it has to conquer.'[2]

These lectures became the publication, *Theism in the Light of Present Science and Philosophy*.

In his essay 'Christian Faith and Unbelief in Modern Scotland', William Ferguson explains why Darwinism in Scotland was more easily accepted than elsewhere and talks of the role Iverach

2 Henry Mitchell Maccraken, *A Propaganda of Philosophy* (New York: F. H. Revell, 1914), p. 41.

played in that: 'In Scotland no one denomination or institution sought to monopolise learning. Diversity of views was possible, indeed inevitable, given the divisions of Scottish Presbyterianism that then existed. It is noticeable for instance that the new standards of biblical criticism and theological study came from the Free Church and the United Presbyterian Church in spite of opposition from the traditionalists who sought to cling to the Westminster Standards. Another factor that helps explain differing attitudes in England and Scotland was the wide range of courses needed for the Scottish University degree. This enabled many Scots theologians to be more appreciative of the work of scientists than was the case with many of their counterparts in England. Scottish Churchmen were also aware of the Scottish contributions to the new science. Thus Darwin's bombshell did not have the same devastating effect in Scotland as it had elsewhere. James Iverach, for example, a minister of the Free Church who had studied Maths and Physics, attempted to work out a modis vivendi between science and religion in such works as *The Ethics of Evolution Examined* (1884) and *Theism in the Light of Present Science and Philosophy* (1900). Iverach accepted Darwin's theory of natural selection as a useful hypothesis whilst rejecting the evolutionary Pantheism of Spencer and Haeckel.'[3]

Settled Years

In 1905 Iverach became the Principal of what was now the United Free Church of Scotland College. Yet again its future had been under discussion in the Church. 'Some felt that the maintenance of three colleges was more than the church should be asked to bear. On accepting the Principalship, Iverach's characteristic word was, "I might respectfully hint to my brethren that they should speak a little less of the college, and pray for it a good deal more."'[4]

---

3 Stewart J. Brown et al., *Scottish Christianity in the Modern World* (Edinburgh: T&T Clark, 2000), p. 82.

4 Alan P. F. Sell, *Defending and Declaring the Faith* (Exeter: Paternoster Press, 1987), p. 120.

In spite of this, the following years were settled ones for the College and most of the business documented in the minute books is concerned with arrangements for the opening and closing of teaching sessions, the timetables, the awarding of prizes and bursaries, and continual correspondence with Edinburgh regarding financial disagreement.

In August 1909, 'The Senatus record their deep sorrow at the death of one of their students, Mr Benjamin Maclean ... who lost his own life in attempting to save the life of another ... The Senatus record their sincere sympathy with the bereaved parents and family on this most sudden and lamented close of an exemplary and hopeful life.'[5]

It seems that he had saved a drowning lad on the shores of the Moray Firth and his bereaved fellow students arranged a memorial tablet for him which was placed on the stair wall of the College.

Alterations were constantly underway to the College building and sketches were submitted showing plans which would provide a smoking room for students. The Senatus Secretary of the time, Professor Cameron, pointed out that there was no money and a call went out to the Northern Presbyteries asking them to support the College. Three months later it is minuted that the smoking room for students had been completed at a cost of £15!

David Edwards, the Secretary of the Financial Board, who had been closely involved with all the legal ramifications connected with the aftermath of the Union of 1900, died in 1910. The Financial Board note this as follows: 'The Financial Board desire to place on record their sense of the loss they have sustained in the death of their secretary Mr David Edwards. In the ordinary administration of the finances of the College Mr Edwards always acted with tact, wisdom, skill and with knowledge. His great business knowledge was always at the service of the board. But in the crisis which ensued at the decision by the House of Lords, Mr Edwards' knowledge was of the highest value. In his evidence before the Royal Commission he set forth the state and destination of the funds of the College with clearness and with thorough

---

5 Senatus Minute Books, Vol. 2, p. 90.

knowledge … And in all the dealings with the Commission and the authorities of the United Free Church he may be said to have represented the interests of the College with the highest ability, tact and skill. He ever had at heart the interests of the College, was ever forward in its defence and ever ready to defend it in all attacks made on its continuance and efficiency. They express their sympathy with the widow and children of Mr Edwards in their sore bereavement and commend them to Him who is the husband of the widowed and the Father of the fatherless.'[6]

Mr James Hastings Edwards MA LLB of the firm Messrs Edmonds and Ledingham Advocates was appointed as the new Secretary and Treasurer, thus continuing the connection with the firm set up by Francis Edmond the same year that the College opened its doors.

Moderator

James Iverach became Moderator of the General Assembly of the United Free Church in 1912 and was the first to pay an official visit to the General Assembly of the Church of Scotland. 'He longed for union and he worked tirelessly on committees concerned with it.'[7]

A newspaper cutting of the time records: 'It is proposed that the ladies of Aberdeen belonging to the United Free Church give a present to Principal Iverach on the occasion of his Moderatorship of the General Assembly of the Church. The students – past and present – of the United Free Church College in Aberdeen are presenting him with the robes of his office; and the congregation of Ferryhill to which he belongs with the hood for the robes. A portrait of Principal Iverach has been painted by Mr Allan Sutherland. This portrait it is suggested would be a most fitting gift to Principal Iverach on this occasion by the ladies of Aberdeen and it is hoped they will contribute to this object. The following ladies are receiving contributions – Mrs Adam Maitland, Rubislaw Den House; Lady Fleming, Dalmunzie, Murtle; Mrs

6 Financial Board Minute Books, Vol. 3, p. 500.
7 Sell, p. 120.

Stalker, 20 Rubislaw Den South and Mrs George Adam Smith, Chanonry Lodge, Old Aberdeen.'[8]

The impressive full-length portrait is now housed in the Special Collection at Aberdeen University. This portrait features in correspondence between the Rev. Dr Henry Sefton, Master of the College in 1986, and a relative of Principal Iverach. This great-nephew, Iverach McDonald, was writing from Oxford requesting photographs of the portrait for himself, his son in Washington DC, a daughter in Stirlingshire and an Iverach cousin in New Zealand. Iverach McDonald was a journalist of international renown, one of the most respected foreign correspondents and editors of the post-war years. His early career was mostly spent in Communist countries for *The Times*. In his letter to Henry Sefton he says: 'Principal James Iverach was always a titanic figure to me as a boy; stories about him seemed unending. Espe-cially memorable was his last intervention in a General Assembly of 1921. He listened to brethren who in arguing against talks about union with the Established Church dwelt on old divisions and old declarations. James Iverach spoke only briefly. He was reminded, he said, of the Northern farmer whose horse and trap were nearly swept away one winter in a swollen river. In summer the horse shied at the same ford although the river was only a stream. "Toot, beastie," cried the farmer, "I doot yir memory's better than yir judgement!" My great uncle carried the Assembly with him it is said.'[9] This story is told almost word for word by George M. Reith, in *Reminiscences of The United Free Church General Assemblies*.[10]

On 8 October 1913 John A. Selbie, Professor of Old Testament, took on the role of Secretary of the Senatus and the minutes become easier to read. The previous Secretary, Professor George Cameron, was conservative in his use of paper and tried to get two lines of text into one line of space. He also had great trouble controlling ink flow and the minutes are scattered with blots and

8 *Aberdeen Press and Journal*, 10 May 1913, www.britishnewspaper archive.co.uk (accessed 05/03/2018).

9 Iverach McDonald writing to Rev. Dr Henry Sefton, Christ's College.

10 George M. Reith, *Reminiscences of The United Free Church General Assemblies (1900–1929)* (Edinburgh: Moray Press, 1933), p. 138.

scorings out. His sudden death was noted, along with a tribute to his 'devotion to duty, his affectionate and helpful consideration for the students ... a privilege to be close to one who walked so humbly with God'.[11]

The First World War

The lecture at the closing of the session in March 1914 given by Principal Iverach was entitled 'Truth and Freedom', and was delivered with an awareness of dark days ahead. War was declared in July but not mentioned in the minutes until the meeting on 7 October, when 'in response to a letter from Major Gordon of the Aberdeen Territorial Association it was agreed to grant the use of a room at 2 Alford Place for the use as a collecting and distributing depot for gifts for the military hospitals in town'.[12]

Just two weeks later, it was reported that two third-year students, Mr Forbes and Mr Knowles, had left to take up military service.[13]

D. S. Cairns writes, 'Into that period of prosperity there suddenly broke the storm of the war. Students had the momentous decision to make between the profession to which they had dedicated their lives and what seemed an imperative call to give their youth, and it might be, their lives, to the cause of justice and freedom.'[14]

On 16 November 1914, it was reported that Messrs Mackay, Crichton and Ross, fourth-year students who had originally intended to take up work in the guild camps, had abandoned that intention and had enlisted in the 4th Battalion of the Gordon Highlanders; and that Messrs Dey, Robertson and Thomson, also of the fourth year, and Mr Andrew Fraser of the second year had enlisted in the same battalion. Mr Cheyne, a third-year student, had after a month's service with the YMCA also enlisted in the

---

11 Senatus Minute Books, Vol. 1, p. 113.

12 Ibid., p. 119.

13 Ibid., p. 121.

14 D. S. Cairns, 'From Union to Union: 1900 to 1929', in *The Church College in Aberdeen* (Aberdeen: Aberdeen University Press, 1936), p. 20.

4th Battalion.[15] That session was closed with Principal Iverach delivering a lecture entitled 'Loyalty: British and German Ideals'.

In March 1915, while the Battle of Neuve Chapelle was raging, the minutes noted, 'A communication was read from Knox College Toronto inviting the Senatus to send a delegate to attend the ceremonies in connection with the dedication of the new building of the College next September. The Senatus regrets that none of its numbers finds it in his power to go as a delegate but resolve to send a congratulatory letter.'[16]

It isn't until 13 October 1915 that the inevitable is minuted.

'The Senatus note with deep sorrow that since their last meeting three students who had taken up Military Service have fallen on the field of battle: (Private) John Forbes Knowles on 5th May; (Sergeant) John Maclean Thomson on 22nd July; (Sergeant) John Keith Forbes on 25th September. The Senatus cherish grateful memories of all these students and desire to place on record their esteem for their attainments and high Xian [sic] character, as well as their appreciation of the conscientiousness and devotion to duty which have culminated in their laying down their lives in the cause of truth and righteousness.'[17]

One of the first to enlist had been the first to die. John Knowles was killed by a sniper's bullet near Ypres. 'His genial sunny temperament made Knowles a favourite with his fellow-students. His exceptional gifts as an elocutionist, combined with his scholarship, pointed to a distinguished career as a preacher. He was an active and successful worker in the Mission carried on by the U.F. students in the East end of Aberdeen.'[18]

His fellow student John Thomson suffered the same fate in the same place less than three months later. 'He was an excellent specimen of what used to be a common type of Scottish student who, faced by serious obstacles, contrived to make their way to a University and professional education ... A student of no mean attainments, he was also an athlete and in every sense a

15 Senatus Minute Books, Vol. 2, p. 123.

16 Ibid., p. 129.

17 Ibid., p. 133.

18 Mabel Desborough Allardyce, ed., Aberdeen University Roll of Honour 1921, www.abdn.ac.uk/library/roll-of-honour (accessed 05/03/2018).

"sportsman" and a "good fellow". His enthusiasm found vent equally in Mission work in the slums of Aberdeen, on the football field, and in the trenches.'[19]

Not long after, John Forbes fell at Hooge. 'A more versatile genius than Forbes never passed through Aberdeen U.F. College. A tireless walker, an intrepid mountaineer, a keen sportsman, a humorist, a skilled musician, a linguist, a scholar – no achievement seemed beyond his capacity. Even in the trenches he pursued his studies, and left behind him singularly able notes on the Book of Job, which to the last he studied in the Hebrew original, with the aid of the latest German commentary.'[20] His name had cropped up numerous times in the Senatus minutes as a winner of the Foote and Eadie prizes.

At the same meeting, 'Principal Iverach also fittingly expressed to Professor Stalker an assurance of the sympathy of his colleagues in the great loss he had sustained through the death of his son Lieut. Frank B. D. Stalker who recently fell in action in the Dardannelles.'[21]

In June 1916, 'It was reported that a conference had been held between Principal Iverach, Professors Stalker and Selbie of this College and Professors Cowan, Gilroy and Fulton, representing the Divinity Faculty of the University as to a possible fusion of classes next session. In view of the small number of students likely to attend and of the advantage of setting free some of the Professors for other service during at least part of the session.'[22] The following month Professor John Selbie, who was writing these minutes, lost his son, Colin, at Longueval. 'For Professors and students alike, the period must have been trying indeed. Two of the former had lost sons and for one reason or another the very few students left were exempted men, separated very unwillingly from their fellow youth.'[23]

The situation at King's College being much the same, the two decided to cooperate and joint teaching began. It was Professor

19 Ibid.
20 Ibid.
21 Senatus Minute Books, Vol. 2, p. 133.
22 Ibid, p. 143.
23 Cairns, p. 21.

Cowan of the Divinity Faculty at Aberdeen University who closed the next session with a lecture entitled 'The Christian Ministry and National Service'.

The minute books do not then keep an accurate record of those going to war and those killed; but later, when the erection of the war memorial is discussed, it becomes clear that eight current students and two former students had lost their lives. At the back of the Senatus minute book is a typed, fragile and browned letter dated 25 December 1917, which reads as follows:

Dear ...

In the name of the Senatus I send you the following message, with the cordial greetings of all the Professors. The message is being sent to all the eight surviving students who are on military service:

The Professors of the college are always thinking of the students who were members of the College when the war began and who in response to the call of God and of their country have gone forth to fight for freedom and righteousness and truth in our far-flung battle line.

They recall with sorrow and yet with thankfulness and pride the fact that many of them have made the supreme sacrifice and have given their lives for this great cause. This roll of honour is very large in proportion to our members and the names on it were those of men of the highest worth and of the greatest promise. We keep their names in everlasting remembrance, and we are persuaded that the public spirit and Christian devotedness of these men will prove an inspiration, a stimulus, and an incentive to duty to Professors and students of the College in all days to come.

The Professors are mindful also of those students of the College who are still bearing the burden of service in the active conduct of war. They feel that they can scarcely realise the conditions under which their students live and work on the battle front or in other fields of service; but they know enough to understand that the work of war demands the whole strength of body, soul and mind if it is to be well done. And they are persuaded that their students will be equal to the call. Those powers of thought and concentration which the Professors knew and appreciated in their students in happier times are now called forth and exercised in the strange work of war, and we are persuaded that the students will endure hardness like good soldiers of Jesus Christ. For work in this war, the Professors are well assured, is work for God, and those students have their share in filling up what is lacking of the sufferings of Christ for His body's sake.

The Professors have followed, with deep interest, your career in the army, and they rejoice that you have taken your full share in this heroic struggle. They pray that it might be yours to show, in the days to come as you have in the past, calmness and courage in the hour of danger, collectedness and presence of mind in all emergencies and a spiritual superiority over all opposing circumstances, which ought to be the quality of those who feel their life-work to be in harmony with the gracious purposes of the living God. We believe that in all possible issues it is well with you, but we pray that you may be preserved to return in safety, and that you will live and come back to place at the service of Christ and His Church the ripe experience of service in the Army, and so to help and guide the church in the great reconstructive work which lies before her in the future.

With affectionate remembrance and kindest regards.
I am, Yours very sincerely,
J. A. Selbie,
Secretary of Senatus.[24]

A total of 2,852 University staff, students and alumni served in the First World War, of whom 341 lost their lives. Their service spanned all branches of the Armed Forces. Many enlisted in the University's U Company of the 4th Gordons; others served with the Argyll & Sutherland, Seaforth, and Cameron Highlanders, as well as other army regiments and corps, the Royal Navy, the Royal Army Medical Service, and the fledgling Royal Flying Corps. They came from all walks of life, all professions and ages – the youngest to die was 18, the oldest was 66. Some died

---

24 Letter in Senatus Minute Books, Vol. 2.

in the first weeks of the war, while others, as a result of their experiences on the battlefield, lived on for some months after the armistice only to die after returning home. Many also returned to the University to continue their studies after the war, young men changed irrevocably by their experiences.[25]

For the complete biographies of nine of those commemorated on the College war memorial see Appendix A. There is no information about Ian Duncan Munro although he is listed as a former student.

After the War

The first post-war meeting of the Financial Board welcomed back its Secretary and Treasurer Mr James Hastings Edwards and congratulated him on his safe return after four and a half years in France.

Discussions were held regarding the war memorial for the students and a subcommittee was formed. It wasn't until October 1919 that the subcommittee reported that they had examined the building [Main Building Alford Place] and made the decision to 'erect a tablet in oak, the upper part of which would be an ornamental celtic brass and the lower part would be reserved for the names in gold letters of the fallen students and the tablet should be erected in the staircase wall'.[26] The dedication service took place on 9 March and 'Sir Thomas Jaffrey[27] very generously undertook to defray the whole cost of the memorial.'[28]

Immediately prior to the War, the Board had agreed to issue an appeal for the Student Dinner Fund. This was not issued and student dinners ceased for the war years. This was re-drafted and re-issued and student dinners were to recommence. It was also

---

25 Allardyce (accessed 05/03/2018).

26 Financial Board Minute Books, Vol. 2, p. 29.

27 Sir Thomas Jaffrey was a prominent citizen of Aberdeen. He worked at the North of Scotland Bank before moving to the Aberdeen Savings Bank in 1892, a post he held for thirty-seven years. He was knighted in the 1920 New Year Honours and created a Baronet in 1931.

28 Financial Board Minute Books, Vol. 4, p. 39.

agreed by the Board that they take over the telephone installed by the Territorial Army Forces Association in the College Library, so the College had its first phone.

There was a definite air of returning to business as usual, and the matter of the portrait of James Lumsden was raised again and finally resolved. The portrait 'had been injuriously affected by the sun shining on it through the west window of the hall'.[29] It was agreed that a curtain would be put over the portrait to keep it screened at all times except when the hall was in use. Soon after, Mr Alex Fraser of Aberdeen Art School repaired this and several other portraits for £30. The matter of the flagstaff, which had blown down in a recent storm, was not so easily resolved as Norwegian spars were unobtainable. The Board accepted that in future when the flag needed to be flown 'they should fix the staff to a chimney as was done on the day the armistice commenced'.[30]

Andrew Fordyce, the janitor, requested a pay rise and found his wages doubled to £104 per year.

Principal Iverach Resigns

In Sederunt 492 of the United Free Church College on 17 February 1920 appears the announcement: 'The College Committee desires to express its deep regret that feeling the burden of the years, the Rev. Principal James Iverach, D.D., Professor of New Testament Literature in Aberdeen College, desires to resign his Chair at next meeting of the General Assembly. Principal Iverach has served the Church with high distinction for the long period of fifty-one years. Ordained in 1869, he was appointed Professor of Apologetics at Aberdeen College in 1887 and Principal in 1905. In 1907 he was transferred to the Chair of New Testament Litera-ture. His books, *Is God Knowable?*, *Evolution and Christianity* and *Theism* were notable contributions to religious thought, and by numerous articles in dictionaries and periodicals he has main-tained his place among leading theologians of the day. Principal Iverach has a strong philosophical cast of mind. He is a serious

29 Ibid., p. 28.
30 Ibid.

thinker, and has approved himself a serious defender of the faith
... The Committee rejoices that Principal Iverach sees his way
to retain the Principalship and hopes he will be spared for many
years to be the Head of the College with which he has been so
long associated and to which his labours have added lustre.'[31]
The Assembly accepted his resignation and James A. Robertson
became Professor of New Testament.

The lack of money in the Student Dinner Fund continued to be
a source of consternation to the Board and there was great confusion regarding the Dinner Fund money being accredited to the
No. 8 Alford Place account. Purchased in 1896, No. 8 had been
let out but was a constant drain on finances. It was suggested
that this be sold. At a Board meeting chaired by Principal Iverach
on 15 September 1921, the secretary, Mr Edwards, reported the
steps he had taken to sell the property and then read the following letter from Professor Stalker on the subject.

'Have you found a customer for the house beside the College?
In reading the advertisement at the door of the house, I have been
allowing my mind to think of the position of theological education
in Aberdeen five or six years hence when the two churches will be
united. It may not be known to the non Professorial members of
the committee what provision for the same presently exists at the
Old Town. It is of the most wretched description. The classrooms
are large, dingy and draughty. There are only one or two of them
for all subjects and the only senate room is so small as to hardly
afford standing room when all the Professors are present. I have
been informed that during the war there was a movement among
the Established Church students to petition for the teaching of
all classes at our college where every class has a separate room
and the size of the room just about what might be expected to
be required. In the present rapid extension of the subjects at the
University there would be a hungry desire for rooms at King's
if theology vacated them. The principle [sic] thing to consider
is the position to be held by theology on the United Church and
there is no likelihood whatever of it securing accommodation in

---

31 Senatus Minute Books, 'Sederunt 492 of the United Free Church
College on the 17th of February 1920', inserted at Vol. 2, p. 173.

Old Aberdeen. Our buildings on the contrary on account of the admirable site would form an ornamental addition to the University plant and would, I should think, be regarded as a valuable asset by the university authorities. Only it makes very questionable any diminution though the sale at the current time is of course a tempting way out of difficulty.'[32]

Professor Cairns pointed out that the vital matter was the state of the Student Dinner Fund, but he was overruled and it was unanimously resolved not to sell the house.

The last minute of that meeting resolved to give the janitor, Andrew Fordyce, a bonus of £10 to enable him to take a holiday. During Principal Iverach's time the employment conditions of the janitor had been greatly improved!

This turned out to be Iverach's last meeting as ill health prevented him from further attendance. At the following meeting it was announced that the Rev. Dr Miller of Buckie, a member of the Financial Board, had left £100 to the Student Dinner Fund which relieved the situation temporarily.

Death of the Principal

James Iverach died on 6 August 1922 and Professor Stalker gave the following tribute on 18 August.

'Principal Iverach's long experience of College administration obtained under Principal Brown and Principal Salmond prepared him for the duties to which he was appointed as Principal in 1905 and it was not difficult for one who at the University had distinguished himself as a mathematician to learn to deal with figures and the details of business. While he delighted in being associated with such veterans as Sir William Henderson and Mr Thomas Ogilvie, he drew round him younger men likely to be interested in the welfare of the College, and in presiding at meetings, he was always genial and good humoured. It was a remarkable demonstration of the versatility of his mind and the variety of his acquirements when in 1907 for the convenience of

---

32 Financial Board Minute Books, Vol. 4, p. 57.

the College he passed from one chair to another showing himself a master in the whole field of Theology. When, during the war, the teaching forces of the Church of Scotland and the United Free Church were combined, he threw himself with his whole heart into the arrangement looking at the experiment as a foretaste of the union of these denominations to which he was ardently looking forward. The losses sustained by the College in the war deeply affected his heart and he denounced the idolatry of the state out of which the aggression of Germany had arisen, yet he was proud of the heritage which the College had acquired with the heroism of those who had gone to the front and especially of those who had made the great sacrifice.

'While ever zealous for the cultivation of scholarship in all branches he never ceased to set before his students as the goal of all their training that they should be powerful preachers of the Gospel and he set them an example not only by being, to the end, a powerful preacher himself but by loving the Gospel which he preached. The loss to his family is all the more poignant because his qualities shone with special lustre in the home and the members of the financial board in sending to the bereaved this expression of sympathy commend them earnestly and affectionately to the God of all comfort and consideration.'[33]

The Senatus minutes record a similar memorial message but add, 'His Colleagues also retain grateful memories of those conversations with the late Principal in the Senatus Room between classes, which were so illuminating. They admired him as a quiet and good man and loved him as a true friend.'[34]

33 Ibid, p. 71.
34 Senatus Minute Books, Vol. 3, p. 18.

6

David Smith Cairns,
the last 'Principal'
1923-37

David Smith Cairns had been teaching Systematic Theology in the College from 1907, and became Principal in 1923 following the death of James Iverach. He led the college through crucial years in its history and remains one of its most distinguished Principals. He was also the last 'Principal'.

He was born in 1862 in Stitchil, Roxburghshire, his father being the village United Presbyterian Church minister. Following his Arts degree in Edinburgh, Cairns went to New College for his Theology studies. He was ordained in 1892 and was a parish minister in Ayton, Berwickshire until his appointment to the chair of Dogmatics and Apologetics at the United Free Church College in Aberdeen. He was deeply committed to church work and played a leading role in the historic World Missionary Conference in Edinburgh in 1910. He was also one of the main speakers of the Student Christian Movement which saw him travelling extensively in America and China. His journey with religion was not always straightforward and twice he had a crisis of faith. D. M. Baillie in the introduction to Cairns' autobiography writes, 'The first was concerned with the stern Calvinism of his background and inheritance and his reaction against it. It began with a great period of misery and gloom, from which he was delivered by reading a simple little book of evangelical outlook which brought home to him the unchanging love of God even for those who neither love Him or believe in Him. At this time, Cairns was still a boy at school but he never ceased to think with gratitude of that obscure little book, and he looked back upon this experience as in some sense his conversion.'[1] The second episode came when he was an undergraduate Arts student at university and was more keenly felt than the first. 'I have a vivid snapshot of myself standing beneath a flaring gas-jet in my bedroom at Lonsdale Terrace, absolutely dismayed. How did I really *know* that anything in that inherited theology, or such a construction of it as I had made, was *true* – what *reason* had I for believing in God or Christ or immortality? I entered then a long dark tunnel of my life from which I only gradually emerged.'[2] It was three years before he was well enough to resume his studies but he did not regard those years as wasted: he travelled and taught and 'he was reading and thinking hard, wrestling with his intellectual problems, working out his faith'.[3]

During his time at Ayton, David married Helen Wilson Craw, daughter of a neighbouring gentleman farmer. Their marriage was very happy and their children Alison and David were born at the Manse in Ayton. Sadly Helen became ill while they were there, and although she had three years with her family after their move to Aberdeen her illness was serious and she died in 1910.

First Lady Student

David Cairns' reputation attracted many students to the College and in 1910, following the Conference in Edinburgh, Aberdeen United Free Church College welcomed its first female student, Caroline Macdonald. When she met Cairns in Edinburgh Caroline was already a respected pioneer with the YWCA in Japan.

Annie Caroline Macdonald was born in Ontario in 1874. Her grandparents were Scottish and her upbringing was steeped in the Presbyterian tradition. Her mother was a founder of the Women's Foreign Missionary Society of the local church. 'Caroline became

---

1 David Cairns, *David Cairns: An autobiography* (London: SCM Press, 1950), p. 10.

2 Ibid., p. 11.

3 Ibid.

active in the Young Women's Christian Association (YWCA), which was at that time an interdenominational evangelical organization that encouraged educated Christian women to work for "the regeneration of society".[4] At the age of 30 she responded to an appeal from the World's Committee of the YWCA to begin an outreach to non-Christian women in Tokyo. Her biographer, Margaret Prang, states that she went to Japan 'with some ease since she had grown up in a family, a church and a student milieu where interest in foreign missions was strong, and had herself been presenting the claims of the mission field to Canadian students. There is no record of conflict or hesitation surrounding her decision.'[5]

Caroline immersed herself in the language and culture and was soon able to teach Bible classes and English literature in a college, and established YWCAs in other places. YWCA secretaries were able to take leave and return home for a furlough period every five years. Caroline's parents were now in London so she spent some time there and also travelled home to Ontario. She attended meetings in New York and a conference in Berlin before travelling to Edinburgh for the World Missionary Conference as an observer for the YWCA. 'To be present at the most representative gathering in the history of Protestant Christianity was an exhilarating experience, not least because of the presence of delegates from eighteen of the "younger churches" in Africa and Asia and for the resolve of the conference to persevere in organised cooperation with the task of evangelising the world. Some of those present including John R. Mott, the mastermind of the conference, realised they were making history in a meeting that would prove to be the beginning of the modern ecumenical movement.'[6]

Caroline decided she wanted to spend some time during her furlough in study, and having heard David Cairns at the Conference she discussed this wish with him. He encouraged her to come to

---

4 John P. Vaudry, 'A. Caroline Macdonald of Japan', https://www. renewal-fellowship.ca/93 (accessed 18/07/2018).

5 Margaret Prang, *A Heart at Leisure from Itself: Caroline Macdonald of Japan* (Vancouver: UBC Press, 1995), p. 19.

6 Ibid., p. 68.

Aberdeen and study at the United Free Church College, 'assuring her that, although no woman had ever done so she would be welcomed'.[7] Her time in Aberdeen was documented in great detail in letters to her sister Peg. She was surprised that her coming to the College had evoked such a great deal of interest and 'even the local press had heard of the lady student who proposed to study theology'. The first lecture she attended was delivered by James Stalker, Professor of Church History, who opened with 'Miss Macdonald and gentlemen'. She was in the midst of these 'gentlemen' for two weeks before they invited her to dine with them. Cairns was always mindful of the Student Dinner Fund which enabled all the college students to dine together at 1pm in the hall where the meal was served to them. He had asked Caroline to join them at this daily dinner but she had suggested she wait until her fellow students issued the invitation so that they would see that she 'had no ambition of intruding'. When she walked into the hall that day she was met with vociferous clapping. She learned later that some of the students had been very against allowing a lady to join them for their daily dinner.

Caroline attended two classes delivered by David Cairns. She enjoyed them immensely and after the 'sheer exhilaration of three hours of lectures in the morning and a good deal of reading she was sure she looked ten years younger'.[8] In her letters Caroline talked frequently of David Cairns and Sunday visits to his home after church to share lunch with him, his children and his sister Jessie who, following the death of his wife, was helping him bring up Alison and David. Caroline describes Dr Cairns to her sister as having a 'clear cut face. He's something of a mystic order and when he begins lecturing ... his hands go through his hair and he draws down his brow and rubs his eyes (he sits when he lectures) and then you are off into the realms of the space where he has gone peering in to see if you can get even a faint vision of what he sees so *clearly*.'[9]

---

7 Ibid., p. 70.
8 Ibid., p. 73.
9 Ibid., p. 74.

Caroline's three months in Aberdeen came to an end in December, and she recounted that the 'theologicals' had given her a great send-off and sang, 'For she's a jolly good fellow'.[10]

Cairns became a lifelong friend and correspondent. He visited her in Japan in 1927 when he was on a Far East lecture tour accompanied by his daughter Alison.

Caroline returned to Tokyo and found her path changing as she became more and more involved with prisoners and prisons following the imprisonment of one of her Bible class students who had murdered his wife and children. She resigned from the YWCA secretary position in 1915 after ten years of service, and started a type of freelance ministry trusting that God would supply her financial needs.

Margaret Prang writes, 'She was convinced that she must learn more about prison work and services to ex-prisoners and their families elsewhere. Her reading and her contacts with Americans in Tokyo persuaded her that in the United States she would find the most advanced models of prison reform and other social services.' Caroline came to believe that 'the cause of crime is the neglect of children'.

Ill health came to Caroline early in 1931 and she returned to Canada to be with her family. She had lung cancer and died in July, a truly remarkable lady who became known in Japan as 'the White Angel of Tokyo'.

Famous Alumni

In 1911, the year after Caroline attended the College, there were two more overseas students from Spain and Austria, who were well known. From Cadiz came Pastor José Felices, who spent only

10 Ibid., p. 76.

a year at the College before departing to Buenos Aires where he was appointed to St Andrew's Scots Kirk. His job was to develop the Spanish work of the Church, holding services in Spanish and starting Spanish Sunday Schools. His mission brought numerous adults and children from many nationalities into the Church.

From Austria came Joseph Luki Hromádka, who had been attracted to Aberdeen to study under the 'strong influence of David S. Cairns. He was impressed by the biblical piety and missionary zeal of Cairns and the Scottish Church.'[11] This led to another lifelong friendship and further notable visits to the College which will be described in Chapter 9.

Hromádka later went on to be a much-beloved Professor of Theology at Princeton Theological Seminary, having been forced to leave his native Czechoslovakia because of his opposition to German Nazism. 'On his return home in 1947, he became a controversial figure for urging reconciliation between Christians and Communists. He became a founding member of the World Council of Churches at the Conference in Amsterdam in 1948. He was also founder and chairman of the Christian Peace Conference, an organisation which served as a vehicle for Christian–Marxist dialogue and communication between Christians in the East and West, and he received the Lenin Peace Prize in 1958.'[12]

Papers for War Time

In 1914 David Cairns contributed to a series of pamphlets called 'Papers for War Time' where he made his stance clear. He was not a pacifist but he felt strongly that the brutality of war should be renounced.

'A man and his wife are sitting peacefully talking together in Antwerp in the quiet of an autumn night. No formal investment or warning of bombardment has been given. A zeppelin sails

---

11 Jan Milic Lochman, 'Josef Hromádka: Ecumenical Pilgrim', Princeton Seminary Bulletin, 1999, http://journals.ptsem.edu/id/PSB1999201/dmd008 (accessed 05/03/2018).

12 Charles West, *Hromádka: Theologian of the Resurrection*, https://worldview.carnegiecouncil.org/archive/worldview (accessed 05/03/2018).

in in the darkness, drops its bomb beside them, and all that is left of them is a falling drizzle of blood. Beside them hundreds are maimed or slain. Again, in a great French city, far from the battlefield, a little girl is playing beside her nurse. A "Dove" sails in overhead, there is a loud explosion, and what remains is a dead woman and a little wailing heap of crippled humanity. The doer of this deed, a strong and bold youth, sails away in triumph to receive military honours and the plaudits of an admiring people. Had that people been in its senses it would have hanged him, and repented in anguish and tears the deed that had stained the honour of a great nation.'[13]

In her *Intellectual Biography of David Smith Cairns*, Marlene Finlayson writes, 'For Cairns, atheism was a nobler thing than a religion that saw such actions as part of God's plan for the world, and he averred that, "If our country is going to do such things and make us complicit in them, then shall we renounce our country and seek admission to some nobler State." ... For Cairns, war was an aberration from God's will by one or more parties. Christians who believed that it was inevitable because of sin indulged in a self-fulfilling prophecy that was tantamount to saying that God must accept defeat of his Kingdom in this world. Because sin endured in the world, it did not mean that war was inevitable. He reminded his readers that at one time slavery had seemed a necessity. In the case of war, people needed to understand that "there is something ignominious and brutal in its very essence". He concluded by calling on the Church to preserve what was noble in patriotism, and to provide a "moral equivalent for war" in promoting the struggle to establish the Kingdom of God. War was a failure to live up to the Christian ideal, and the answer to militarism would only be found in the active embracing of the values of the Kingdom of God, which transcended all national boundaries, and provided the basis for all human morality. The quest for world peace as obedience to Kingdom values was now firmly established in the social dimension of his theology. For him, the end did not justify the means, and the bombing of civil-

---

13 David Cairns, *An Answer to Bernhardi*, Papers for War Time, No.12 (London: Oxford University Press, 1914).

ians and the practice of espionage were intrinsically reprehensible practices.'[14]

Due to the decision between the Divinity Faculty and the United Free Church College to share teaching in view of the small numbers of students, David Cairns was able to go into full-time war work in 1916 in the YMCA camps in France. His children Alison and David were living with his sister Jessie in Edinburgh where the extended family provided a stable and loving setting for the children, then aged fourteen and twelve.

Cairns led a YMCA interdenominational inquiry looking at the effects of this war on the religious life of the nation and attitudes towards the Church. 'When the men were questioned, it became clear that the main causes for their disengagement from the Churches were their denominational divisions, their failure to meet the social and physical needs of working people, and the perceived selfishness and materialism of church members. It was also clear that the men lacked much understanding of Christianity, raising concern about the quality of the religious teaching they had received.'[15]

The report, *The Army and Religion,* was published in 1919 and became one of D. S. Cairns' most important works. He speaks of the Churches' failure to engage with the young men at the Front and the feeling from them that the churches in general could have done more to prevent the war. Cairns was hopeful that much could be learned to enable the Church to be more effective in modern post-war times.

'The report noted an awakening of conscience throughout Christendom, in which attitudes to war were changing, partly due to the scale and horror of the recent conflict, but also because of "a deepening sense of individual freedom, of the rights of human personality" and to the idea that these will prove to be incompatible with militarism.

'The whole structure of world society has become so interwoven that world war is an anachronism. Mankind cannot

---

14 Marlene Elizabeth Finlayson, *An Intellectual Biography of David Smith Cairns,* Thesis, Edinburgh University, www.era.lib.ed.ac.uk/handle/1842/11739, p. 156 (accessed 01/09/2017).

15 Ibid., p. 239.

face the repetition of such things unless it is prepared to face dissolution. The men who used to think that world peace is an impracticable ideal are beginning to see that the alternative way is impracticable also.'[16]

Cairns' years at the front had shown him the conditions and sacrifices of the fighting men, so when he was awarded an OBE for his war work he commented that he felt that 'something especially irrelevant had befallen me'.[17]

The Calm Before the Storm

Following the death of Principal James Iverach on 6 August 1922, the following General Assembly appointed David Cairns as the fifth Principal of the Aberdeen College. His induction by the Presbytery took place on 10 October and on that day he delivered his first opening lecture as Principal entitled 'Theology and Life'.

At the same time he was also Moderator of the General Assembly of the United Free Church, and the Senatus agreed that 'Mr Niven of Causewayend would conduct the work of his classes every Monday'.[18]

Through Senatus minutes and Financial Board minutes it becomes clear that Principal Cairns was concerned with raising the standards of living for students and Professors alike. Meetings were held on a more regular basis and the Financial Board agreed to a memorandum from the Colleges Committee in Edinburgh for salaries to be brought into line with what had been set at the General Assembly in 1900. 'The Board, while agreeing to the proposals were of the opinion that there is no reason why the Principal and Professors of Aberdeen College should not receive salaries of the same amount as the Principal and Professors in the other colleges and resolves the right to raise it in the future.'[19] Married Professors at other colleges were to be paid £708 per annum while the Aberdeen staff were only receiving £680.

16 Ibid., p. 169.
17 Ibid., p. 180.
18 Senatus Minute Books, Vol. 3, p. 26.
19 Financial Board Minute Books, Vol. 4, p. 104.

In 1924 Professor Stalker, Chair of Church History and Christian Ethics and Practical Training, resigned and was replaced by the Rev. Adam Fyfe Findlay. He was welcomed to the Senatus. At the same meeting Professor Cairns told the Senatus that 'the widow of the late Professor McEwan of New College, Edinburgh had presented through him to the College a handsome table used by her husband which has now been placed in the Senatus Room where it will be a great service'.[20] The table had originally belonged to Principal Cairns' late uncle, Principal Cairns of New College.

The practice of sharing the opening and closing lectures with the Divinity Faculty, which had started during the war, continued but had never been clarified. At a Senatus meeting on 14 October 1926 it was agreed that in future the rotation should be fixed and the lectures alternate. When it was the turn of the United Free Presbyterian College these were to be delivered in King's Chapel at the University and when it was the turn of the Church of Scotland Divinity Faculty at the University they were to be delivered in the College. This was the first major cooperation between the two bodies.

In February 1927 Principal Cairns asked the Senatus to release him for the remainder of the session to enable him to visit the mission stations and educational institutes in Manchuria. Travelling with his daughter Alison, he was able to spend a week with Caroline Macdonald in Japan. The Rev. Niven was to undertake his classes again. At the next meeting in October his safe return was welcomed and he was congratulated by his colleagues on the success of his mission in the Far East.

Later that month, a special Senatus meeting was held to discuss the Library. The Rev. William Cruickshank, the Librarian, reported that he had made an examination of the Brown Lindsay collection and part of the Thomson Library (see Chapter 1). He was 'very cordially thanked for the pains he had taken to collect so much valuable information'.[21]

---

20 Senatus Minute Books, Vol. 3, p. 36.
21 Ibid., p. 69.

The Library was in future to be made accessible for reading to ministers other than those of the United Free Church at an annual cost of five shillings.

It wasn't until the beginning of the following year that '[t]he librarian reported that an expert sent by Thins, Edinburgh had finished a valuation of the whole contents of the Library. This was ordered to be kept in retertis by the Librarian.'[22] There must have been items of considerable value as the Principal was then going to confirm with the Financial Board regarding getting a safe to store them and looking at an 'adjustment of insurances'. The work on the Library must have taken its toll on Rev. Cruickshank as he had to resign in November 1928 due to serious trouble with his eyes. The Library continued to be discussed at each Senatus meeting with additional material constantly being added.

Meanwhile, the Financial Board was taken up with the usual problems of the Professors' salaries, having been told by Edinburgh that there was not enough in the funds available to maintain the stabilised salaries so the Colleges would have to subsidise these. On a lighter note they dealt with a request by the Post Office to place a telephone kiosk on the west side of the main College building. The Board agreed to this and requested a minimum rent of 5/- a year. This was not acceptable to the Post Office and despite their lack of funds the Financial Board eventually accepted a rental of 1/-. This remained the same until 1984 when the equivalent value was 5 pence a year.

The Great Union

Page 89 of the third volume of Senatus Minutes begins, 'The following minutes are subsequent to the union of the United Free Church with the Church of Scotland consummated at Edinburgh on the 2nd October 1929.'[23]

---

22 Ibid., p. 72.
23 Ibid., p. 89.

This Union was primarily facilitated by the passing by the British Parliament of the Church of Scotland Act 1921 which recognised the full independence of the Church in spiritual matters. The further hurdle concerning property and endowments was sorted in 1925.

The minutes of the meeting on 10 October state that 'as arranged by the Union Committee, the work in this College is meanwhile to be conducted on the same lines, separately from the classes controlled by the Divinity Faculty of the University'.[24]

However, that status quo was not long lasting and, while the Union had been remarkably straightforward and cordial, the resulting discussion between the Aberdeen College and the University of Aberdeen became considerably more complex and acrimonious.

Meetings or 'conferences' were taking place with the Divinity Faculty regarding 'joint' classes and agreement was finally reached about the fees and finances for the students.

On 31 March, page 109 of the minute book, the scribe changes from years of J. A. Selbie to the most neat, precise but difficult-to-read script of Adam Fyfe Findlay. The following meeting has the Senatus tribute to John Selbie who died at the end of April: '[H]e gave himself with such unselfish devotion to the work entrusted to him that his going has left the College immeasurably poorer. The Senatus gratefully remember his gifts of learning and insight into the word of God ... and acknowledge the warm sympathy and the individual care which he exercised in dealing with his students, by whom he was honoured and loved, not less for the humility and friendliness of his nature than for the clarity and helpfulness of his teaching.'[25]

A letter was read from the Education for the Ministry Committee in Edinburgh recommending that the Old Testament teaching of Professor Selbie be taken over by Professor Gilroy at the University, 'in view of the proposed amalgamation of our Colleges with the University Divinity Faculties'.[26]

---

24 Ibid., p. 90.
25 Ibid., p. 111.
26 Ibid., p. 112.

Then the Fight Begins

At this point the name 'Mr Butchart', Secretary to the University, crops up frequently as the University looks into the situation with the College. In the Senatus meeting of 19 November 1931, the committee read a letter from solicitors Messrs Davidson and Garden which had been received by the Financial Board. Mr Butchart had contacted the solicitors suggesting that it was the right of the University Court to claim the funds left to the College by Mr Thomson of Banchory, 'in consequence of the fact that no appointment had been made to the chair which had become vacant on the death of Professor Selbie. The University Court has expressed the opinion that as the College was not now in a position to provide a full course of training to students for the ministry, as stated in the papers of the Thomson bequest and therefor, "The monies fall to be conveyed and made over to the University of Aberdeen."'[27]

The reply from Secretary James H. Edwards makes the College position quite clear. 'I am instructed to say in reply that the opinion expressed by the University Court seems to rest on a misapprehension of the true state of affairs. The decision of the General Assembly of the Church in May last not to make an appointment to the chair occupied by the late Professor Selbie was due solely to the desire not to complicate the arrangements which will fall to be made when on the passing of the University Bill measures are taken to institute a larger faculty of divinity in the University.'[28]

The Secretary goes on to expand the explanation, citing the facts that Professor Gilroy had been paid by church funds to continue Professor Selbie's teaching and that on his untimely death the same arrangement was put in place with the Rev. Stiven. 'It is accordingly, not the case that the Church College in Aberdeen no longer provides a full training for its students.

'Further may I respectfully point out that the question as to whether the Church College provides a full training for its students is one for the Church and not for the University Court.

27 Ibid., p. 125.
28 Ibid., p. 127.

'I am accordingly instructed to inform you that in the judgement of the College Authorities the claim of the University for the reversion of the monies under the Thomson Trust is not well founded and to express the hope that in view of the facts I have stated the claim will be withdrawn.'[29]

Early in 1932 the announcement from the conference between the two committees for training for the ministry came, suggesting that there should be six chairs at St Andrews and seven at Aberdeen. Also, 'This Committee after some discussion, agreed that – On the passing of the Universities (Scotland) Bill, the University Theological staffs and the College staffs at Edinburgh, Glasgow and Aberdeen should be amalgamated.'[30]

The College responded that they wished the chairs to be: Hebrew and Old Testament Literature and Theology; New Testament Language, Literature and Theology, Practical Training; and two each in Systematic Theology and Church History. They also confirmed that the College could be altered and reconstructed at a much smaller cost than building a new College.

Business continued much as normal, with bursaries, grants and prizes being awarded and appointments being made for the Thomson and Warwick lectures. In September 1933 Principal Cairns wrote to the Committee on Training for the Ministry requesting the committee's help with the ongoing discussions surrounding the place of teaching after the amalgamation of the University Divinity Faculty and the Church of Scotland College.

At a meeting of the Senatus on 2 November 1933, 'Professor Robertson reported the great satisfaction which was felt by the Senatus and students of the College of the honour done to the Principal by the University of Edinburgh in bestowing on him the degree of Doctor of Divinity on the occasion of the 350th anniversary of the University.'[31]

It wasn't long before the University Secretary upset the Senatus again by writing to all the College students, 'Dear Sir, With reference to your attendance at Divinity classes this session, I have to inform you that all students studying for the degree of B.D. are

---

29 Ibid., p. 129.
30 Ibid., p. 132.
31 Ibid., p. 155.

required to pay an inclusive fee of £42, payable in three annual instalments of £14 each, in addition to the matriculation fee of £2.2/- which you paid this session.'[32]

This caused panic among the students. They approached Professor Findlay who reassured them that the matter would be dealt with by the Senatus. It did so with a three-page letter reminding the University Secretary of the agreement reached previously concerning the finances of joint teaching which made this demand erroneous. 'In the past three sessions our College students have attended the united Divinity classes, whether held at King's College or at the College, Alford Place, on these agreed conditions and although in that period several of our students were studying for the B.D. degree no question of this obligation to pay the inclusive fee of £42 was ever mooted.'[33]

At the next meeting the Secretary of the Senatus reported that he had received a letter from the University Secretary accepting the previously agreed conditions.

At the Senatus meeting on 24 April 1934, 'The Principal reported with reference to the future place of teaching the Divinity classes after the amalgamation of the College with the University that the Committee on Training for the Ministry under Dr Frew were to recommend to the General Assembly that a special committee should be appointed to negotiate with the Aberdeen University Court as to the place of teaching.'[34]

The College Under Threat Again

In October 1934 the Principal received a request from Mr Butchart to 'set forth the views of the Senatus with reference to the future place of teaching the Theological classes'.[35]

In a document of about 2,000 words the College obliged, outlining the importance of keeping the teaching in the Alford Place College (part of this is recorded in Appendix B).

---

32 Ibid., p. 157.
33 Ibid., p. 158.
34 Ibid., p. 166.
35 Ibid., p. 175.

The University came back with a proposal to erect a new building in Old Aberdeen at a cost of £13,000 where all the theological teaching would take place.

'Principal Cairns said the Senatus objection to this was two, constitutional and practical. Dealing within the first, the fundamental objection was that there would be complete absorption of the College in the university and the building at Old Aberdeen would be part of King's College and not a separate College with a Principal at its head as was the case in Edinburgh, Glasgow and St. Andrews. The practical objection is that there is a strong feeling not just in the Senatus but in the Presbytery that the teaching of Divinity and the training of students could be carried out more effectively in the College at Alford Place than in a building in Old Aberdeen. Professor Findlay said that the University Court had stated 3 reasons why the teaching should be given in a building at Kings College.

1 It was very desirable that the divinity school should be near King's College Chapel.
2 It was desirable that the students should share in the full current of university life.
3 It was desirable that the University Divinity Faculty should not be housed in a Church College.'[36]

The Board agreed the following answers:

1 That the attendance at the daily service in King's College Chapel was only 30–40 out of the students' strength of 500. Moreover it was proposed that if Alford Place is to be reconstructed, to have a chapel there.
2 The only university life outside the classroom is at Marischal College and it would be as easy for students at Alford Place to go to Marischal is it would from King's.
3 If the teaching was to be at Alford Place it would be proposed that a new name be given to the College and this College as an integral part of the university system, although owned by the

---

36 Financial Board Minute Books, Vol. 4, p. 192.

Church, would house the University Faculty of Divinity. There has been no difficulty in Edinburgh and Glasgow. Students of all denominations, particularly post graduates, attend the classes at New College, Edinburgh and Trinity College Glasgow.[37]

It seems that the College was right not to accept the proposed new building as it turned out that it was going to house many other offices and classrooms with only a few reserved for the teaching of Divinity. The University intended to dispense with a College janitor and saw no need for provision of a College dining room; students were to eat in Elphinstone Hall.

On 10 May 1935 a lengthy document was minuted at a Senatus meeting to be sent to the Committee of the General Assembly under Dr Frew which was negotiating with the University Court. 'We feel that our position in opposing the proposals to make King's College the one seat of all theological training in Aberdeen may very easily be misunderstood by those not intimately acquainted with the locality. It may well seem to them that the mere site of such teaching is a matter of altogether secondary importance and that our sustained opposition and our preference for the Alford Place site is due to mere conservatism and denominational preference.'[38]

It appears that the Church Committee had been coming round to the University's way of thinking, as the 5,000-word document stating the case closes with: 'We believe that a sacrifice so unnecessary and unjustifiable on the part of the church would shock the feeling and thought of very many of the best of the people of the North East of Scotland. We have good reason to believe that there is strong feeling among representatives of the civic and business life of the city against the proposals to make King's College the centre of the teaching. We need hardly refer again to the unanimity of the Presbytery but we submit that we have here an expression of the local feeling that the Church can hardly ignore. The college has its roots deep in the past of the city as well as of

37 Ibid.
38 Senatus Minute Books, Vol. 3, p. 204.

its present. It is regarded with affection and reverence by present and past students and we believe that its forcible disappearance against the considered judgement and the common will of so large and so representative a body of its ministers and citizens is something to which the Church ought not to give its consent. We have tried to show in this memorandum that there is here something which is worth preserving, which there is no adequate reason for throwing away and which in the future may be of the greatest value to the reunited Church of Scotland.'[39]

Strong words which saved the College.

In 1936 the Financial Board and the Senatus were given the 'Report of the Special Committee on the site of Theological teaching at Aberdeen'. A compromise was being put forward which suggested that the academic teaching required for the BD degree would be given at King's and all teaching specifically for church purposes would be based at the College site in Alford Place.

'After a full discussion, the Board approved of the memorandum.'[40]

So again the history of the 1850s Aberdeen Church College changed direction. Although the governing bodies hadn't achieved their initial proposals they had, against heavy odds, managed to retain a College at Alford Place.

Laws of Livingstonia

At what was to be the last meeting of the body known as the Senatus, a letter was read from Miss Laws, daughter of the late Very Reverend Robert Laws of Livingstonia. 'A bronze plaque was being presented by the natives of Nyasaland as a memorial to her father in Livingstonia, and offering to present to the College a bronze coloured replica of the plaque with suitable inscription. The Secretary was instructed to write to Miss Laws expressing the deep gratitude of the Senatus for her very kind offer and stating that they would count it a great honour to have the replica of the

---

39 Ibid., p. 220.
40 Financial Board Minute Books, Vol. 4, p. 216.

plaque as a memorial to Dr Laws who for a time had a been a student in the college.'[41]

Robert Laws was born in Aberdeen in 1851, son of a cabinet maker. He was educated at the Free East Church School, Aberdeen, then became an apprentice cabinet maker while studying in the evenings for university entrance qualifications. He read Arts and Medicine at the University of Aberdeen, and attended Hebrew classes at the Free Church College. His Theology was actually studied later in Edinburgh along with further classes in Medicine. In 1875 he was ordained by the Presbytery of Aberdeen, having graduated in Edinburgh with a MB ChB, and the same year was appointed as a missionary of the Free Church of Scotland Mission, to be sent to Livingstonia, Nyasaland (now Malawi).

Laws joined the new mission as a medical officer but just two years later found himself heading up the Mission where he stayed until his retirement in 1927. He married his Aberdeen church sweetheart, Margaret Troup Gray, in Blantyre, Nyasaland in 1879. Their only surviving child, Amelia – the Miss Laws who was to offer the plaque to the College – joined the nursing forces in France in the First World War. She later returned to Edinburgh and studied medicine, becoming a doctor in 1930. The Livingstonia Mission was a great success and many College graduates have worked there over the years. Robert Laws developed a Christian community of 60,000 including African pastors, and founded over 700 schools which, on his death, were educating 44,000 pupils. In 1928 he received the Freedom of the City of Aberdeen. He died in London in August 1934 and is buried in St Machar's Cathedral churchyard in Old Aberdeen, which now also houses the bronze plaque.

The discussion of the plaque drew to a close the final meeting of the Senatus. Written in red at the end of the page is: 'The above minute is the last of the College Senatus and with the following begin the minutes of the College Council.'[42]

---

41 Senatus Minute Books, Vol. 3, p. 50.
42 Ibid.

Name Change

On 29 June 1936 it is minuted that the General Assembly accepted the Report of the Special Committee on the site of theological teaching at Aberdeen. The report is copied out in full in the minute book, with blanks left for the name of the College which was later agreed to become Christ's College. Other names proposed were St Devenick's College or Emmanuel College. To avoid any confusion with the University body of the same name, the Senatus became the College Council and was to be 'presided over by one of its members to be appointed by the Church of Scotland under the designation of "The Master"'.[43]

Apocryphally it is thought that the then Principal of the University of Aberdeen, William Hamilton Fyfe, who had been appointed the previous year, had taken great exception to the thought of there being another 'Principal', claiming that there would only ever be one Principal at Aberdeen and that would be him.

Now that these years of debate were settled the Board went on immediately to discuss the 'reconstruction' of the College and the funding thereof. The improvements needed were listed as:

1 Common Room for Students
2 A reading room
3 Improved lavatory accommodation
4 Heating and lighting for the library
5 Additional furnishings[44]

A later meeting added the request for the old benches in the lecture rooms to be replaced with seating. At this stage the College did not have surplus funds so they applied to the University Court to use the accumulated income from the bursary accounts for the reconstruction. After a year of discussion with the College Council it was agreed to ask only for £2,500 from the accumulation and the rest to remain for the bursaries. At the same time that these momentous moments in the history of the College were unfolding, the teaching of theology and day-to-day busi-

43 Financial Board Minute Books, Vol. 4, p. 220.
44 Ibid., p. 222.

ness continued. After twenty-seven years the janitor, Mr Andrew Fordyce, was resigning for health reasons. He was given a generous pension of £1 a week and was replaced by Edmund Merson who was to remain at the post for the next twenty-six years and who must have seen many changes as the College entered the 1960s. Mr Merson's weekly wage was still £2 but he was also receiving a free house with free coal and gas. Annually he would receive £7 for rough cleaning and £20 for him and his wife to provide the students' dinners. It was also decided that he should have a uniform. Principal Cairns was called to consider submitted patterns and chose a uniform of a jacket, two pairs of trousers and an appropriate cap.

Karl Barth Visits

In 1937 the German theologian Karl Barth was called to deliver the Gifford Lectures.[45]

He was hosted in Aberdeen by Principal Cairns who invited him, along with College staff, to an evening in his house at 139 Desswood Place on 9 March 1937. David Cairns' son, David, who was a minister in Bridge of Allan at the time, attended the get-together and subsequently typed up four pages of notes about the conversation that night.

'Barth – "The amazing thing about the Confessional Church is that it has put up so strong a resistance [to Hitler]. I had never expected anything of this kind. The trades unions were a very strong body but have gone down like ninepins ... People who one would have expected to stand firm have collapsed, among them orthodox and conservative theologians. Liberals who were suspect have stood firm ... The Bishops have been weak, but that is not because they were Lutherans, but because they were Bishops, and have always pursued regional politics."'[46]

Principal Cairns asked what Karl Barth thought the Church of Scotland through its Assembly could do regarding Nazism. Barth replied 'that the influence of our protests, would have depended

45 www.giffordlectures.org/overview/history (accessed 05/03/2018).
46 David Cairns papers, MS3409 no. 38, 4 typed sides.

on the grounds given for protest. If the C. of S. protest because they are all for toleration, they will not have much influence ... We in Germany have got the impression that the C. of E. and perhaps the C. of S. are not confined to this pure Gospel, but are preaching also a god of race – God and the Empire, God and Nature.'[47]

At this point David Cairns Junior steps in and starts a theological debate with Barth which becomes heated at times. At one point, Cairns Junior notes, 'here my father swung in to defend me',[48] but it appears that Barth ignored the intervention and continued his hypothesis. There was laughter at times in the conversation. At one point Barth is reported as saying, 'You are all really Catholics!'[49] To which David S. Cairns retorted: 'Judged by your criterion, then so was Calvin and so was Paul, Karl Barth (laughing) Nein, Nein, Nein!'[50]

Handwritten by David Junior at the side of the typed notes is added: 'At 11.50p.m. when, long after the other guests, Barth left the house, I went downstairs with him, and with my hand on the front door handle in the hall said, "You must excuse me Herr Professor, if I spoke too impulsively." He answered "yes of course, I too was a bit lively. But obviously I did not understand the most of what you were saying" – with which delightful twist of my tail he departed into the night.'[51]

End of an Era

Principal Cairns chaired his last meeting on 30 April 1937, after fourteen tough years at the helm but years which set him firmly in place in the history of the College. He was the first of the College Principals to retire, rather than dying in service.

The tribute from the Financial Board of the newly named Christ's College was made by Professor Adam Fyfe Findlay, who succeeded him and became the first Master of the College.

---

47 Ibid.
48 Ibid.
49 Ibid.
50 Ibid.
51 Ibid.

'The Financial Board desire to put on record their huge appreciation of the invaluable services which Principal Cairns, who demitted office as head of the college last autumn rendered to the Board during the long period of 30 years for nearly half of which he presided over their deliberations. They recall with affection and pride their association with one who held so large and distinguished a place in the life of the Church and had done so much to maintain the honourable traditions of the College in Aberdeen. They greatly acknowledge their sense of privilege in having been admitted to his friendship and their admiration not only for his personal qualities but also for the wisdom and breadth of outlook with which he guided the administration of the business affairs of the College. In particular they remember with what ability and resolution he upheld the interests of the College when its very existence was in danger and for this as well as his many other services they desire to express their deep and lasting gratitude. Now that his connection with the Board has been severed they are conscious of the personal loss which they have sustained and they would assure him that he is followed into his retirement from college life by their warm affection and esteem.'[52]

David Smith Cairns died in 1946 but the Cairns name continued to be linked with theological teaching in Aberdeen through his son David, who returned after the war to become Professor of Practical Theology at Christ's College. 'David Smith Cairns was one of Scotland's leading theologians, internationally renowned and respected for his apologetics, which for many breathed new life into the Christian religion ... Ecumenism was certainly a defining characteristic of Cairns, and it was in the ecumenical spirit, combined with a rigorous search for truth, that he made his distinctive contributions in three major areas during the first four decades of the twentieth century: the science–religion debate; the search for a new paradigm for mission; and the response to the events of the First World War.'[53]

---

52 Financial Board Minute Books, Vol. 4, p. 243.
53 Finlayson (accessed 05/03/2018).

7

Adam Fyfe Findlay – The First Master and the War Years

1937–47

Professor Adam Fyfe Findlay was appointed to the Chair of Church History and Christian Ethics at the United Free Church College of Aberdeen in 1923. Prior to that he had been a parish minister in Whithorn, Arbroath, Edinburgh and Linlithgow. In the First World War he served as a chaplain with the Scottish Horse and Highland light infantry in Egypt and Palestine. After the war he was appointed to the Kerr Lectureship at Glasgow University where he delivered a course of lectures entitled 'Byways in Early Christian Literature'.

On 3 July 1937 in the College Council Minutes, Professor Cairns, in the name of the Council, congratulated Professor Findlay on having been nominated by the Church's Nomination Board as the Master of the College. The third period truly began with the appointment of the first 'Master' of the newly named Christ's College.

At this point Professor G. D. Henderson, who had occupied the Chair of Church History since 1924, became the Secretary of the Senatus, hereafter referred to as the Council, and a huge deterioration in handwriting ensued. Adam Fyfe Findlay had an exact style of handwriting and minute book keeping which was precise and particular. It was, however, difficult to read. The new Secretary was easier to read but showed a completely different approach to the job in hand. Scorings out, blots and gaps start to appear regularly and the prose is more mundane. The pages are no longer numbered so go by date alone.

Bursary Funds Fight

In 1937 Findlay had to take up where Cairns left off in the negotiations with the University and the Court of Session regarding
use of the accumulated bursary funds. A wordy and somewhat
aggressive response had been received from the Court of Session.
'What is the petitioners' reply to the respondent's statement that
they have offered to provide all the necessary accommodation for
Divinity students but that this offer has been declined?'[1]

So it seems that the compromise of 1936 had, after all Principal
Cairns' polite and politically correct insistence on the cordiality
between the two, left a sour taste with the University. Another
clause asked, 'Is it the case that Divinity students due to lack of
funds undertake paid work during their academic course to the
detriment of their health as well as of their studies?'[2]

In February 1938 the Financial Board minutes are as follows:
'There was submitted a letter dated 22nd instant from the Secretary of Aberdeen University on whose behalf objections had been
lodged in court to the petition for the authority to utilise a portion
of the accumulated revenue of bursary funds for reconditioning
the College building from which it appeared that the University
was of the opinion that the whole of the accumulations should
be used for bursary purposes and for these purposes only and did
not see that any good purpose could be served by the conference
asked for by the Council of the College unless the council were
prepared to discuss the utilisation for bursary purposes alone of
the total accumulations. After consideration and discussion the
Board resolved in view of the uncompromising attitude of the
University and the condition laid down that no good purpose
would be served by a conference and the secretary was instructed
to reply accordingly.'[3]

The Council response minuted on 27 April was typical of G. D.
Henderson's secretarial style: 'some discussion took place as to
the situation raised by the withdrawal of the petition to the Court

---

1 Council Minute Books, Vol. 4, 13 January 1938.
2 Ibid.
3 Financial Board Minute Books, Vol. 4, p. 242.

of Session with regard to the accumulated bursary fund'.[4] No details are given but a few months later the Master submitted a draft letter to be sent out in connection with the proposal to raise money for the reconstruction of the College as a memorial to the work of Principal Cairns. At the same meeting a letter was submitted by Dr George MacLeod requesting a meeting with ministers, probationers and students to be arranged in order that he might explain his Iona scheme. It was agreed to have the meeting at the College and to issue invitations and provide tea.

For the rest of the year the meetings focused mainly on entrance exams, length of courses, prizes and final certificates. There was consternation that some students had not attended the elocution classes with sufficient regularity and must repeat them in the next session.

On 29 March 1939 it was noted by the Financial Board that contributions to the Cairns Commemoration fund stood at £785/18/3. It was therefore agreed to go forward with the 'reconditioning of the College with money from the fund being set aside for a portrait or other commemoration of Cairns'.[5]

The portrait was commissioned in February 1940 and in October it is minuted that the painter, Mr Gordon Shields, 'had died but fortunately he had been able to complete the portrait'.[6]

The Second World War

There is no sense in the Board or Council minutes of the looming world crisis. The first mention of the war is on 21 September 1939: 'The Council authorised the Master of the College to write to Divinity students with regard to the opening of the session, pointing out the importance of due provision for the spiritual needs of the nation at this time and after the war and therefore of having now an adequate supply of men training for the Ministry.'[7] It was a long meeting during which the Council agreed to provide

4 Council Minute Books, Vol. 4, 27 April 1938.
5 Financial Board Minute Books, Vol. 4, p. 254.
6 Ibid., p. 266.
7 Council Minute Books, Vol. 4, 21 September 1939.

a suitable shelter under the Library to be used for air raids. It was decided that college dinners were to start as usual and be continued throughout the session if it was possible.

'Permission was given to the Church of Scotland Life and Work committee to use part of the College buildings for a military canteen purpose.'[8]

'Intimation was made that George P. Jack, Charles B. Edie and Thomas J. T. Nicol had left to obtain Army commissions. The Secretary was instructed to write to them expressing the interest and good wishes of the Council.'[9]

'In view of the special circumstances this session, the Council decided that instead of the usual opening lecture for which arrangements had been made, a religious service with communion in King's College Chapel on Wednesday 18 October at 10am would be conducted by the Master.'[10]

College dinners continued until October 1940 when it was deemed advisable to discontinue them due to the present war circumstances. It was agreed to give the janitor an ex gratia payment of £20 to compensate for the loss of his wife's earnings as cook.

At that meeting, it was also noted that Charles Edie was now a prisoner of war.

In March 1941 the arrangements for fire watching and firefighting were discussed by the Council, and the following month they were discussed by the Board along with the protection of the College and Library buildings against bomb damage. Later that year the books in the College were insured for £3,000 and the furnishings for £600 under the War Damage Act. Moreover, 'The portraits undernoted had been removed from the college and were now at the following addresses

1 Dr. R. J. Brown and Dr. Robertson Smith with Colonel Simpson, Kirkville, Skene.
2 Principals Lumsden, Cairns and Dr. David Brown with General Hamilton at Skene House.

8 Ibid.
9 Ibid.
10 Ibid.

3 Sir William Henderson, Principal Salmond and Dr. Edmond with Dr. Watt at Culter House.'[11]

After this the Financial Board rarely met until the end of the war although they did annually approve and 'doquette' the accounts. In 1944 they recorded with sadness the deaths of two great servants of Christ's College.

Dr Kelly had been a member of the Board for twenty-five years. 'Dr. Kelly laid his outstanding professional gifts freely at the service of the College and in particular he was unremitting in the care of the College buildings. It may be fitting to recall that the beautiful tablet in memory of the students of the College who fell in the last war was designed by him.'[12]

The Board was also saddened by the death of 'Mr. James H. Edwards who for over thirty years acted as Secretary and Treasurer of the Board a position held for many years by his father before him. This inherited interest in the affairs of the College was highly regarded by Mr. Edwards as he frequently testified and he spared himself no trouble in order that everything affecting the material well-being of the college should be administered to the best advantage. The Board acknowledge with deep gratitude the invaluable service which he ungrudgingly rendered and the generosity with which he declined to accept any remuneration for what for him was a labour of love. Further they wish to express the high esteem in which they held Mr. Edwards for his personal qualities his wise council and his unfailing courtesy.'[13]

The Board agreed to appoint Mr Clement Marshall, MA LLB, advocate in Aberdeen, to be the Secretary and Treasurer of the Board. This was the first Secretary who was appointed only because of his employment with Edmonds and Ledingham rather than a personal connection to the College.

The Council had continued to meet every few months during the war. In October, estimates for the blacking-out of the College were sought and the Secretary reported that he had seen Dr

---

11 Financial Board Minute Books, Vol. 4, p. 274.

12 Ibid., p. 298.

13 Ibid., p. 299.

Edwards, who agreed that as the matter was urgent it need not await a meeting of the Financial Board.

In March 1942 it was reported that the 'Education for Ministry Committee was anxious to make the most adequate use of manpower in the present emergency and to economise in expenditure'.[14] The Council appointed the Master and the Secretary to attend meetings in Edinburgh. Later that month, 'a full and frank discussion took place with regard to possible readjustment in the interest of financial economy and the best use of manpower in the Colleges'.[15] Again Secretary G. D. Henderson uses few words but it says a lot about the mood of the meeting and leaves no doubt that the College might once again be fighting for its individual existence.

On 16 February, Professor Fyfe Findlay reported that 'representations had been made to him with regard to the Spiritual tone of the Divinity classes due mainly to lack of personal contact between staff and students. The Council, while recognising that personal contact had been rendered more difficult by war time conditions resolved that an endeavour should be made during the summer term and thereafter to arrange meetings between teachers and students outwith class hours.'[16]

At a meeting on 23 October 1943 it was agreed that all classes except elocution be at King's for session 1943–44 as a war measure only.

There is a minute from that meeting as follows: '[I]t was remitted to the Master to see what could be done about again sending books to C. B. Edie, prisoner of war in Germany.'[17]

By 1944 first and second years were being taught together and all classes were at King's. From November 1943 the meetings were concerned with discussion about transferring income from various prizes and funds for Emergency Ordinance. The Privy Council agreed to this but it was noted, 'The General Assembly might require to know to what special purposes it was proposed

---

14 Council Minute Books, Vol. 4, 12 March 1942.
15 Ibid., 23 March 1942.
16 Ibid., 16 February 1943.
17 Ibid., 23 October 1943.

to apply the surplus from the Bursary Funds. The Council agreed to propose that the funds be applied:

1 To reduce the College's indebtedness to General College Fund
2 To increase endowment of student dinner fund
3 As all College funds are tied to special purposes, to form a small fund which would be available for College purposes for which no other fund can be used such as a payment of expenses of students attending conferences.'[18]

On 7 August it was reported that the accumulated bursary funds were now at the disposal of the Council. Of the £1632/4/9 available, £632/4/9 was to go to the Education for Ministry Committee.

The staffing of the Library had been an issue of concern throughout the war years but on 12 May 1944 the Council agreed to appoint the Rev. A. M. Watt, late of Clatt and now of 10 Albert Terrace, to be Librarian from 1 June at a salary of £50 per annum. The Library was to be open Monday – Friday 2pm – 4pm.

The war ended with no mention of such in the minutes, but in June 1946 'the Master of the College read a letter asking whether the Christ's College replica of a bust of Dr Wisely, late of Malta could be handed over to the King George V Merchant Seamen's memorial hospital, Malta with which he was long associated to replace the bust destroyed by enemy action. The Council gladly agreed to this request.' [19]

George Wisely entered the Free Church College in Aberdeen in 1846 so will have left before the building was completed. He may, however, during his student days in Aberdeen, have been aware of the Free Church establishing itself in Valletta, Malta

---

18 Ibid., 7 April 1944.
19 Council Minute Books, Vol. 4, 27 June 1946. There is no documentation concerning this replica bust, who gave it or when. The hospital mentioned was closed in 1967 and the bust's present whereabouts are unknown.

to serve the regiments of Scots soldiers stationed there. Congregations rose quickly and by the time George Wisely arrived as the new minister in 1854 there were as many as 600 worshippers on a Sunday and nowhere big enough to hold them in one session. He had been ordained in Leghorn, Italy, now known as Livorno, where he also married Jessie Millar, the daughter of the Senior Minister of the Free Church in Europe. He and his wife began fundraising as soon as they arrived in Malta and soon gathered £2,000 made up of donations ranging from sixpence to one of over £100 from a wealthy Valletta merchant. Building of the new church, designed by George Wisely himself, started in 1856. The building remains the same to this day despite suffering bomb damage in the Second World War. St Andrew's Scots Kirk in Valletta was dedicated on 30 November 1857 and George Wisely continued his ministry there for a further forty years.

On the fiftieth anniversary of his arrival in Malta the *Daily Malta Chronicle* of 5 May 1904 carried a glowing tribute. 'There is a Reverend gentleman who is ever met moving about amongst us wearing a frock coat made of worthy black broad cloth. His step must have been elastic and vigorous once, for his feet to bear him even now so easily after all his going in a busy life. His hair is white and seems more blanched than it really is with age from contrast with his sable garment. He is stooped a little, perhaps with the burdens of others as much as with the weight of his own many years. He is a hale old man, who manifests an interest in life, in the life of the young above all, still keen ... Our thoughts are of a widely respected man who has now withdrawn from the scenes of his greatest activity and passes a green old age in the retreat of his choice at Boschetto. We speak of the Reverend Dr Wisely. Just 50 years ago this venerable ecclesiastical gentleman, this good old Dr Wisely, first came to Malta. His activity was mostly displayed amongst those of his own faith. To guide them as the pastor he was called hither. To them he chiefly belonged. But Dr Wisely was too enlightened a man, too broad-minded, too truly Christian to suppose that it was not his duty to do good in the world wherever he could. And no movement in the last fifty years was ever set on foot to further the material, the mental, or the moral condition of men in Malta, of whatever creed, of whatever race, which had not his good wish and his hearty and ready cooperation.'[20]

While Malta had become his adopted country he had maintained contacts in Aberdeen and received an honorary doctorate from Aberdeen University. A few years after the death of his wife in Malta he moved to Kent, where he died in 1917. Following his instructions his body was taken and buried in St Machar's Cathedral graveyard and we assume that this must have been his preferred place of worship in his Aberdeen years.

The Council were no doubt delighted, although there is no minute for such a sentiment, that Charles Edie had returned from his incarceration in a German POW camp, and at a meeting on 20 December 1945 it was agreed to grant him a final certificate. Charles Edie continued in the ministry until his retirement in 1984. He died in 2001.

'A lifetime of service to others came to an end with the passing on January 28 of the Rev. Charles Benjamin Edie. Charles took ill on his way to worship at St Ninian's Old Parish Church and died later in Stirling Royal Infirmary.

'Born at Bieldside, Aberdeen, on June 20, 1916, Charles's early years were spent in Cape Town, South Africa, where his father was professor in biochemistry at the university there. Following Dr Edie's death in 1927 Charles returned to Aberdeen with his mother and his sister, Kitty. He was educated at Robert Gordon's College and later at Aberdeen University, where he studied theology.

'At the outbreak of the Second World War Charles volunteered to serve in the army rather than complete his divinity course. He became a lieutenant in the King's Own Scottish Borderers and was posted to the regimental headquarters at Berwick-on-Tweed. It was there that he came into contact with a young lady named Eileen Kirk, who had enlisted in the Territorial Women's Transport Service and was working as an ambulance driver.

'They became engaged to be married in February 1940, but in April of that year Charles was sent on the ill-fated defence of

20 http://website.lineone.net/~peterbidmead/index.htm (accessed 05/03/2018).

Norway as part of No. 1 Independent Company, the forerunners of the Commandos. On May 10, he was wounded and taken prisoner by the Germans. After treatment in a Norwegian hospital he was transferred to a prisoner-of-war camp in Germany, and there he remained until released by the American Army in May 1945.

'On his return home Charles and Eileen were married on July 17, 1945, and thus began a long and happy partnership of 55 years. Eileen died four weeks before Charles on Sunday December 31, 2000.

'Charles was ordained into the ministry of the Church of Scotland in January 1946 after serving as assistant to Dr J. W. Baird at St Machar's Cathedral in Aberdeen and he was inducted to the rural charge of Eddleston in Peebleshire. In 1950 he was called to St Margaret's Parish Church, Juniper Green, Edinburgh, and then in 1955 the Edie family moved to Stirling, where Charles became minister of the historic Church of The Holy Rude. During his ministry in Stirling, Charles was active in the presbytery, being convener of a number of committees and serving as Moderator. He was chaplain to the High School and Stirling Royal Infirmary and for many years also to the Stirlingshire battalion of the Army Cadet Force ... Following his retirement in 1984, Charles remained active and served as locum in a number of churches throughout the Presbytery of Stirling. He was also for seven years a pastoral assistant at St Columba's Church in Stirling. His gifts as a preacher were considerable and his faithfulness as a pastor was greatly appreciated by many. He had a remarkable ability to relate to people, and his kind and cheerful nature made him a most approachable and likeable individual ... [I]t can certainly be said of Charles B. Edie that he lived and enjoyed his life to the full, and in the course of his life he touched and enriched the lives of a great many people.'[21]

Thomas J. T. Nicol returned from the war and became a parish minister but in 1947 returned to army chaplaincy. Twenty years later he was to receive the degree of Doctor of Divinity from Aberdeen University. At this point he was Assistant Chaplain General

---

21 Gary J. McIntyre in *The Herald*, 3 March 2001, www.britishnews paperarchive.co.uk (accessed 05/03/2018).

Sir Francis Edmond

Principal James Lumsden

Principal David Brown

William Robertson Smith

Mr and Mrs Thomson of Banchory

John Knox's watch

Tollohill Monument

*Gift bracelet from
Queen Victoria*

Sir William Henderson

Principal James Iverach

First World War Memorial

Principal David Cairns

Class of 1939

St Andrew's Church, Malta

4

Plaque: James Hastings

Plaque: Laws of Livingstonia

Rev. Professor Jim McEwen

Rev. Professor Alan Main and Rev. Dr Henry Sefton

The Alford Place Church

Four Masters: Ian Dick, John Swinton, Henry Sefton and Alan Main

Very Rev. Professor Sir Iain Torrance with the Duchess of Rothsay and Sir Ian Diamond

The College Bar

John Swinton and Clare Davidson

Scottish Command and had been decorated in the Korean War. He was described by Brigadier Bernard Ferguson as the 'ideal regimental padre'.[22] Of the other serving student mentioned, George P. Jack, there is no mention until his death notice in the Aberdeen Divinity Bulletin of 1966 as follows: 'May 16th. The Reverend George P. Jack of Edinburgh Charteris-Pleasance. George P. Jack was a man of compassionate heart and adventurous spirit. Whether on the field of sport, in the discussion of ideas, new and old, and in the work, to which he was called, he gave his all, willingly, for Christ's sake.'[23]

Aberdeen University lost 182 men in the Second World War, considerably fewer than in the First World War, and Christ's College was not as affected by loss as it had been in the Great War. In an entry added to the roll of honour at the University of Aberdeen, the death of a former student appears whose father was one of the early students of the then Free Church College in Aberdeen, arriving in 1858 and noted as becoming a medical missionary in Kashmir.

Douglas Emslie
Rank: Chaplain to the Forces
Regiment: The Gordon Highlanders
Biography: Son of Rev. William Emslie, China Inland Mission, and of Jessie Douglas Emslie (nee Cuthbert); born China, 15 March 1899; educated in China. In the First World War he served with the Argyll and Sutherland Highlanders and won the M.M. Desiring to enter the church, he took the modified course in Arts and Divinity from 1930 to 1935, and subsequently became minister of the West Church, Crieff. At the outbreak of war he became a Chaplain to the Forces and was posted to the Gordon Highlanders. In May 1940 he was drafted to France when the fighting was at its height and died of wounds in an Advanced Dressing Station on 12 June 1940.
Honours: Military Medal
Date of Death: 12 June 1940

22 Aberdeen Divinity Bulletin No. 11 (1968), p. 5.
23 Aberdeen Divinity Bulletin No. 9 (1966).

Burial Details: Buried at St Valéry-en-Caux Franco-British Cemetery, C, 33.[24]

Details of other students who survived both wars are found in subsequent obituaries in the Divinity Bulletins.

Lewis L. L. Cameron died in 1973. 'During the First World War he was discharged from the Gordons with wounds so serious "that he was never likely to work again". He took his degree in Agriculture in Aberdeen and for a time taught in Leeds. But his real love was the Kirk and after his Divinity course, he ministered with uncommon success in such varied types of parishes as St Ninian's Aberdeen, Mortlach and Bo'ness. He rose to become the Church's first Director of Social Service. It may be confidently asserted that the phenomenal expansion of this great work was due to his indefatigable energy, his organising acumen and his genuine love for all sorts of conditions of men, women and children. During the Second World War, Dr Cameron served as Secretary of the Committee on Huts and Canteens and as administrative Welfare Officer in Scottish Command. He was awarded the M.B.E. for his war work and honoured with both the O.B.E. and the honorary D.D. for his church work.'[25]

Charlie Gibson died in Australia, also in 1973. 'During the War he served as a combatant officer with the 2nd Gordons in Malaya and was captured at Singapore. He spent most of his time in captivity on the infamous Burma railway where he resumed his position as a minister and buried many of his fellow prisoners of war. On his return to Scotland he visited many of the relatives of his comrades who fell. He held the charges of Knox's, Arbroath and Eckford near Kelso prior to emigrating to Australia where he served for twenty years. Charlie was a blyth spirit and a valiant soldier of Jesus Christ'[26]

John Ross died in Torphins in 1972. 'Despite a physical handicap, John served as an Army chaplain in the late war. He was one of a group of chaplains who entered the notorious Belsen

24 Aberdeen University Roll of Honour 1952, www.abdn.ac.uk/library/roll-of-honour (accessed 01/09/2017).
25 Aberdeen Divinity Bulletin No. 15 (1973), p. 7.
26 Ibid.

prison camp and set up a bureau and post office by means of which thousands of prisoners were able to make contact with their relatives. He was made an MBE for his services in Northwest Europe. John Ross who was a native of Stornoway was a most exemplary parish minister and in the administration of the church was both most diligent and wise of counsel. No man was ever in doubt as to where John Ross stood – it was at the side of his Master.'[27]

Death of Principal Cairns

On 11 September, 'The Council agreed to minute in the following terms their sense of loss at the death of Emeritus Principal D. S. Cairns and to send a copy to his family.

'The church in Aberdeen and the whole Church Of Scotland and Christians in other denominations and countries deplore the recent death of Principal David Cairns: but outside of his family group none can feel themselves more sadly bereaved than those who as colleagues and students have been associated with him in the life of Christ's College. This was the centre from which for so many years his influence went forth. Here he taught and it was as Professor of Dogmatics and Apologetics in this College and later as its Principal that he was known throughout the world. We are proud of the fact that his name and that of our College will always be connected, proud also of the portrait in our Hall which will perpetuate his memory for other generations.

'Those who served with him in the College Council and the many ministers of our church and of foreign churches who had the benefit of his instruction and inspiration remember him as the most loveable, approachable and sympathetic advisor, a man of strong conviction, determined principle and high spiritual tone, an earnest scholar, widely travelled, a persuasive writer and an experienced soul-friend with a particular gift of entering into the problems of others to their unfailing benefit. We thank God for

---

27 Ibid., p. 8.

the long career of distinction and Christian usefulness that was granted him.'[28]

William Robertson Smith Centenary

In 1946 a major event was being planned in conjunction with the University to commemorate the centenary of William Robertson Smith's birth. Sixty-five years after his ignominious departure from the College, the great and good were gathering in his honour. The event was held on his birthday, 8 November, and on the previous Saturday the *Aberdeen Press and Journal* ran the first of two articles written by G. D. Henderson under the heading, 'Old, unhappy, far-off theological battles are recalled by the Centenary of the birth of William Robertson Smith – a name still well remembered – whose querying of Old Testament fundamentals provoked the fight.'[29]

The main lectures were delivered by the Rev. Charles Earle Raven, Master of Christ's College Cambridge and Regius Professor of Divinity in Cambridge, and Professor Stanley Cook, a former student of Smith's.

The day after the event, the *Press and Journal* ran with, 'Scholars honour memory of "Martyred Professor". A dramatic link with the expulsion of Professor William Robertson Smith from the chair of Hebrew in 1881 was shown to a company who assembled yesterday to celebrate the centenary of his birth. It was a manuscript containing in his own writing, the Professor's answers to questions put to him by Aberdeen Free Church Presbytery when he was "on trial" for writing views on the bible that the church would not accept. Yesterday in the Assembly Hall of Christ's College from which he was expelled, it lay on the desk at which he had worked during his 7 years at the College.

'Above it was a portrait of William Robertson Smith painted from memory after his death by his great friend the late Sir George Reid.

28 Council Minute Books, Vol. 4, 11 September 1946.
29 *Aberdeen Press and Journal*, 2 November 1946, www.britishnews paperarchive.co.uk (accessed 05/03/2018).

'"We are proud to have that picture on our walls" Professor Adam Fyfe Findlay Master of Christ's College told the gathering. "It reminds us and will remind all who come after us of the most illustrious teacher the College ever had". Professor Fyfe Findlay described the event of sixty-five years ago as a tragic decision which all deplored today.'[30]

On 21 November the minute reads, 'A reception had been held in the College to which were invited the Church of Scotland ministers in the city, the staff, members of the Financial Board with the wives of all these, the students, Principal and Lady Fyfe, the guests from other universities and colleges, relatives of William Robertson Smith and others.

'The Master of the College presided and spoke of the association of William Robertson Smith with the building, a message from New College, Edinburgh was delivered by Professor O. S. Rankin, and a paper on the work of William Robertson Smith in Cambridge was read by Professor Stanley Cooke, a surviving pupil of William Robertson Smith.'[31]

The same minute finishes with the single line, 'It was decided to permit smoking in the Dining Hall and in one room of the College.'[32]

College Equality

At the start of the following year the Council was again wrestling with the Committee for the Education for the Ministry and trying to ensure equality between the Colleges. 'The Council reminds the committee that prior to 1929 the four University Divinity faculties each had four professors. Since 1929 Edinburgh and Glasgow have had the full services of the combined university and college staffs available while although the number of students in Aberdeen is small, the same curriculum has to be provided there, to the same standard without a second Hebrew Chair, a second

---

30 *Aberdeen Press and Journal*, 9 November 1946, www.britishnews paperarchive.co.uk (accessed 05/03/2018).

31 Council Minute Books, Vol. 4, 21 November 1946.

32 Ibid.

New Testament Chair or lectureship and a second church history chair or lectureship.'[33]

A favourable response was noted at the next month's meeting. 'A letter was read from Education for the Ministry committee intimating that the committee had agreed to the appointment of a lecturer in Hebrew and Biblical Criticism. For a period not exceeding 5 years from the date of appointment at a salary of £600. However they also asked Christ's College to draw to the attention of the University court that in the 3 other centres the university provides for the teaching of elementary Greek and Hebrew in the faculty of arts and suggest in the view of the limited resources of the committee the same practice might be put into operation in Aberdeen.'[34]

In June the Master conveyed to Professor Henderson the congratulations of the Council on his appointment by the General Assembly to be Master of the College from 1 October. It was also noted at that meeting that following considerable debate and negotiation it had been decided to appoint a Professor of Practical Theology at Christ's College who would be a part-time lecturer at the University and a member of faculty of Divinity. A further step forward had been achieved to support the role of Practical Theology within the University.

In July Professor Findlay chaired his last Financial Board meeting, at which it was agreed to proceed with the scheme for heating and lighting the Library and accept the estimate from J. T. L. Parkinson which would include fluorescent lighting.[35]

Farewell to Professor Findlay

George David Henderson became the second Master of Christ's College and began his first meeting with the following:

'In connection with the retirement of Rev. Prof. Adam Fyfe Findlay from office in the College, the council desires to place on

---

33 Ibid., 30 January 1947.

34 Ibid., 25 February 1947.

35 J. T. L. Parkinson later initiated an endowment fund for overseas students.

record its grateful appreciation of his long, varied and diligent service as Professor of Church History and Christian Ethics from 1924 to 1935, as Professor of Christian Ethics and Practical Theology from 1935 to 1947 and as Master of the College from 1937 to 1947.

'Dr Findlay was a distinguished student of Aberdeen University and had a prominent place in university athletics and public life. Ordained to the ministry under the United Presbyterian church, he held in succession several charges coming into prominence as a scholarly and business like minister who took his full part in the work of the church and of the Christian community. His Kerr lectures were published in 1923 and this special evidence of patient scholarship was naturally soon followed by his selection for a professor's chair.

'His versatility has been noteworthy. His extensive ministerial experience made him a trusted advisor to successive generations of Divinity Students.

'His kindliness and personal interest were always much appreciated by those who studied under him. He was for many years a painstaking and methodical secretary of the College Council thoroughly familiar with all the affairs of the institution and careful of its interests. As Master of the College he admirably discharged the duties and maintained the dignity of his office: and the value of his friendly guidance and experienced leadership through a somewhat difficult period is cordially acknowledged by his colleagues. The members of the council desire to express their best wishes for his years of retirement and would also like to record very grateful and most respectful good wishes to Mrs Findlay.'[36]

In researching Adam Fyfe Findlay, a letter to his wife was discovered, written by Mary Mitchell Slessor, who was born in Aberdeen and brought up as a mill-girl in Dundee. In 1876 she was accepted for training by the United Presbyterian Mission Society and sailed to Calabar, now part of Nigeria. In 1888 she began the mission at Okoyong, which made her reputation as a pioneering missionary, a reputation she enhanced by writing

---

36 Council Minute Books, Vol. 4, 9 October 1947.

articles published in Britain praising the abilities of the African peoples she lived among. In 1903 she moved to Itu and for the next twelve years until her death moved continually inland. In this letter, describing another move, her single-minded courage and dedication are evident. 'You know I think I have been exercised in heart about these towns lying in wickedness and sin up in this remote district. Well, when I came over as far as Ido & Ikpe I just opened out the camp bed Mrs Peacock loaned me, & sat down in the Government Rest House & said, I'm not going farther on any journey till I have it out with those heathen chaps who so bitterly are opposing the Gospel message.'[37]

The laureation address given by Professor Taylor on the occasion of Professor Findlay's Honorary LLD gives more information and tells us of his athletic side which was never apparent through years of solemn minutes. 'It is many years since Professor Findlay entered the University from Aberdeen Grammar School of which he was gold medallist. In the field of sport he soon took an outstanding place. Representing the university in army athletics at Aldershot he won the 100 yards against competitors drawn from the whole British Army. He played in the first rugby match at the opening of the King's playing field. He was secretary of the rugby club, the SRC and played in the cricket XI. In taking farewell of our colleague we recall with pleasure his kindly face and the quiet wisdom he brought to our Council and we like to think that in his retirement that same sanity and vigour which we have known here will continue to be available to the university and to the community which he has served with so much acceptance and distinction.'[38]

37 Letter from Mary Slessor to Mrs Findlay, 20 February 1914, www.scran.ac.uk/database/record.php?usi=000-000-579-132-C (accessed 05/03/2018).

38 Thomas Murray Taylor, Collection of Addresses delivered at Graduation Ceremonies in the University of Aberdeen 1946–1962, MS 2843/3.

The Morrocco Portrait

The final paragraph is born witness to by a gentle and soulful pencil drawing of an elderly Adam Fyfe Findlay, drawn by the now-famous Scottish painter Alberto Morrocco. There is no information as to why Morrocco came to draw Fyfe Findlay. The portrait was loaned to Christ's College by his grandson, Andrew Steven, in 2001. He wrote to then Master, the Rev. Professor Alan Main, 'We wondered if the College might like to have this on loan for appropriate display ... Among the family items I discovered, were photographs of my grandfather in the University cricket and rugby teams of 1885 ... In his closing years, he would wear in our house in Old Aberdeen – the Forestry Manse – his university rugby cap of 1889. These were in days before central heating!' [39]

---

39 Letter, Andrew Steven to Alan Main, Christ's College, 2001.

8

G. D. Henderson and Collegiate Life
1947–57

George David Henderson

Although he was presiding as Master Designate, G. D. Henderson started making changes at his first Council meeting in October 1947. It was agreed to hold a weekly Chapter every Monday at 12:20. This innovation was to make a lasting difference to College life and would normally consist of a short devotional service and a discussion on some topic of interest. The Master suggested and the Council agreed to meet henceforward on the first Thursday of every month during term and that the newly appointed Librarian, Mr Watt, was to be invited to join the meeting for a short while for the discussion of Library business.

The new Master also proposed the production of a College handbook. This then appeared annually until the turn of the century when data protection and printing costs became a concern.

The Council agreed that when any members were to travel on College business, their expenses should be met by the McHardy Bequest and the accumulation funds; the claims to be initialled by the Master before going to Edmonds and Ledingham for payment.

There is a clear impression that Professor Henderson had been waiting eagerly in the wings for some time. He had been appointed to the chair of Church History in 1924 at the young age of 36 out of a strong field of twenty candidates. He brought with him experience in parish ministry and had served as an army chaplain during the First World War. The Rev. C. E. Forster wrote in the

Aberdeen Press and Journal: 'Professor Henderson is a preacher of outstanding merit, and his students will learn something not only from his lectures but also from his pulpit ministrations. There are people who expect a Professor to be dull in the pulpit, and they are sometimes disappointed, but one can wager that our latest divinity professor will surprise many when he appears in our city pulpits. He can preach. Lest anyone might misunderstand this, let's say that Henderson is a thinker as well as a scholar. He has interests out and beyond the routine theological subjects he will have to teach. The whole life of the University, and the civic life of our city will both be enriched by his coming.'[1]

The short article finishes with an amusing remark by the author: 'Professor Henderson is a little, a very little man, and there may be some who will be inclined to despise his inches. Those who look for quality service will not be disappointed.'[2]

He had been 'Master in waiting' since 1937 when he became Secretary of the Senatus under Professor Adam Fyfe Findlay. The new Secretary of the Council was Professor A. M. Hunter and the writing becomes neater. At his second meeting the Master announced future plans for the College Chapter and for speakers at College lunch. 'The Common Lunch should be used to strengthen contacts among the students, between students and Professors, between students and representatives of the church and between students and people outside, city laymen and also students who might become Divinity students.'[3] Mr Watt was in attendance. New books were suggested and the Council agreed to think of ways of making the Library more attractive and useful for ministers in the district. It was agreed to recommend to the Financial Board that the salary of the Librarian to be raised from £50 to £100.

The Council agreed to invite David Cairns, the new Professor of Practical Theology and son of former Principal D. S. Cairns, to give the inaugural lecture at the opening of the spring term, and

---

1 *Aberdeen Press and Journal*, 30 August 1924, www.britishnewspaperarchive.co.uk (accessed 05/03/2018).

2 Ibid.

3 Henry Sefton, Divinity Alumni Association Newsletter no. 15 (Winter 1995/6), p. 8.

100 invitations were to be sent out to ministers and interested laymen. It was agreed that a retreat should be held and Professor Cairns was to arrange this.

Professor Henderson chaired his first meeting of the Financial Board, not in the offices of Edmonds and Ledingham as was the norm but in the College itself to allow an inspection of the facilities to take place. It was agreed to provide nameplates at the College door, to remove the doors from the bookcases in the Library, to modernise the toilets and to provide a lounge and equipment for the students. That was the end of business for 1947.

Shuttle Lane Mission

Early in 1948 the future of the Shuttle Lane Mission came up for discussion. Professor Henderson gave a brief résumé of the Mission's history, constitution, etc. After considerable discussion the Council decided to record their opinion on the whole matter in the following terms: '[T]he Council of Christ's College is unanimously of opinion that the construction of the Shuttle Lane Mission has become anomalous and in many ways unsatisfactory both from the point of view of mission work and from that of the students and staff of the College; that the erection of the Board of Practical Training by the General Assembly has made it impracticable and undesirable for the students to accept responsibility any further for work of this special type and that the Presbytery should bring to an end the connection presently existing between the College and the Mission and take steps to safeguard the spiritual interests of all persons connected with the several organisations still active.'[4] This was the start of the end for Shuttle Lane which had been part and parcel of the students' lives from the beginning of the Church College in Aberdeen (see Appendix C).

---

4 Council Minute Books, Vol. 4, 4 March 1948.

Accommodation Problem

Another weighty subject was aired at that meeting. Just over ten years after the protracted discussions and subsequent compromised agreement, the subject of the 'accommodation problem' came up again. The Council unanimously agreed on the following resolution, which they decided to send to the Education for the Ministry Committee for submission to the General Assembly. 'That the scheme for the division of teaching of Divinity in May 1936 be rescinded and the following substitute agreed on by the University Court and the Church of Scotland.

'The division of the teaching of Divinity at Aberdeen will be a matter of arrangement from time to time between the University Court and the Church of Scotland committee on the Education for the Ministry on the understanding that the use made of Christ's College shall not be less than that indicated in the present scheme.'[5]

A later Master, Henry Sefton, wrote, 'Professor Henderson prepared a memorandum for his colleagues in which he suggested that they should make the most of the two sites of theological education. On the one hand they should encourage their students as fully as possible to enjoy the privileges and face the responsibility of belonging to the whole student body. On the other hand they should try to develop the Christ's College site so that the students would have increasingly such privileges as are more commonly associated with the denomination theological seminary in the Church of Scotland elsewhere ... In this same memorandum the Master says, "I am particularly anxious to bring all the students together for one hour a week as a collegiate body when as Master of the College I can have them all before me as a group and when any matter of general concern can be vented."'[6]

On 6 May it was reported that the first Retreat organised by Professor Cairns had been successful and this annual event continued until 2012. It was also reported that the College improvements were well on the way to completion. The heating was already in operation and a suite had been installed in the common room.

---

5 Ibid.
6 Divinity Alumni Association Newsletter, no. 15 (1995/6), p. 8.

It was resolved to get an architect's opinion on the possibility of converting the far end of the Library into a temporary chapel as, according to Professor Henderson, 'A Theological College should have a chapel as part of its normal equipment.'[7]

At that meeting the Council also approved the Master's suggestion for sending a College Christmas card to alumni. This continued for many years and varied from photographs of the college to a fine collection of line drawings by Professor James McEwen's wife Patty, many of which are still in existence.

The minutes of the following meeting give nothing much of note except for the dramatic change in presentation which coincided with the introduction of the use of ballpoint pens, and despite Secretary Hunter's best efforts the book becomes very messy!

The meetings in 1949 continued to arrange classes, guest speakers, Chapter services and prizes, and the work of reconstruction continued. Mr Watt was making improvements to the Library which included the start of a card index system. The space earmarked for the Chapel was currently occupied by the Natural History Museum which was part of the Thomson of Banchory Bequest in the early days of the College. The Free Church had considered that Natural Science should be included in the course of training for the Ministry but, as this was no longer the case, Professor Henderson had been in discussion with University departments where he felt the contents better belonged. Professor Wynne Edwards of the University Zoological department was agreeable to house the collection of birds and Professor Lockhart to find room in the University Museum for the anthropological specimens. At this point the Council also agreed to lend the orrery to the Geography department from where it seems to have disappeared.

---

7 Ibid.

Silver Wedding

Luckily, by November the Secretary seems to have purchased a better quality Biro! This year, 1949, also saw the occasion of the twenty-fifth wedding anniversary of the Master and his wife, as reported in the local paper.

'That he had built up a reputation as a churchman and scholar of integrity both at home and abroad, in the churches of America and on the Continent, was said of Professor G. D. Henderson by Professor John Graham last night. Professor Graham was speaking at the annual gathering of the professors and students of Christ's College, when Professor Henderson was presented with a brief case, a desk lamp and a wallet of notes to mark the celebration of his silver wedding. The gifts were a mark of appreciation from students and professors who had worked under Professor Henderson. Professor Henderson held an honoured position in the history of the Church of Scotland, said Professor Graham. His work was marked by the ideal of completeness and a remarkable fairness of mind – giving the fairest possible appraisement to any movement in the Church, whether he had any interest in it or not. Professor Henderson had made history a living study. In recent years he had become Master of Christ's College, exercising the function of a leader of a community. "He must have found our ignorance and carelessness very trying", added Professor Graham. Speaking on behalf of the alumni, the Rev. E. Duncan said he thought semi-jubilees were usually marked by a reference to age. "Here is an old boy who simply refuses to get old", he said. Mr Duncan emphasised the profound debt owed by students to Professor Henderson's capacity to make his subject supremely alive and interesting. He was not only a scholar and a teacher but, above all, a great friend. Mr W. P. Drummond, representing the students, said they were grateful for his sound advice. Many of them would forget history but all would remember the sound advice given. Professor Henderson thanked the professors and students for their kindness. In view of their eloquent orations he felt a sense of embarrassment, he said. He had been brought up in Airdrie and had adopted the motto, "Airdrie's no dune yet." There was a decrease in the power of reading, he said. If people did not use their own brains they had to use others. That was not always successful. "I would like to put some people in prison and compel them to use their brains", he added. The appreciation of former students was expressed by Professor A. M. Hunter, who read letters of congratulations.'[8]

The next year, 1950, brought authorisation for Professor Cairns to arrange short courses of lectures to be given on such subjects as mental health and teaching methods, the expenses thereof to be paid for out of the accumulations fund to a limit of £30. The Committee on Education for the Ministry had refused to fund this suggestion.

The annual deputation from the Education for Ministry Committee reported the following student requests: 'more instruction on church music; guidance on the use of a film projector; more tutorial classes and some interchange of divinity students among the various theological colleges during the summer term'.[9]

College Centenary

A major milestone in the history of the College was approaching. The Council agreed that the centenary of the College should comprise a service, a civic luncheon and a reception in the afternoon. The Moderator of the General Assembly had agreed to preach. But it was not to be and again the College found itself fighting for its existence. Not this time in the debating hall of the General Assembly but in the inner fabric of the building itself: dry rot!

Urgent repairs were necessary, so much so that the opening lecture was cancelled and the centenary celebrations had to be postponed.

However, the event was not long delayed. The *Aberdeen Press and Journal* on 22 November ran the following announcement: 'More than eighty former students of Christ's College, Aberdeen, many of whom are distinguished figures in the Church of Scotland, will take part in the centenary celebrations on November 30

8 *Aberdeen Press and Journal*, 15 December 1949, www.britishnews paperarchive.co.uk (accessed 05/03/2018).

9 Council Minute Books, Vol. 4, 2 March 1950.

to mark the opening of the college. The alumni of the College, who will come from many parts of Scotland, will be entertained to luncheon along with present students. The Rev. R. G. Philip, one of the oldest surviving alumni, will preside, and the Rev. Professor A. Fyfe Findlay, Emeritus Master of the College, one of his college friends, will be one of the speakers. The Rev. Dr Robert Mackintosh, Edinburgh, secretary of the Home Board, a former student of Christ's College, and Mr Alan O. Robertson, Stonehaven, a divinity student, will also speak. A civic luncheon will also be given to a representative company, when the speakers will be Lord Provost Duncan Fraser, the Rev. Professor D. Cairns, son of a former Principal of the College, and the Very Rev. Principal G. S. Duncan, St Mary's College, St Andrews, last year's Moderator of the General Assembly.

In the morning a service will be held in King's College Chapel at which the preacher will be the Very Rev. Principal John Baillie, New College, Edinburgh, a former Moderator of the General Assembly. During the war years Principal Baillie was convener of the Commission on the Interpretation of God's Will in the Crisis, which gave the Church guidance on problems facing the country. The Rev. Professor G. D. Henderson, Master of Christ's College, will conduct the service and the lessons will be read by Principal T. M. Taylor, Aberdeen University and Lord Provost Fraser. The Rev. Professor A. M. Hunter, Dean of the Faculty of Divinity, will lead the prayers. At a reception in the College in the afternoon the Rev. Professor W. D. Niven, an alumnus of the college, and a former minister of Causewayend Church, Aberdeen, will be one of the speakers. Other speakers will be the Rev. Principal William Fulton, Trinity College, Glasgow, and the Rev. Dr T. Caldwell, convener of the Church of Scotland Committee on Education for the Ministry.'[10]

At the next meeting it was noted that the day had been a great success and that Mr Merson, the janitor, was to get an ex gratia payment of £10 for all his extra work.

---

10 *Aberdeen Press and Journal*, 22 November 1950, www.britishnews paperarchive.co.uk (accessed 05/03/2018).

Last Council Minutes

Early in 1951, Professor Cairns suggested to the Council that they consider the possibility of acquiring a 'voice recording apparatus'. The Council agreed that Professors Henderson, Macleod and Cairns be given power to hear some of them in action and, if they thought one suitable, to buy it. The College seemed to be moving slowly but with great deliberation into the 1950s. However, finances were becoming an issue and the provision of a proper College Chapel was still on every agenda. It was agreed that this should be high on the list of priorities in the event of College funds becoming available.

The Council decided to hold the weekly Chapter service on Fridays at 12:25pm and empowered the Master to make arrange-

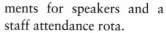

ments for speakers and a staff attendance rota.

On 7 February 1952, in the absence of the Master, Professor Kennedy took the chair and after a reference to the death of King George VI led the Council in prayer for the royal family. Following illness the Librarian, Alex Watt, had resigned and the Rev. Mitchell Hughes was appointed.

At this point we come to the end of the Council Minute Book which began in 1935 and there are no further minutes of Christ's College Council meetings available until 1970. Somewhere there must be a book of minutes undiscovered; the search continues.

This section ends with a wonderful statement at the last documented meeting when it was agreed to 'invite staff wives to the next council meeting in order to get their advice about the proper cleaning of the college'.[11] And that ends an amazing piece of history.

The Christ's College Chapel was finally built and dedicated at the opening session of 1954/5. The cost had been in the region of £2,000. It featured on the 1954 Christmas card.

Moderator Designate of the General Assembly

The year 1954 saw Professor Henderson appointed Moderator Designate of the General Assembly of the Church of Scotland for 1955. 'That the Master of Christ's College will discharge his duties as Moderator with *eclat* none of us doubts for a moment. He has all the gifts needed: quickness of mind, spirituality, experience of men and a remarkable flair for business and the practicalities. His knowledge of Presbyterianism, attested by many books, is unexcelled and is to be found at its most readable in *The Claims of the Church of Scotland*. But "G.D." is no ivory-tower *guru* permanently retired from the hurly-burly of our modern world: he is a man of affairs *par excellence*, direct, lucid minded and impatient of cant and inefficiency. We have heard him say that every university ought to have a Chair of Common Sense. None would fill it better than himself.'[12]

The Presbytery of Aberdeen launched a fund for his Moderatorial attire. 'The sums of money which have been rolling in to the Moderatorial Robe Fund recently opened speak much for the esteem in which the Rev. Professor G. D. Henderson is held, in the spheres of Church, town, and gown. Those robes which include the magnificent Court dress with breeches worn by Moderator of the General Assembly of the Church of Scotland on great occasions are extremely costly I am told by the clerk of Aberdeen Presbytery, the Rev. John Mowat. There are also the top robe and the fine lace ruffles and cuffs. To give an idea of all-over cost, says Mr Mowat, the ruffles and cuffs of Moderatorial

---

11 Council Minute Books, Vol. 4, 6 March 1952.

12 A. M. Hunter, 'The Moderator Designate', *Life and Work*, December 1954.

lace cost £25 alone. But the money for them won't have to come out of the local fund. They are being made in Kalimpong; at the Church of Scotland mission there, and will be presented by the Colonial and Continental Committee of which Professor Henderson has been convener.' [13]

The Assembly of 1955 attracted a lot of media attention due to the attendance of Billy Graham on his Crusade to Scotland. It is only just over sixty years ago but the press style of reporting has changed significantly. In these days regular columns were spent on Presbytery meetings and large coverage given to the annual General Assembly. The following is from the *Aberdeen Evening Express.* 'More colourful than anything Hollywood has ever dreamed of, pageantry of Old Scotland came to life in Edinburgh today at the opening of the General Assembly of the Church of Scotland. Many visitors to the city watched the stream of ministers and elders entering St Giles for the service which traditionally precedes the Assembly. It was conducted by the retiring Moderator, the Right Rev. E. D. Jarvis, DD. His successor installed in office in one of the first acts of the Assembly, is the Very Rev. Professor G. D. Henderson, of Aberdeen.

'Brilliant sunshine broke through grey curtain of cloud half an hour before the ceremonies started. Thousands of people lined the High Street and watched the procession. Waiting in the courtyard of St Giles was a guard of honour from the 1st battalion Gordon Highlanders with their regimental band and pipes and drums. Immaculate in their dark green tunics, kilts and white sporrans, spats and bells, they formed an impressive background of the pageantry to come. There was an expectant hush as the guard completed their final rehearsal of presenting arms and then in constant stream came notabilities from every walk of Scottish life and from abroad. From the city chambers, walking slowly up the High Street came Lord Provost John Banks, of Edinburgh, with the magistrates and councillors and then followed the Lord Provosts of the other Scottish cities. Close on their heels arrived the Court of the Lord Lyon, a touch of mediaeval splendour

13 *Aberdeen Press and Journal*, Wednesday, 20 April 1955, www.brit ishnewspaperarchive.co.uk (accessed 05/01/2018).

about their multi-coloured tabards. There was elbow nudging and excited chatter as the American evangelist, Billy Graham smart in a morning suit and carrying top hat got out of a black limousine which had brought him from the Palace of Holyrood House. At his side was his wife, trim and dainty in a grey costume and white hat. The group stood at the entrance to the Cathedral and watched while the Lord High Commissioner – the Duke of Hamilton – accompanied by Lt-Gen. Horatio Murray, G O C in-C. Scottish Command, inspected the guard. That over, they filed into the great church for the opening service, while outside The Gordons marched off to the Castle, the strains of the pipes floating down to the dispersing crowds. There was a slight hitch in the normal split-second timing of proceedings. As the retiring Moderator came in, everyone stood up. The Very Rev. Dr E. D. Jarvis took his place in the chair and glanced up expectantly to the gallery above, but the Lord High Commissioners had not yet arrived. The gathering remained upstanding for fully a minute and then Dr Jarvis turned and sat down. But the delay was soon over and voices swelled in the singing of Psalm 24.

'With due ceremony a letter from the Queen to the Assembly was read. In it she welcomed the opportunity given her to assure the Assembly of her sincere concern for the well-being of the Church of Scotland and her keen interest in its many activities. "We willingly reaffirm our determination to retain her historic rights and liberties," wrote the Queen. The Church of Scotland in her vigorous evangelism at home, her work overseas, and by her participation in the councils of the Christian Churches through-out the world, had shown her awareness of the challenge of the times, and of the need to meet it by renewed and universal accep-tance of the fundamental Christian truth, her letter continued.'[14]

As Moderator, Professor Henderson undertook the many duties required accompanied by his Chaplain the Rev. Dr J. W. Baird, Minister of St Machar's Cathedral in Old Aberdeen where 'GD' served as an elder.

In December he led the dedication service of the new St Colum-ba's church in London, the original having been destroyed by

---

14 Aberdeen Evening Express, Tuesday, 24 May 1955.

bombing in the Second World War. At the exact time as the church burnt down, the incumbent minister Dr Fleming died. A dark day for the Church. The dedication service led by Professor Henderson was broadcast on the BBC.

It was also reported that he addressed a few hundred potential school teachers at the Aberdeen Training Centre saying, 'One of the most important agents for good in human society is a school-teacher who is a Christian.'[15] Professor Henderson then confessed that, although he had been teaching for thirty years, he was one of that despised class – the unqualified teacher. He continued, 'My mission for you would be that you should become such centres of firm and happy influence.'[16] Professor Henderson said that a new crusade was on, 'a crusade against the devil and all that was meant by that. Those who are under our care in school and church will be out in the thick of the fight. What is going to happen to them? Will they perhaps quickly conclude that they have been let down, that they have been allowed to start without proper and adequate preparation, without armour of defence or weapon of attack, or supplies to sustain them? We have to realise what we are sending them into, no child's game, but the battle of life. Together, church and school. We must equip them for life not just to earn an income. I think we ought to co-operate and can.'[17]

An address entitled 'A century ago ... and now' was published and sold at one shilling and sixpence. In it The Right Reverend the Moderator of the General Assembly asks: 'What warnings and encouragements has a picture of one hundred years ago to give us? Much is just as it was; much has changed. But are we better orientated today in Scotland than in 1855? Are we more what we should be, more Christian or less? I turn to the records of that year with some personal interest for my father who became a minister of the church of Scotland was born in 1855. It is remarkable how many notes of our time were struck in 1855. Norman Macleod was writing "Nothing can exceed the present

---

15 Ibid., Wednesday, 1 February 1956.
16 Ibid.
17 Ibid.

complexity of the politics of the world. This war [the Crimean War] is drawing all nations slowly into a huge maelstrom" ... A Free Church Minister in Aberdeen complained in 1855 of the way in which on the slightest excuse people stayed away from church and also of the spirit of indifference among the young and so many nominal members making a sudden appearance at Communion time ... 1855 had no cinemas, aeroplanes, wireless and television, electric lighting, gas stoves, typewriters and typists, motorcars or bicycles, telephones, central heating, old age pensions, eventide homes, Sunday papers, illustrated magazines, organized sports, football pools, crossword puzzles, detective stories, compulsory elementary education, youth movements, afternoon tea or morning coffee. For women there were no votes, nor university degrees, nor cigarettes, nor places in public life or in church courts or guilds.'[18]

While Professor Henderson was on his year of Moderatorial duties A. M. Hunter, Professor of Biblical Criticism, chaired the Financial Board meetings. On 20 March 1956 he welcomed a new auditor to the Board and this afforded board members the opportunity to question the layout of the accounts which 'were not as readily understandable as they might be'.[19] This resulted in a streamlined version of the accounts in the future which was greatly appreciated. There had been a lot of spending in the last ten years and funds were low. It was therefore suggested that as the lease of Number 8 Alford Place, which was still causing a drain on finances, was due for renewal this might be a good time to sell. 'After much discussion it was felt that the College might have use for part of the building with the reorganisation of the Library.'[20]

---

18 G. D. Henderson, *A Century Ago ... and Now* (Edinburgh: Church of Scotland, 1955).
19 Financial Board Minute Books, Vol. 4, p. 407.
20 Ibid.

Sudden Death

A year later, on 12 March 1957, there was still debate about the reconstruction of the Library and difficulties had arisen as to the disposal of certain volumes both in the Library and in the College. The Council was tasked to form a plan accessible to all for the disposal of certain volumes.

It turned out that was the last meeting that Professor G. D. Henderson attended. He died on 28 May during the General Assembly of 1957, and in the tribute in the second edition of the Aberdeen Divinity Bulletin, which he had launched the previous year, it says: 'He had been there during the long sittings of the previous day and on the day before that had made a notable contribution to the proceedings. It seemed incredible that we should see him no more, the small slight figure who like so many men of that build, had an energy and alertness that suggested years of life and achievement still to come ... On first acquaintance the man himself seemed reserved and aloof and even a trifle forbidding. Certainly not for him, we felt, the conventionalities of social intercourse: consequently students hesitated to engage him in small talk (one remembers the embarrassment of a bus journey from Christ's to King's in the days of long ago – an embarrassment that seemed as acute on his side as on ours). Despite this apparent aloofness – which was really just shyness – he followed a student's career with unfailing interest, taking a deep delight in any successes though careful to conceal this from the man himself. The truth is that G. D. Henderson was a man of large humanity and great kindness. He had only to discover a case of need among his students to be moved instantly in an act of succour.'[21] He was remembered as a great teacher: 'The bell at the end of the hour surprised you in his class'.[22] 'He was always down to earth, "Church History," he would say, "is not a set of mythical legends. The men of the early church were very much like our own church leaders." In an aside he would remind us that St Paul had a bald head and bandy legs.'[23]

---

21 Aberdeen Divinity Bulletin No. 2 (1957), p. 1.
22 Ibid., p. 2.
23 Ibid., p. 1.

There were no further meetings of the Financial Board until 11 March 1958, when 'Professor Hunter said he was sure the meeting would wish him to put on record the sense of great indebtedness they felt to the late Professor G. D. Henderson, not only for his work as chairman of the Financial Board but as Master of Christ's College. The College would feel the loss of Professor Henderson for many years to come for in the ten years during which he had been Master he had made his own particular mark on the work of the College.'[24]

The work he had initiated in the Library was to continue: detailed plans were laid before the meeting and after much discussion were agreed. The estimated cost was £2,980. Professor Hunter 'had pleasure in intimating that Mrs Henderson was to donate the sum of £100 to assist in the renovation of the Library in memory of her husband, and it had been agreed that one of the bays in the Library should be called the "Professor Henderson Bay" and that a suitable plaque be placed there'.[25] She also donated all his books and a lectern for the Chapel in memory of her husband.

In his article 'Theological Education in Aberdeen', Henry Sefton writes: 'Professor Henderson entered on his new duties with considerable zest and proved an enthusiastic and indeed innovative Master of the College.'[26] Dr Sefton suggests that G. D. Henderson provided the framework which continued for many years giving the students a great and lasting collegiate experience.

'GD' was remembered with affection by a student who was interviewed for the oral archive of Aberdeen University. 'Professor G. D. Henderson was the most excellent Master. He was a little man, smaller than I am, used to stand on tiptoe and say "Very important point, Gentlemen."'[27]

Another student who reminisced about Professor Henderson, shortly before she died in 1996, was Beatrice D. Bonnar. She was the first woman to graduate at Aberdeen University with a BD

24 Financial Board Minute Books, Vol. 4, p. 427.

25 Ibid., p. 428.

26 Divinity Alumni Association Newsletter no. 15 (1995/6), p. 8.

27 Stephen Goodbrand, interview recorded on 7 September 1990 by Colin McLaren. MS 3620/1/91.

in 1937. 'Though he was small in stature, the students were rather afraid of him. No one ever dared play truant from any of his classes. I was most grateful to him as he was keen to have women ordained to the ministry. I remember attending a meeting on the subject of the ordination of women when one person in the audience stood up and said, "Jesus never had a female as one of his disciples." Prof Henderson's reply was: "if you are going to be exact as that you should have a Judas in every Kirk Session" and as he sat down he whispered to me, "No doubt there is one."'[28]

In 1996, when the belongings and all the furnishings of the Chapel and College were being offered to suitable new homes on the sale of the last remaining Alford Place building, the then Master, Professor Alan Main, wrote to the incumbent minister of St Machar's Cathedral to offer the lectern donated by Mrs Henderson. It is still used by St Machar's when services are held in the Church Hall in Dunbar Street.

Of the many legacies of Professor Henderson's time as Master the starting up of a newsletter has been the one that has helped to preserve the history of the College and its people, and its current annual publication reaches nearly a thousand alumni and friends.

In his first letter in the first edition Professor Henderson wrote:

Dear Alumni,

When you write to a friend you instinctively concentrate upon what you and he have in common, whether places, people or interests. This Bulletin will go out to some hundreds who all have in their hearts King's College and Christ's College, those who were their fellow students and teachers during a short but

---

28 Divinity Alumni Association Newsletter no. 15 (1995/6), p. 4.

critical period of their past, and a calling to which they have alike responded and which is unique amongst callings. It will do everyone good to have a reminder of what they thus share.

No one has forgotten the first day he went into King's or took his place in a Divinity classroom as an accepted candidate for the ministry. The fellowship of college years makes a permanent impression which cannot be reduced to a list of lecture headings or of subjects solemnly or frivolously discussed at midnight.[29]

---

29 Aberdeen Divinity Bulletin No. 1 (1956), p. 1.

9

Changing Days
1957–82

From the late 1950s the Financial Board Minutes become more
business-like and lack the colour and verbosity of previous years.
The Council Minutes are missing until 1970 so there is a period
when there is an overall dearth of material. However, the Masters are now in living memory; many former students remember
A. M. Hunter, Professor of New Testament, who became the
eighth head of the College succeeding Professor G. D. Henderson.

Born in 1906, Archibald Macbride Hunter was a prolific writer
and many of his books became standard references for teachers,
students and ministers. *The Work and Words of Jesus* was first
published in 1950 and he wrote in the preface, 'This book was
written ... to serve a practical purpose ... our New Testament
scholars are not writing "Lives" of Christ; and when I looked
around for a short one, embodying the results of recent scholarship, to put into the hands of my divinity students, I found none
suited to my purpose. This is a very modest attempt to supply the
want.'[1]

Writing his first letter from the Master to the Alumni in
Bulletin No. 3, Professor Hunter mentions student numbers as
the College's main problem. 'Last year we had barely twenty and
this year with seven new men entering, we are not likely to have
many more. Surely ten men in each of the three years is not an
impossible target to reach. If we had a real religious awakening in
our land, I am confident the problem would solve itself. But these
things are not in our control – we cannot command the tides of

---

1 A. M. Hunter, *The Work and Words of Jesus*, revised paperback edition (London: SCM Press, 1973), Preface.

the Spirit. What we can do is by our prayers, by our writing and by our Christian propaganda, to enhance the dignity of Christ's College and thereby hope to attract young men to it.'[2]

Church Union?

Shortly after becoming Master of Christ's College, A. M. Hunter found himself in the limelight following a controversial decision by the General Assembly. The question of Church Union was at the forefront of proceedings again and the Assembly of 1959 was receiving the feed-back of Presbyteries considering what became known as the Bishops' Report.

'From this report it was envisaged that if union could be agreed upon by the Episcopalian and Presbyterian Churches then the Presbyterians would accept a form of Episcopacy known as "Bishops in Presbytery". The report had been the result of several years toil by a committee consisting of Anglicans and Presbyterians. Many Presbyterians felt that their representatives had been drawn too much from the University Divinity Professors and that ordinary ministers and laymen had not been sufficiently represented.'[3]

The response from the Presbyteries was entirely negative. The Inter Church Relations Committee at the Assembly suggested a compromise with a motion stating that the report was not acceptable in its present form. This led to a furious and lengthy debate which eventually threw out the conciliatory motion and bluntly declared that the report was unacceptable. Dr A. C. Craig, the Convenor of the Committee for Church Union, resigned over this decision saying that it meant a reversal of the Church's policy over the last ten years and a retreat into 'spiky Presbyterianism'.[4]

Tradition had it that two representatives from the Church of Scotland attended the Episcopalian Council during the week of the General Assembly. 'It was rather a tense moment when the Bishop of Moray escorted the Presbyterian delegates, the Rev.

---

2 Aberdeen Divinity Bulletin No. 3 (1958), p. 1.

3 Thomas Veitch, 'As Edinburgh Went, So Might Have Gone the World', *The Living Church*, Vol. 138 (14 June 1959), p. 20.

4 Ibid.

Professor A. M. Hunter, of the Chair of Biblical Criticism in Aberdeen University and the Master of Christ's College and Sir Hugh Turnbull into the hall. The Primus, Dr Hannay, Bishop of Argyll and the Isles welcomed the delegates. He said that the decision of the previous day had shown that the churches were not so close together as many had hoped, yet such interchange of visits were worthwhile even as a matter of good manners and courtesy. He said we must not sit down miserably under the decision but begin all over again to work for unity and go on praying tirelessly for it.'[5] It fell to the Master of Christ's College to send the Assembly's greetings; and he was reported to say that 'the decision might well have been a wise one. A premature move towards unity might have caused further splits in both the Episcopalian and Presbyterian Churches and done more harm than good. There were many questions upon which people were not clear and much further threshing out of problems would be worthwhile.' But he went on, 'most of us feel that this is not the end – we must go on talking to each other and go on working for unity and not resist the leading of the Holy Spirit and capitulate to un-Christian despair.'[6]

The reporter, the Rev. Thomas Veitch, had titled the piece 'As Edinburgh went, so might have gone the world'. He felt '[t]he importance of Scotland in this whole matter of union is very great for by action here in this ancient ecclesiastical storm centre, unity between Episcopalians and Presbyterians all over the world might be achieved'.[7]

At a Financial Board meeting on 17 March 1959, Professor Hunter welcomed Professor James (Jim) McEwen to his first meeting and it was finally agreed to rent out all of No. 8 Alford Place and not to sell.

---

5 Ibid.
6 Ibid.
7 Ibid.

Adult Education

Professor McEwen was quick to make his mark by providing Adult Education classes on the Bible and Church History. These were attracting large numbers. It was also around this time that '[m]en over 25 who had chosen to enter the ministry were at present accepted as modified curriculum men into the Arts Faculty of the University. Owing however to the pressure of places in the Arts faculty the University could no longer accept these men and the Committee on Education for the Ministry of the church was considering setting up pre-training courses which would be conducted by the church consisting of two years attending classes.'[8]

A year later the Master commented that 'Christ's College was now being used on a scale far wider than he himself had ever experienced. The pre-divinity courses had been instituted and the Adult Education classes were proving very popular.'[9]

However, student numbers were seen as low. One alumnus, Grahame Bruce, writes an entertaining article in the fifth bulletin. 'Christ's itself seems to be in good order save only that the very stones seem to cry out for more men to fill its walls – more students intent on offering their lives to him whose name the College proudly bears.'[10]

In the Divinity Bulletin of 1961, Professor McEwen in his position as Dean of the Faculty writes, 'I am glad to report that there has been a rise in the number of students entering the Faculty in the past session and the prospects for next session look quite good. We are still, however falling well short of really adequate numbers.'[11]

In the same edition, alumnus Peter Youngson recalls the voices and characters of the staff, including 'the rich deep voice of Nimrod, the "Mighty Hunter". It was a voice which might reasonably have been expected to show signs of wear at times, for the Master's life is a full one. Yet this voice was heard inspiringly in worship, stimulatingly in classroom, and constantly dealing

---

8 Financial Board Minute Books, Vol. 4, p. 448.
9 Ibid., p. 453.
10 Aberdeen Divinity Bulletin No. 5 (1960), p. 3.
11 Aberdeen Divinity Bulletin No. 6 (1961), p. 1.

sensitively and practically with the flow of problems an impor-
tunated student body always produces ... Professor McEwen is
a man whose enthusiasm for his subject is infectious and whose
subject is therefore always alive. We were also fortunate to sit
under a man who patiently weighed the value of the Red Herrings
we trailed through his lectures and dealt simply and lucidly with
them if they merited it ... the voice of Professor Cairns, patient
and tolerant as he conducted us through a course filled with those
so essential intangibles which are hard to learn and testing to
teach. Then the voice of Professor Graham coolly arbitrating
even when feelings ran high in the heat of debate on pacifism or
some other equally emotionally charged ism ...'[12]

In 1962 the College lamented the sudden and tragic death of
the University Principal Thomas Taylor and the Master initiated
work on a publication of his sermons and graduation speeches.
A. M. Hunter knew him well and admired him greatly. He
corresponded regularly with Lady Taylor, writing to her about
his proposal, 'so that those of us who knew and loved the Principal may have a record of the spiritual wisdom and signal felicity
of phrase we all in part remember'.[13]

He wrote elsewhere, 'He was indeed a Principal of principles
and to us in the Divinity Faculty a tower of strength. In the fourteen years he guided the destinies of the University not only did
he bring lustre to his Alma Mater by his superb gifts of speech
and mind but by his fearless Christian witness and by his valiant
support of all good things Scottish.'[14]

Doric Memories

In October 1966 a student called David Ogston entered the
Divinity Hall and later wrote his memoirs in Doric. 'If King's is
oor intellectual hame, Christ's is the spiritual for a hail variety o
reasons. The student body is aa convened ilka Friday for Chapter,

---

12 Ibid.
13 Correspondence between Helen Taylor and W. Douglas Simpson,
MS 2843/31/1-28/11.
14 Aberdeen Divinity Bulletin No. 7 (1962), p. 1.

faar we are sermonised an catechised an treated to the rainbow
splurge o doctrinal colours and fyles some gweed aul-fashioned
oratory fae invited spikkers. The bonus is lunch in the common
room aye wi the preacher at the service up at the seats in the win-
dae wie Professor Cairns, the rest o's at twa lang tables. We hiv
wir ain Sacrist, Jimmy Davidson, an his wife daes the cookin for
the Friday meal: she maks sure us singal loons hiv a real tichtener
tae mak up for all the pies and cheese pieces that we resort till
that are neither balanced nor fullin. There is table tennis across
the road, nae a gweed idea efter Mrs Davidson's mince and
tatties ... I hiv heard there is elocution lessons up at Christ's an
aa, obligatory nae less, tae plane oot yer rollinn Rs tae something
less roch, or tae sort oot yer sibilants and yer labial fricatives ...
There is a library tee, under the eagle eye o the Presbytery Clerk
Jake Mowat. Tae say the books is fooshty is gey near the mark
bit naebody daes.'[15]

Library Issues

The presence of the Presbytery Clerk as Librarian caused certain issues: it was commented at a Financial Board meeting
that ministers were seeking him out on Presbytery business and
disturbing those studying. John Mowat had taken over after the
retirement of Mitchell Hughes in 1965. Hughes had been in post
since 1952 following many successful years in various parishes.
In a tribute to him following his death in 1968, A. M. Hunter
writes, 'No member of our staff was more widely loved. He
quickly established himself as the *genius loci* and under his regime
the Library became, as Barrie would have put it, "the place that
likes to be visited". Students, ministers, laymen now came to
use it as it had not been used for years as the chair by the desk
became a kind of confessional with Mr Hughes father-in-God
to old and young. Nor was it only our Scottish lads who sought
his advice; hither also came men from the Continent and from
America, to be guided in their reading, helped with their sermons,

---

15 David D. Ogston, *Grey Stone Zion* (St John's Kirk Perth, 2008),
p. 12.

and encouraged by his counsel. One of these, the German, Gotthard Bode spoke for them all when he said: "Mr Hughes was one of the great experiences I made in Scotland". Thirteen years of devoted service ended to our keen regret in December 1965 when increasing frailty forced our grand old man's retiral.'[16]

In the Aberdeen Divinity Bulletin of 1967 it is noted that student numbers have greatly increased and the facilities of the College were now under strain. 'When fifty or more men attend the various classes and do research work in the College, attendance at the weekly lunches has to be limited and accommodation is sometimes a problem ... those who have attended our College in other days will appreciate what it is to worship in Chapter and Chapel with so great a throng.'[17]

New ground was broken at a meeting of the Financial Board in May 1967. 'Professor Hunter explained that he had been approached by Mr Edwards on the matter of the keeping of the College accounts. Mr Edwards had explained that the day to day transactions over the year were of considerable volume and by no means decreasing and he had suggested that a payment might be made to his firm to go towards meeting some of the overheads involved. The figure of 150 guineas had been suggested and the Council of the College were agreeable to recommend this sum. Mr Edwards explained that there would be no question of payment for his personal services and these would always be at the disposal of the College for what they were worth.'[18] Mr James Gordon Hastings Edwards was the third member of his family to serve as Secretary of the Financial Board of Christ's College. His grandfather, David, took over the role in 1895 following the death of John Edmond, son of the original benefactor of the College, Francis Edmond (see Chapter 1). He in turn was followed by his son James Hastings Edwards, who died in 1944. His son was not able to succeed him immediately due to war service, so Clement Marshall of the firm stepped in for a few years until James Edwards once again took up the family mantle.

16 Aberdeen Divinity Bulletin No. 1 (1968), p. 2.
17 Ibid., No. 10 (1967), p. 2.
18 Financial Board Minute Books, Vol. 4, p. 474.

The agreement to pay the firm for doing the books continued into the next century.

John Knox's Watch

At this same meeting Professor Cairns brought up the matter of John Knox's watch. He explained that he had been approached by the organisers of an exhibition in Edinburgh related to John Knox, requesting the loan of the watch. This had been part of the Thomson Bequest in 1870. When the items were given over to the University following the removal of the Museum in 1949 to allow for the construction of the Chapel, the Thomson Trustees had consented to the item being given to the University on permanent loan. 'Professor Cairns was apprehensive of the future destination of this watch as he felt it was far more appropriate that it should be in the custody of the college or in any event the Church. Mr Edwards undertook to look into the terms of the Trust.'[19] In George Smeaton's memoir he quotes Mr Thomson, 'The unvarying family tradition is that this watch was the property of the great Reformer and further that it was presented to him by Queen Mary on some occasion when she wished to show favour to him and it has ever since been preserved as an heirloom in the family.'[20]

How it came into the possession of the family is not documented but Alexander Thomson spoke of seeing a portrait of John Knox with this watch, 'an old but coarse picture, very black, rather more than three quarters length representing the Reformer standing beside a small table and on the table lay a rude figure of this watch'.[21] The watch remains on permanent loan to Aberdeen University.

---

19 Ibid.

20 George Smeaton, *Memoir of Alexander Thomson of Banchory* (Edinburgh: Edmonston and Douglas, 1869), p. 3.

21 Ibid., p. 408.

Joseph Luki Hromádka

The year 1968 saw another visit to Christ's College from Joseph Luki Hromádka. Hromádka, born in Moravia in 1889, had studied at the United Free Church College in Aberdeen in 1911. He had been drawn there by the strong influence of David S. Cairns (see Chapter 6), being impressed by the Biblical piety and missionary zeal of Cairns and the Scottish church.

After his year in Aberdeen, Hromádka had become a pastor in the Czech Lutheran Church and then a military chaplain in the First World War. His teaching career began at the Charles University in Prague, and from 1920 to 1939 he was Professor of Systematic Theology at the Jan Hus Theological Faculty in Prague. 'Without hesitation Hromádka joined the struggle against the emerging danger of German Nazism. His name appeared on the Gestapo list. After the collapse of Czechoslovak democracy in 1938 as a result of the Munich agreement, Hromádka had to leave his country and found refuge in the Princeton Theological Seminary where he became a much loved teacher.'[22] Hromádka made the choice to return to Czechoslovakia in 1947, to accept the Communist coup d'état in 1948, and to work as a Christian within the framework of a Marxist-dominated socialist society. 'I am in no sense a Communist,' he wrote, 'but I take part in this revolution from the point of view of my Christian faith which sees the work of the forgiving grace of God in the midst of changes that are coming about.'[23]

He became a controversial figure for urging reconciliation between Christians and Communists. He was a founding member of the World Council of Churches at the Conference in Amsterdam in 1948. He was given a DD from Aberdeen University the same year and preached at King's Chapel on a number of occasions. He was also founder and chairman of the Christian Peace Conference, an organisation that served as a vehicle for Christian–Marxist dialogue and for communication between Christians in the East and West, and he received the Lenin Peace Prize in 1958.

22 Charles West, 'Hromádka: Theologian of the Resurrection', https://worldview.carnegiecouncil.org/archive/worldview (accessed 05/03/18).
23 Ibid.

Hromádka came to Christ's College for the last time in January 1968. He had lunch with the students and received a Christ's College tie which he later wore during a television interview. 'He recalled his coming in 1911 to study under David S. Cairns. "Fresh from his German studies and full of Teutonic 'heresies' and Higher Criticism he found his time in Aberdeen a wholesome corrective. One day, he told us, Professor Cairns suggested

they might sort things out together theologically, in a long walk. At the end of it, he turned perplexedly, to the Professor, 'Do you think I am a Christian – or a pagan?' David Cairns thought for a long moment before replying in his deep voice, 'Hromádka – I think you are a Christian – but you don't show much enthusiasm for it!"'[24]

In a piece entitled 'In Remembrance' in the Aberdeen Divinity Bulletin of April 1970 Professor John M. Graham, Dean of the Divinity faculty, writes, 'History has not yet given a verdict on this great man, whose last public act before his death just after Christmas 1969 was to resign from the movement which he had founded in protest against the attacks made on its present secretary by the hard line communist reactionaries. But his faithfulness to God and his record as a Christian must stand untarnished whether his work bear immediate fruit or not.'[25]

Hromádka's name appears again in the transcript of David H. Cairns' farewell address to the College. 'One of the most invigorating things that Professor Hromádka said to me just before his death during his last visit to Aberdeen was an answer to a comment I made to him. I had said "Most of the people one sees in church these days are so old, I begin to wonder what will happen

---

24 Aberdeen Divinity Bulletin No. 12 (1969), p. 4.
25 Ibid. No. 13 (1970), p. 3.

in the future. In ten years' time, most of us will be gone. How much church will there be left?" He answered, "Well then you and your contemporaries have ten years in which to set it right." I hope we may be able to respond in some degree to this challenge.'[26]

First Female Minister Ordained

In 1969 a momentous event took place in Aberdeen with the ordination of Miss C. McConnachie as a Minister of the Word and Sacrament. It was the first ordination of a female by the Church of Scotland, and one of the first among the European national churches. This is not minuted by the Financial Board but would probably have been discussed by the College Council. There is a letter in the archives from a future Master of Christ's College, the Rev. Henry Sefton, in his position as Secretary of the Committee on Education for the Ministry. He writes to the Rev. John Mowat, Aberdeen Presbytery Clerk, 'I note that the Presbytery of Aberdeen has received an application from Miss C. McConnachie BD DCS. I have been in touch with Miss McConnachie and invited her to fill in a schedule of application. What we do next I am not quite sure!'[27]

Catherine McConnachie was a student of Christ's College, completing her BD in 1959, more than twenty years after the first female student. She served in the diaconate before applying successfully to be Assistant Minister in St Georges,' Tillydrone, a new parish lying between Woodside and St Machar's where she was ordained and remained until her retirement. She died in a Church of Scotland nursing home in 1990.

In the Divinity Bulletin of April 1970 Professor John Graham, Dean of the faculty, writes, 'Now we have three young women among our students – two of them straight from school and like a number of their male fellow students, taking the first year of the new four year "first degree" BD. This new presence in our

26 Ibid. No. 15 (1973), p. 3.
27 Letter of 5 July 1968 to the Rev. John Mowat, Devanah Gardens, Aberdeen, MS3241/3/6/3.

classrooms is refreshing.' Looking back, Catherine Macdonald's presence in the classrooms of 1910 was indeed remarkable (see Chapter 6).

The College at Risk Again

Also in April 1970, calls to redecorate the College were rejected at a Financial Board meeting due to the uncertainty of the future of the College. In 1969 the 'Ad Hoc committee on the Recruitment and Training for the Ministry' had reported to the General Assembly recommending the dissolution of the colleges in Edinburgh, Glasgow and Aberdeen. The commissioners of the Assembly agreed the need for a special committee to 'consult with the respective colleges and faculties in Scotland to consider the implications and advisability of such a step and to report to the next General Assembly'.[28]

The interim report in 1970 stated that the most satisfactory way forward was to report on each college individually. So the colleges had to wait another year to learn of their fate and little upgrading was done on the Christ's College buildings.

The Sanderson Report was the result of these consultations and a typed copy of it was sent to Professor Hunter, the plain brown envelope addressed simply to The Master, Christ's College, Aberdeen. The letter, dated 24 February 1971, asked for amendments and comments by 5 March at the latest to the Very Rev. Dr W. Roy Sanderson, Haddington.

The report took issue with the assertion by the committee of 1969 that the work of the colleges had been taken over by the divinity faculties. This was rejected as false as the faculties had been solely responsible for the academic teaching. Practical theology and elocution were taught in the colleges.

The report added that in 'each of the three centres, there are residual elements of former colleges which still prove useful'.[29]

---

28 Sanderson Report, MS3241/9/5.
29 Ibid.

The 1969 committee had stated, '[W]e believe that it is better to have one body responsible for the students';[30] this was seen as confusing by the Sanderson Committee. 'There can never be one body wholly responsible since theirs is not only an academic but also a vocational training.'[31]

One point made in 1969, that the dissolution would make possible fuller integration of the students, was examined by the Sanderson Committee in discussion with the staff and students of the three colleges.

There was general opposition to the readjustment although Professor John MacIntyre, Principal at New College, did feel that this move might be favoured by 'a very few members of the Faculty who were not adverse to the removal of the Church of Scotland's interests in the Faculty operations'.[32] The committee recommended no action in Edinburgh. Staff and students in Glasgow wanted to keep collegiate life with prayers and societies; but as College lunches had been discontinued 'they were already using the facilities at the university and it was found that the Divinity students were no different from those in other faculties as they tended to sit at the same table as those from their own faculty!'[33]

A students' questionnaire run by the Divinity Students' Council in Aberdeen showed the majority of students vehemently opposed to the dissolution of Christ's College.

The conclusion of the committee was in favour of continuing the present arrangements in Aberdeen, but it felt that 'in view of the fairly extensive use of the buildings made by Presbytery, a considerably greater contribution from this source might be made towards the upkeep of the College'.[34]

The Assembly of 1971 accepted the Sanderson Report and Christ's College was spared again.

---

30 Ibid.
31 Ibid.
32 Ibid.
33 Ibid.
34 Ibid.

The Next Master – James S. McEwen

In 1972 Professor Hunter retired from the University and from his position as Master of Christ's College. The next Master was Professor James Stevenson McEwen. He had been minister in three parishes before going to a lectureship in New College, his alma mater, where he had been a star pupil. 'In 1936 in New College Edinburgh, a dull and routine occasion turned into something dramatic and prophetic. Professor John Baillie was returning to his students their class essays. He paused. The class fell silent. Baillie held in his hand one essay. "Just once or twice in a teacher's lifetime one comes across as essay which is perfect; it says everything which can usefully be said about the given subject. Such an essay is this one by Mr McEwen. What can one add? There is only one comment. I give it an Alpha." Prof. Baillie's words confirmed what we his fellow students, always had known about Jim McEwen – that he was head and shoulders above the rest of us ...

'McEwen proved it again when some months later he gave his valedictory address as the retiring president of the theological society. His subject was "Justification by Faith". In half an hour he told us more about this central subject than we had learned in years of theological study.'[35]

After lecturing in New College he moved to the Church History chair at Aberdeen in 1959. 'There he joined a team of men who in the 1960's made Aberdeen the foremost Theological Faculty in Scotland.'[36]

At his first Financial Board meeting as Master in November 1972, Professor McEwen announced the sudden death of Mr James Gordon Hastings Edwards who had been Board Secretary since 1949. He welcomed Graham Cran Hunter, advocate, of Edmonds and Ledingham, who was unanimously appointed to the position.

Christ's College has a lot to be thankful for due to James McEwen. Not only had he already extended the use of the building

35 William M. Macartney, 'Obituaries and funeral eulogies', MS3757/3/16.

36 Ibid.

for adult education and pre-divinity classes but in so doing he had increased the public profile of the College. Although the future of the College would come up time and time again, what Professor McEwen did next helped to secure it financially to enable a series of renovations and improvements – a decision which caused him personal strife.

Book Sales

The Master reported in June 1972 that 'the College had far more books than it could accommodate and their condition was deteriorating. The only thing to do was to get rid of non-theological books.'[37] These would have been part of the Thomson bequest.

Sotheby's became involved and said that certain items might be of considerable value, so it was decided that, due to the high cost of insurance and the lack of a secure location, these manuscripts and books should be sold. At the next meeting, 'It was agreed to put on record the Council's gratitude for the outstanding services rendered by Dr James Wood in classifying the Library's treasures and to appoint him as the College representative at the sale due to be held in London in November. It was agreed to meet in full his and Mrs Wood's expenses in respect of travel and accommodation. The Council's thanks were also expressed to the Master, the Librarian and the Sacrist together with various students who had worked so hard.'[38]

The sale raised over £34,000 and that sum, together with the proceeds of the eventual sale of No. 8 Alford Place, led to the setting up of an Investment and Finance subcommittee.

It was reported in July 1973 that £5,000 was to be designated 'The Master's Fund' to be used at the discretion of the Master. This fund is still in existence and is of vital importance to the College and its students. There was further upgrading of the facilities in the College building, including the long-awaited new oil-fired central heating system. Also in July the Council authorised the Master 'to make a written statement to the Committee

37 Council Minute Papers, 19 June 1972.
38 Ibid., 12 October 1972.

on Education for the Ministry on the sale of books from the Library'.[39] It appears that Church of Scotland Headquarters was not happy that the Master had taken it on himself to arrange the sale of these rare books and some felt that this should have been discussed with the Department. This rumbled on, and the Master's letter to Alumni the following year shows the depth of feeling engendered. 'Our buildings which were becoming too out of date and dilapidated for effective teaching to continue in them have been transformed into an efficient well equipped teaching College. This has all been achieved without cost to the Church, but not without causing heartburnings among the ecclesiastical establishment who have an innate dislike of resolute and un-orthodox action; but of this we shall say nothing lest we pour petrol on the smouldering embers.'[40]

Professor McEwen received a letter from George Hewitt, Convenor of the Church's Committee on Education, in October 1974 asking him to meet to discuss the issue: 'It seems to me that we could achieve a great deal and clear up much of the confusion that exists if we could all meet round one table as a group interested in and concerned for the welfare of Christ's College and its Library. Relationships seem so tangled and the issues are so obscure that we think clarification would be best secured through discussion. Frankly Jim, I was moved by that last letter you wrote and the terms in which it was couched and I should like to think that we will be able to get together and resolve any difficulties whether apparent or real.'[41] This is the last documentation on this issue.

The students certainly appreciated the improvement of their surroundings. In the Aberdeen Divinity Bulletin of 1974 the President of the Divinity Students' Council, J. P. Renton, wrote: 'I am sitting in the Study at Christ's College. My surroundings are bright and modern, in fact this room might not be recognisable to any past student. This is only one of the many improvements in the College which have materialised by the sale of some valuable books. The recreation room, known better as the table-tennis

---

39 Ibid., 3 July 1973.

40 Aberdeen Divinity Bulletin No. 16 (1974), p. 2.

41 Letter from the Rev. G. B. Hewitt, General Secretary, Church of Scotland Department of Education, to the Master.

room, now has facilities for making coffee which is supplied by the College. The class room next door is now a lounge with easy chairs and tables. Gone are the old desks of the Practical Theology room which have been replaced by tables and chairs. We are indeed grateful for what has been done which supplements the lack of facilities for many who live in digs and flats. Other changes have taken place this year. The new courses in B.D. and L.Th. are in operation and most students seem to be happy with the options available. Of course the removal of compulsory Greek and Hebrew requirements are thought to be a sad loss to some. However the greatest advantage might be the reduction of lecture hours for each subject allowing more time for reading and study.'[42]

On Wednesday, 20 October 1976, the College Council met and it was reported that the Secretary 'was instructed to enquire whether minutes required to be written by hand in the Minute Book'.[43] This must refer to the missing book. There is authorisation at the next meeting on Friday 18 February 1977 for the minutes to be kept in loose-leaf typescript form. That is how they were kept in various folders until 2002 when no more appear. At that meeting, 'Professor Gray referred to the Master's serious illness and expressed the Council's prayers for a good recovery.'[44]

James McEwen had suffered a very sudden coronary thrombosis. His apologies were given at the next meeting in June; and in the October meeting: 'The Council place on record their appreciation of the services rendered by Professor J. S. McEwen as Master of the College and also as member of the Council for almost twenty years. The transformation of the interior of the main building will be a lasting reminder of his Mastership but still more permanent will be his wise guidance and relevant teaching of successive candidates for the Church's ministry. His services to the Pre-Divinity School and to many courses of Adult Christian Education and his pastoral care and concern for his students in all of these contexts will always be recalled with affection and gratitude.

42 Aberdeen Divinity Bulletin No. 16 (1974), p. 3.
43 Council Minute Papers, 18 February 1977.
44 Ibid.

'Mrs McEwen has been his support in all of these but made her distinctive contribution to the life of the College and its Alumni by the delightful series of Christmas cards designed by her. To both the Council offer thanks and good wishes for a long and happy retirement.'[45]

In a tribute appearing in the Aberdeen Divinity Bulletin in May 1978, Professor John Gray writes, 'At the beginning of this session Professor McEwen was a notable absentee, sadly missed as a loyal and agreeable colleague and as a warm hearted friend and pastor to students over the nineteen years during which he occupied the chair of Ecclesiastical History in the University of Aberdeen for the last six years of which, as Master of Christ's College, he guided the affairs of the College with ability and distinction.

'His lectures in the Faculty and in Adult Education will be long remembered for their erudition, sound judgements, and their relation to the living situation, of which Professor McEwen was always keenly aware. In all his work he had the individual needs

---

45 Ibid., 19 October 1977.

of all his students and the practical problems of their future pastorate ever before him, and they knew it.'[46]

He died in 1993, and a fellow student from New College days wrote: 'What sort of man was J. S. McEwen? He was tall, thin and at first glance looked indeed like a Professor of Church History. For he had a quiet demeanour and a rather solemn cast of countenance. Until that is one noticed a twinkle in his eye. I can say without hesitation that the most amusing letter I have ever received was from Jim. It was not witty, it was not waggish it was just uproarishly funny. It produced what the Americans call "belly laughter". The one thing about J. S. McEwen that infuriated us his friends was his reluctance to publish. At the time of the 1972 Knox celebrations, Jim emerged from his accustomed quietness and wrote and spoke with unquestionable and impressive authority.

'Away towards the end of his academic life, however, a splendid thing happened to Dr McEwen. He undertook to give a course of six evening lectures to elders from a group of Aberdeen churches. Such courses of lectures as is well known begin with an audience of around thirty, dwindle in numbers and after the New Year slowly die of anaemia. But not this series – again on the Apostles' Creed. When the course ended the Aberdeen elders themselves decided with enthusiasm to publish the lectures. They took the initiative, carried through their intention and *I Believe* remains a memorial to the crystal mind and sincere faith of that most loveable man, James Stevenson McEwen.'[47]

He had hoped to attend the College's 150th Anniversary celebrations but died just before the event. 'The Master [Professor Alan Main] paid tribute to the work of former Master Professor McEwen who passed to his rest at the beginning of May this year. An eminent Minister, churchman and scholar, his long service in this College as Professor of Church History and Master will be remembered with real affection by many. His warm, friendly and welcoming personality ensured that his door was open to all who came to him for advice and wisdom – and none were

---

46 Aberdeen Divinity Bulletin, no. 19, May 1978.
47 Macartney, 'Obituaries'.

disappointed. His quiet sincerity of faith commended itself to all with whom he had to do and was an inspiration to those who sat under him, in congregation and class. The funeral was led by the Master and former Master [Henry Sefton] and was a celebration of a life well lived, service generously given, and rest well-earned and was attended by a large and representative congregation which gathered to honour a very fine Christian.'[48]

The Next Master

Robin Barbour joined the staff of Christ's College as Professor of New Testament in 1970.

He was born in 1921, the son of the philosopher and theologian George Freeland, Laird of Bonskeid. 'His mother, Helen Hepburne-Scott was known for her warmth and generosity. She brought the traditions of social reform to his background of Christian Mission and it was on these foundations of intellectual rigour, strong faith and generosity of spirit that Robin was to stand.'[49]

He served with an artillery regiment during the war and was awarded the Military Cross. After the war he completed his studies at Oxford University, then Edinburgh before studying Divinity at St Andrews and Yale. He was chaplain to overseas students in Edinburgh before joining the New College staff to lecture in New Testament.

Soon after moving to Christ's College it fell to Professor Barbour to write the letter to the Alumni in the Divinity Bulletin. He comments on the honour of being asked to do this as he had only been in position for sixteen months. 'But so many angels have left the premises that the fools just have to rush in.'[50] He was speaking of the departure of Professors Hunter, Graham and Cairns in the previous twelve months. In the same bulletin, under Personalia, 'The Reverend David Steel DD Minister of St Michael's Linlithgow has brought lustre to our alma mater by

48 Council Minutes Papers, 26 June 1993.
49 James A. Simpson, Obituary, *Life and Work*, December 2014.
50 Aberdeen Divinity Bulletin No. 15 (1973), p. 1.

his nomination as Moderator Designate of the General Assembly of 1974. Our hearty congratulations and our prayers go out to and up for David Steel as he prepares to undertake this high responsibility.'[51]

So in 1977 Robin Barbour became the tenth head of the Church College in Aberdeen. At this point he was also Convener of the Church of Scotland 'Committee of Forty' which had been set up to look at the mission and membership of the Church, and to consider what changes could be made to stop decline. Those who were against reform referred to it as 'Ali Barbour and the Forty Thieves'. Professor Barbour was then seen as an important leader with a commitment to reform. In 1978 he was appointed Moderator Designate and became the youngest serving Moderator at the age of 58.

Just before he took up these duties he was able to write his first report as Master. 'I owe more than I can say to Dr Henry Sefton, Secretary of the College Council and indispensable factotum, whose energy and enthusiasm in the service of the College knows no limits. Last year I was preoccupied with being Dean and convening an unruly body called the Committee of Forty as well as with many other things; this year I am about to go off for an extended period on another series of jaunts. Through it all he keeps the wheels turning. The College owes him a very great debt.'[52]

Later in the report he writes, 'Christ's College we think, ought to be a centre for the education not only of candidates for the ministry of Church of Scotland and other churches but also of the

---

51 Ibid.
52 Ibid. No. 20 (1979), p. 4.

whole church and its members. A live church must be an educated church, and Christ's College should have a broader part to play in that at least so far as the north-east of Scotland is concerned.'[53]

During his first year as Master, Professor Barbour received a letter from David H. Cairns, son of the late last Principal. 'Some time ago an art gallery sub-committee, under Andrew Walls, decided that plaques should be put up in public places connected with Aberdeen's eminent citizens of the past who have not yet been brought before the public. I was astonished to read in the *Express* that my father had made it among the first six. When they asked me where the plaque ought to go, I had no hesitation in saying, "The outside of Christ's College," where he mainly taught and where the public will most easily see it. My father is to be commemorated as a "pioneer of the Ecumenical Movement" which I think most suitable in view of his whole life and in chief in view of his function as chairman of the fourth Commission of the 1910 Edinburgh Conference. He would certainly have scoffed at the whole idea but I need not say I am tremendously pleased and I think my sister, Alison, would have been too for I was under the impression that he was now under the eyes of a generation that knew not Joseph, a largely forgotten figure.'[54]

It is ironic that as a life-long abstainer Cairns' only visible public memorial is on the outside wall of what is now a pub, albeit known as the College Bar.

---

53 Ibid.
54 Handwritten letter in Christ's College files.

Academic Aid Fund

During Professor Barbour's Moderatorial year it became clear that the future was again looking uncertain for the College. Henry Sefton wrote: 'The recent cuts in public expenditure have seriously affected the University and have resulted in every post that becomes vacant being "frozen". The chair of Hebrew and Semitic languages will be no exception. The University has made it clear that there is no desire to abolish the chair but it cannot afford to make a new appointment unless financial help is forthcoming. Negotiations are now in progress to see whether the Church of Scotland can contribute more than it presently does to academic salaries here.

'It is clear that a new stage is being approached in the relationship of the Church with Universities ... It is unrealistic to expect the universities to train ministers without support of this kind.'[55]

An urgent working party was set up with various Church committees and in April 1980 it was reported that '[t]he committee on Education for the Ministry had agreed to make a grant of £3,000 per annum for three years to the Council to assist it to make a grant to the University of Aberdeen. The grant had been made on the clear understanding that the College reconsider the College assets and take full responsibility for any grant from 1st January 1984. It was agreed that the Acting Master should write to the Principal of the University undertaking to make a grant of £5,000 per annum towards Divinity salaries during the incumbency of the new Professor of Hebrew and Semitic languages.'[56]

The money had to be found and it was agreed to ask the Financial Board to launch an appeal for an endowment fund for the College. It was also agreed that Aberdeen Presbytery should increase their contributions for use of the building.

The Academic Aid Fund was duly set up with a generous donation by the Novum Trust and transfers from other funds held by the College. There were also donations from Board members, alumni and friends of the College.

---

55 Aberdeen Divinity Bulletin No. 21 (1980), p. 3.
56 Council Minute Papers, 30 April 1980.

In February 1981, Professor William Johnstone was welcomed to the Chair of Hebrew and Semitic Languages and the Rev. Dr Alan Main, former Chaplain to the University, was welcomed to the Church Chair of Practical Theology. Professor Barbour was congratulated on his appointment as Dean of the Chapel Royal, a position he held for the next ten years.

The day-to-day work of the College continued and student numbers were high, but alongside this there was constant concern about the future. The building at 2 Alford Place needed work and a new member of the Financial Board was asked to undertake a survey of the buildings.

Mr James Kelman's report did not make pleasant reading. He felt that considerable expenditure would be required to bring the building up to a reasonable standard. He also expressed his opinion that the building was of no great value on the market as there was no parking and the rates were very high. He valued it at £45,000.

A small group was appointed with representatives from the Department of Education, the Presbytery and the College Council to discuss the future of the buildings.

The Master Retires

Before they had time to report back the College was rocked by the resignation of the Master. Professor Barbour had taken the decision to retire early. Writing in 2012 he said, 'I retired from my post at Aberdeen on reaching the age of 62. I didn't want to retire early but the university was in considerable difficulty at the time because Mrs Thatcher's government had greatly reduced its grant and one of the ways of saving money was by reducing salaries.'[57] Luckily for the Department, the University was able to retain Professor Barbour for three days a week until he reached the normal retirement age.

His had been a troubled Mastership due to external issues and it is ironic that in 1899 his grandmother had contributed to the

---

57 Alumnus Newsletter, 2012.

appeal for funds for the Professors' salaries (see Chapter 4). As he announced his retirement in 1978 he wrote in the Bulletin: 'I am all too aware of how little I have done and how much I have left undone during the short years since I was appointed. That only increases my gratitude to those who have been my colleagues in the College's life and work. I am thinking especially of Henry Sefton ... he knows it all and had the College's every interest at heart ... and now before we go to press comes the news that the General Assembly has appointed Dr Henry Sefton of the Department of Church History to be the next Master. Everyone who knows him, and everyone who knows anything about the history of Christ's College in recent years will be delighted at this news.'[58]

58 Aberdeen Divinity Bulletin No. 23 (1982), p. 4.

Two Masters, Two Sales
1982–2001

The appointment of the Reverend Dr Henry Sefton was a popular one and made history as he was the first Master who was not a Professor. 'No one knows the College's affairs better than he, no one has delved more deeply into its history, no one except those actually living there finds more time to be present within its walls, no one has greater determination to ensure its welfare in difficult times and no one knows more about its students or cares more for their welfare.'[1]

Henry Sefton was a son of the Manse with considerable intellectual qualifications. He not only had direct ministerial experience in parish work in Glasgow, Wishaw and Newbattle, but went on to become the secretary responsible for the Committee on Education for the Ministry at the Church of Scotland offices at 121 George Street, Edinburgh. He was appointed lecturer in Church History in Aberdeen in 1972 where he soon became Secretary of Christ's College Council and played a leading role in College affairs thereafter. He was greatly involved in the politics of the University cuts in the early 1980s as he was President of the Association of University Teachers. The Reverend James C. Stewart delivered the charges at his induction service as Master and explained why the title of the office is Master not Principal. 'In the 'thirties that title [Principal] was given up, apparently in deference to the University with which the College was entering into a new relationship consequent upon the union of the Churches in 1929. Perhaps it was felt that your predecessor of that day constituted a threat to the dignity of the resident head

---

1 Aberdeen Divinity Bulletin No. 23 (1982), p. 5.

of the University if he retained the old title. If you constitute any kind of threat to the present-day Principal it will not, I think, be as Master of Christ's College but on the grounds of another of your offices.'[2] A reference to his AUT position which no doubt raised a gentle laugh among the congregation.

At his first meeting as Master and Chair of the Council he suggested, and it was agreed, that Professor Barbour be invited back as a member of the Council for the period of his part-time service at the University. Dr Wood, Honorary Librarian, was also to be invited to join the team. The main business was concerned with a report presented by the Reverend Professor Alan Main and Dr Wigglesworth, lecturer in Practical Theology, on their visit to St John's College in Nottingham to study their scheme of Theological Education by Extension. They submitted 'a possible outline of a similar scheme which might be attempted, based upon Christ's College'.[3]

The North Building

A meeting of the Financial Board in March 1983 heralded the beginning of the end for the College buildings. 'The Master reported that a meeting had taken place with representatives from the Committee on Education for the Ministry. It had been made clear that the Committee will not wish to renew the arrangement under which £3,000 has been made to the College to assist with the annual payment which the College in turn makes to the University to assist with expenses in the Faculty of Divinity. The Committee had also expressed its concern at the level of contribution by the Committee to college funds as compared with the contribution made to other colleges in Scotland and, in particular, the suggestion had been made that serious consideration should be made by the College Council and Financial Board to the possibility of disposing of the building on the north side of Alford Place comprising the Chapel, Library and Sacrist's flat.'[4]

2 Ibid. No. 24 (1983).
3 Council Minute Papers, 27 October 1982.
4 Financial Board Minute Papers, 2 March 1983.

The response by the members of the Board was to note that the sale of this building would necessitate finding alternative accommodation for the Chapel, Library and flat. They agreed on a joint meeting with the Council.

By the time the Council met again in May, Dr Sefton had attended two further meetings with the Committee on Education for the Ministry and the Committee was now referring to the '[i]nvestigation into the maintenance of double-site locus of theological education in Aberdeen. After a lengthy and exhaustive discussion of all of the facets of this complex issue a consensus emerged amongst Council members that enquiries should be initiated by the Faculty on behalf of Christ's College with a view to relocating the work of the College and Faculty in Old Aberdeen and moving towards an orderly disengagement from the buildings at Holburn Junction over a period of years, always with the proviso that satisfactory accommodation be secured before any irreversible steps be taken to dispose of the present properties.'[5]

So, just fifty years on from the troubles over the buildings with Mr Butchart (see Chapter 6), the College found itself again in a position of debate with the University over its future.

Before the end of 1983 it had been ascertained that the issue of the selling of the buildings would have to come before the General Assembly. The North building title was in the names of the local trustees but the titles had contained an 'Allocation Order which seemed to suggest that in the management and disposal of the property the trustees were subject to the regulation and direction of the General Assembly'.[6]

Theological Education by Extension

So, with this on the back burner until the Assembly of May 1984, College work continued with Chapter services, prizes, retreats and lunches. Professor Main's work on Theological Education by Extension (TEE) continued and resulted in the groundbreaking setting up of a framework for a pilot programme. However,

5 Council Minute Papers, 10 May 1983.
6 Financial Board Minute Papers, 24 June 1983.

there was no slack in the system for existing members of staff to undertake this work so it was agreed to offer part-time employment for two years to further the research work and construct a pilot programme.

In the meantime the Financial Board, following the advice given by Graham Hunter, the Board's Secretary and Treasurer, were agreeing that, as the General Assembly of the Church of Scotland only met annually, it might be sensible if the approach to that body concerned both buildings, not just the North one. However, just prior to the General Assembly of 1984 the Master reported that he had met with representatives of the Committee on Education for the Ministry and it had been agreed that discussion around the sale of the North building be delayed until the General Assembly of 1985.

On a lighter note Graham Hunter told the Board that the College received an annual payment from British Telecom of five pence because two telephone kiosks were situated on College grounds. Due to administrative costs it was not worthwhile collecting this sum so British Telecom had offered to give the College £20, representing a £1 fee for the next twenty years, on the understanding that their tenure of the two sites would be guaranteed. The Board could not give this assurance so the annual figure of £1 was accepted!

In June 1984 Professor Main was able to report that the Rev. Dr Kenneth Dupar had accepted a contract to work as consultant on the Theological Education by Extension (TEE) project for the next two years.

For Sale

Finally, in June 1985 it is reported: 'The General Assembly authorise the Trustees in whom the Library or North Building of Christ's College Aberdeen is vested, to sell or otherwise dispose of the same at such price and on such terms and conditions as may be decided by the Financial Board and direct that the net proceeds of the sale shall be held and applied by the Financial Board for the furtherance of theological education associated with the main Christ's College Building, such use to include the possible application of funds for fabric purposes in connection with that building.'[7] The wording of this deliverance has been of great importance since then.

A meeting of the Council on the same day agreed that nothing would be done about selling the building until early 1986 and conversations began about the procedures for dealing with the contents. In October, the Master reported that well over 1000 volumes and most of the bound periodicals had been transferred to the Divinity departmental libraries at King's College. The Council agreed to offer the Communion table and chairs in the College Chapel to the Minister and Kirk Session of Inverallochy and Rathen East for use in the church in Inverallochoy. The Minister there, R. F. Yule, had been a student representative on the College Council and on the Board of the soon to be formed Alumni Association.

Henry Sefton writes in the Aberdeen Divinity Bulletin of 1985, 'Over the last ten years there has been a marked tendency for our activities to take place increasingly in Old Aberdeen. Our daily prayers and weekly chapter services are held in the University Chaplaincy Centre and King's College Chapel. With mixed feelings we asked and obtained the General Assembly's permission to dispose of the Library building at 2 Alford Place."[8]

This was the last Bulletin to be produced. Mention of it is made in future minutes but the pressures on the Master and lack of secretarial time rendered it impossible to continue despite repeated efforts. The Master and Professor Main had managed to secure secretarial help from the Sacrist's wife and, in June 1986, '[t]he Master was given the authority to buy a word processor if that seemed appropriate, and to engage supplementary secretarial help as necessary'.[9]

---

7 Ibid., 21 June 1985.

8 Aberdeen Divinity Bulletin No. 26 (1985), p. 2.

9 Council Minute Papers, 20 June 1986.

A Library Assistant

Due to the transfer of some of the books, and the intended transfer of the rest, from Christ's College Library in Alford Place to
join the departmental collections at King's, it was agreed that
'curatorial' services would be required. A Library Assistant, Mrs
Ina Strachan, was appointed and with 'effect from 1st August
1986 would be employed on a regular basis at a salary of £150 a
month provided that the figure involves no liability for National
Insurance Contributions. It was also agreed that proper procedures be put into place to give effect to any PAYE responsibilities.
Since Mrs Strachan's work is to be carried out in the Faculty
Library at the University it was also agreed that further efforts
should be made to ensure that contributions are made from each
of the five departments.'[10]

Christ's College has continued to pay the salary for this position so it seems that negotiations with heads of department did
not go well!

The meeting in June also reported that the Department of Practical Theology had moved to Old Aberdeen and that Aberdeen
Presbytery was looking at the possibility of taking over the running of the main building in Alford Place. So the writing was on
the wall for that building as well. A year later it was noted that
the Presbytery 'had intimated that it was not feasible for it to
assume sole responsibility for the maintenance of upkeep, heating
and lighting etc. of the main building although they might be prepared to consider some scheme of shared use. Unless a scheme for
shared use could be agreed then the intention of the Presbytery
was to cease using the Building in June 1988.'[11]

Sale Concluded

Finally, in October 1987, a closing date was held for the sale
of the North building. Discussion had previously taken place
regarding a possible restriction against the building being sold to

---

10 Financial Board Minute Papers, 20 June 1986.
11 Ibid., 11 March 1987.

be used as a licensed premises. The Board had rejected this with Professor Marshall asking for his dissent to be minuted.

In the event, despite high bids being received from three agents representing owners of potential public houses, an agreement was reached with the Free Presbyterian Church to purchase the building for £100,000. The highest offer was from Temleaf Limited for £174,589, so church over pub cost the College over £74,000. However, all involved will look back at this being the right decision as the building is still used for regular worship and the Sacrist's flat still provides accommodation.

'Future of the College Buildings' still appeared in the agendas of the Financial Board and College Council but alongside this the College activities continued to thrive with ever-increasing numbers of students but no new teaching staff. TEE had taken off with over 150 students enrolled and seven courses being offered and regulations were being looked at to provide a Certificate in Christian Education; this is still in existence under the heading of Distance Learning. Dr Dupar was appointed Programme Director and due to the success of the programme it was decided to delay a decision about selling the main building.

The FAITH Fund

The economic climate of the time was still causing financial difficulties for further education. In the Financial Board Minutes of 20 April 1988, 'Professor Torrance made reference to the serious threat to the future of theological education in the North-east of Scotland resulting from the proposed university cuts. He suggested that it was essential that efforts be made by the College to raise funds on its own behalf.'[12]

The Board agreed that efforts should be made to raise awareness of the situation with friends of the College at home and in North America. Mr Hunter was to look into the possibility of being able to claim back tax if donations were made by Deed of Covenant. It was also agreed that any funds raised should be 'at

12 Ibid., 20 April 1988.

the disposal of the Trustees without any direction either from Aberdeen University or from the Department of Education of the Church of Scotland.'[13]

It took two years and much discussion before the FAITH Fund was agreed under the leadership of a post-graduate student, Mr Scott Rodin. Proposals for a four-year programme were put forward; and although there were anxieties concerning expenditure and risk, and at the great reluctance of Mr Hunter, the Endowment Appeal was launched.

One of the first things Scott Rodin initiated was a Faculty of Divinity Alumnus Association and newsletter, the first of which was produced in winter 1990, five years since the last Bulletin. Christ's College has funded this newsletter ever since. All the department staff were introduced in the first edition and publications by staff and alumni are listed along with an appeal for contact details of 'lost Alumni'. The editorial explains, 'It is with great anticipation that we start this task of communicating with our graduates, former students and staff and friends of the Faculty of Divinity. Our graduates now number in the many hundreds. They are located on all five continents and date back to the graduating class of 1934. There are several important reasons why we have decided to begin this rather large undertaking.

'First the size of our Alumni population has grown considerably during the sharp increases in enrolment over the past ten years. We felt it was time to provide a vehicle whereby we could exchange information and keep you up to date on the happenings in Aberdeen. Secondly we hope to create a means by which our graduates can obtain information concerning the work, writings and whereabouts of their fellow graduates as well as the new publications available by members of staff. We hope the result will be a renewed network of contacts for each of our graduates as well as strengthened ties to the staff in Aberdeen. Thirdly, as we face an exciting and challenging future we felt it most appropriate to seek the guidance, help and support that can only come from a close network of men and women who know first-hand the benefits of a University of Aberdeen education. Your experi-

---

13 Ibid.

ences with us in the past make you an invaluable asset as we seek to build a secure and dynamic future.'[14]

The editor waits until the second issue to launch the Divinity FAITH Fund. 'During the past decade, the time of greatest activity and growth in the Faculty, the public funding for staff, library resources and grant aid have been seriously cut by the national government and the future for public funding looks even worse. To meet this challenge a group of Faculty members banded together and created FAITH, the Fund for the Aberdeen Initiative in Theology.'[15] The areas of highest priority are outlined as scholarships for overseas post-graduate education especially for third-world students, staff funding and library resources.

The Main Building

It was at a meeting of the Council in June 1990 that the future of the remaining building was decided. The stage had been reached where no one was using it other than for storage, vandalism was becoming a problem and the costs of upkeep would increase. 'After a full discussion it was unanimously agreed with great regret to recommend to the Financial Board that the General Assembly be petitioned to authorise the sale of the building with the strongest possible representation being made that the monies realised be applied for the furthering of the original intent of the benefactors, namely the developing and supporting of tertiary theological education in the North East of Scotland.'[16]

The meeting the following year gave the Master power to deal with the disposal of the contents of the College building. The Master further reported on the funding of Mrs Strachan, drawing the attention of the Council to the fact that much of her work was for the University but Christ's College was still paying her salary.

The new Alumni Association was congratulated for its work and the Rev. Ronald Yule and Mrs Edna Pyle were particularly thanked. There had been three reunions in the past year, one

---

14 Divinity Alumni Association Newsletter, 1990.
15 Ibid.
16 Council Minute Papers, 26 June 1990.

in New Orleans and one in Aberdeen which had a tour of the Library followed by a Communion service in the Chapel and then a five-course dinner in the Senior Common Room. The third was a lunch gathering of some sixty Alumni during the General Assembly in Edinburgh. This tradition continues.

A Spanner in the Works

It was not until the General Assembly of May 1992 that the deliverance requesting permission to sell the main building was presented to the Commissioners, and then something totally unexpected happened. This was reported back to the Council and Financial Board as follows: 'The Master reported that authorisation for the sale of the College Building had not been granted by the General Assembly but the matter had been postponed until such time as consultation had taken place with the Presbytery of Aberdeen.'[17] The members of the Board were astonished and 'somewhat dismayed'[18] by this. Mr Hunter reported that he had received a letter from Mr R. A. Paterson, Solicitor of the Church, indicating that correct procedure had not been followed prior to the General Assembly and requesting that the title deeds of the main College building be sent to him. Mr Hunter was instructed to advise Mr Paterson that the Presbytery had been fully consulted and had indicated quite definitely that they did not have any further proposed use for the building. In addition neighbouring Presbyteries and also the Synod had been consulted and had not shown any interest. It was also pointed out that there had been a series of meetings over a number of years with the Department of Education at which the future of the College building had been very much discussed. It had been indicated at these meetings that an approach would be made by the Board to the General Assembly for authorisation to sell and there had been no indication at that stage that this was other than the correct procedure.

The next day, Professor Alan Main in his position of Secretary to the Council sent a letter to the Secretary of the Church of Scot-

17 Financial Board Minute Papers, 6 July 1992.
18 Ibid.

land Trust, with whom the Board had been instructed to deal, regarding the 'vexed matter of the possible sale of the College Building'. He explained that the deliverance was 'opposed by the Clerk to the Presbytery of Aberdeen, whether acting on his own as a commissioner, or as representing the Presbytery, we know not'. He continued with the following points:

1   The title deeds to the College are in Edinburgh and we would wish sight of these to see what the funding provisions were in connection with the building, its use and purpose.
2   In recent years, since we ceased using the College building for teaching purposes, wide-ranging consultations <u>were</u> held with representatives of Aberdeen Presbytery, of surrounding Presbyteries, the Synod of Aberdeen and delegates from the Department of Education, principally its then General Secretary, the Rev. Alasdair Morton. From these no positive suggestions emerged as to possible utilisation of the College Building.
3   To this point, as far as our records tell, the Presbytery of Aberdeen has never made any claim to share in the proceeds from any possible sale of the building.
4   Our clear and unwavering understanding has been and is that Christ's College was established after the Disruption through generous local sponsorship for the behoof of Theological Education in the North East of Scotland. We in Council have simply adhered to that wish in putting to the Assembly our desire that should the building be sold, any monies accruing should be applied to the maintenance and furtherance of theological education in the North East.[19]

The Financial Board meeting must have been a long one as the FAITH Fund came up for lengthy discussion before it was agreed that another meeting was necessary to look in more detail at the operation of the fund and its future. Plans for a William Robertson Smith Congress and the 150th anniversary of the College were also discussed. The final item in the minutes read: 'Dr Sefton

---

19 Letter in Council Minute Papers dated 7 July 1992.

intimated to the Board that he would be retiring from the University as of 30 September 1992 and that he would also be retiring as Master on the same date. He advised that the General Assembly had confirmed the appointment of the Reverend Professor Alan Main as the new Master of Christ's College.'[20]

At Henry Sefton's last meeting in September, Professor Main said, 'All those connected with Christ's College owed a great debt of gratitude to Dr Sefton for all his work on behalf of the College over his 20 years of association with it. During the whole of that period he had worked very hard for the benefit of the College and had been unfailingly helpful and thoughtful.'[21]

His work on behalf of the College continues (at the time of writing) in an advisory capacity as a Board member.

The induction of Dr Alan Main (centre), held in Christ's College, Aberdeen, with (from left), the Rev. Peter Davidson, the Rev. A. Stewart Todd, the Very Rev. Professor Robin Barbour, and the Rev. Professor David Cairns.

A New Master

Born in Aberdeen in 1936, Alan Main went to Robert Gordon's College before studying Divinity at Aberdeen University. He was ordained in 1963 and served as minister at Chapel of Garioch Parish Church, before being appointed Chaplain to the University

20 Financial Board Minute Papers, 6 July 1992.
21 Ibid., 1 September 1992.

of Aberdeen in 1970. His appointment as Professor of Practical Theology in 1980 paved the way for him to take over from Henry Sefton, becoming the seventh Master or twelfth head of College in nearly 150 years.

The anniversary of the College foundation was cause for celebration and a big event was planned. 'On Friday 1st October a notable event occurred at Christ's College. The College building which had lain dormant since all teaching had to be moved to King's in 1986, came back to vibrant life with the celebration ... Dr Henry Sefton, former Master of the College "launched" the programme with a lecture chronicling highlights in the history of Christ's. This was followed to universal acclamation by five cameo picture presentations of life at the College spanning the decades and calling to mind the personalia and happenings of yesteryear. A magnificent buffet was then served in the College Hall, the fruit of the endeavours of staff wives and an able company of students. The climax of the occasion was a service of thanksgiving in the former chapel, conducted by the Master with Professor Robin Barbour as preacher and Dr Bill Macmillan as celebrant. There amidst a very real sense of "The communion of saints", the company was reminded of its origins and encouraged to reflect on collegiate future in the service of the Lord.'[22] The event was attended by 130 people.

The Assembly of 1993 discussed again the 'vexed question' of the sale of the building and Professor Main circulated copies of the deliverance anent the sale which was finally approved by the General Assembly. 'The net proceeds of the sale shall be transmitted to the Committee on Education for the Ministry to be applied by that committee in consultation with the Financial Board of Christ's College, Aberdeen for the purposes of theological education in Aberdeen and the North-East of Scotland.'[23] Finally the Board had the wording they wanted to enable the proceeds of the sale to be used in the spirit of the founders, but the sale was to be overseen by the Church of Scotland Trust and the Committee on Education for the Ministry.

22 Divinity Alumni Association Newsletter, 1993.
23 Reports to The General Assembly (Edinburgh: St Andrew Press, 1993), p. 634.

It was felt 'extremely unlikely that planning permission for change of use to commercial or residential would be given'.[24] This was due to its status as a category B listed building situated in a conservation area and the lack of parking facilities. 'A development for licensed premises might be possible as the guidelines on parking are not so strict.'[25] The Church of Scotland had indicated that it would not be imposing any restrictions on the building to be used as licensed premises. The Board had already had a note of interest from the British Legion although the property had not yet been put on the market. 'Mr Hunter also reported that it transpired that birds – particularly pigeons – had been gaining access to the top of the Clock Tower in considerable numbers over a long period of time and that as a result of this certain repairs to flooring and the stairs would be necessary as well as some general cleaning.'

Professor Johnstone hoped that the Centenary Robertson Smith Conference in April 1994 could still be held there. 'Aberdeen District Council had expressed an interest in erecting a commemorative plaque on the exterior of the front wall relating to William Robertson Smith and it was unanimously agreed to ask the Trust to bear both those points in mind when negotiations for sale are taking place.'[26]

The William Robertson Smith Congress

Over seventy delegates from ten countries attended the Congress to commemorate and evaluate the work and influence of William Robertson Smith, Professor of Hebrew and Old Testament Exegesis, for too short a time, in the Free Church College (see Chapter 3). He died on 31 March 1894 so the gathering took place 100 years and one week later.

---

24 Financial Board Minute Papers, 10 December 1993.
25 Ibid.
26 Ibid.

'The Congress programme, spread over three and a half days, was divided into five sections corresponding to the phases of Smith's career: the late nineteenth century context of Smith's life and work; Smith as Biblical scholar; Smith's international connections and influence; Smith as Encyclopaedist and Social Anthropologist; Smith as Arabist and Orientalist.'[27] There were keynote speakers from across the country and, in all, thirty-one papers were delivered and discussed. There was also a visit to Smith's birth and burial place at Keig and the unveiling of the plaque installed by Aberdeen City Council to accompany that of D. S. Cairns on the other side of the front door of the main building. Both plaques remain on the wall to this day. Professor William Johnstone, organiser of the Congress, commented, 'The interdisciplinary nature of the Congress held coherently together by the focus on the one figure was particularly successful and refreshing. Many appreciative comments were received.'[28]

Sale Concluded

A month after the event the sale of the building went to a closing date and the highest bid of £343,000 was accepted, conditional on obtaining planning permission and licensing consent for a bar on the ground floor and a restaurant on the first floor. Mr Hunter advised the Board that this would take some time and it might be into 1995 before it was concluded. In the meantime moves would have to be made to empty the building. This was to be the last meeting held within the College buildings. 'The meeting was then closed with a prayer appropriate to the circumstances.'[29] Later Professor Main wrote in the newsletter: 'On Friday 17th June another sentimental milestone was reached with the last meeting of the Council and its Financial Board to be held in the Christ's College building. It will be a wrench to part with our old home, but needs must with the impending sale, which is still progressing

---

27 Divinity Alumni Association Newsletter, 1994.
28 Ibid.
29 Financial Board Minute Papers, 17 June 1994.

LEDINGHAM CHALMERS

CHRIST'S COLLEGE, 8 ALFORD PLACE, ABERDEEN

GRANITE 'B' LISTED BUILDING IN TUDOR GOTHIC STYLE WITH CLOCK TOWER
GROSS INTERNAL FLOOR AREA OF 6796 SQ. FT. APPROX COMPRISES (G.F.)
ENTRANCE HALL AND VESTIBULE, FIVE ROOMS, LADIES AND GENTS TOILETS.
(U.F.) SUPERB ASSEMBLY HALL WITH VAULTED CEILING, THREE
ROOMS/OFFICES. OUTSIDE: BOILER ROOM/STORE.

Granite 'B' listed building in Tudor Gothic style with clock tower. Gross internal floor area of 6796 sq. ft. approx. Comprises (G.F.) entrance hall and vestibule, five rooms, ladies and gents toilets (U.F.) superb assembly hall with vaulted ceiling, three rooms/offices, outside: boiler rooms/store

tortuously past a variety of hurdles. One can report that in terms of the disposal of the contents of the building, everything has been done "decently and in good order", with new homes being found for the College Hall paintings (the University), the Laws plaque and the bookcase and the G. D. Henderson lectern (St Machar's Cathedral), the Thomson desk and John Brown chair (the office of the Master of the College), books and furniture in various directions – right to the College handbell (now reposing in Ledingham Chalmers as a reminder of the firm's long association with us). The final meeting was suitably concluded with a prayer of thanksgiving for all that has been over the past 150 years and a rededication of ourselves towards the future yet to be.'[30]

So it was the end of an era – but not, as many thought, the end of the College.

---

30 Divinity Alumni Association Newsletter, 1994/5.

North East Theological Fund

As agreed in the Deliverance of the Assembly in 1993, the net proceeds of the sale were passed to the Treasurer of the Church of Scotland. 'Mr Hunter pointed out that although the major part of the ground involved in the sale had been vested in the Church of Scotland Trust including all of the ground upon which the actual College building was erected, a small strip of the ground had been vested in the local Trustees for Christ's College. Mr Hunter submitted that, on a strict interpretation of the Deliverance, then there should now be an apportionment of the net proceeds of the sale with the major part being retained by the Committee on Education for the Ministry and the appropriate portion of the sale being repaid to the local Trustees. It had been provisionally agreed between Mr Hunter and the Solicitor to the Church of Scotland that since the process of carrying out the apportionment would be somewhat difficult, time consuming and costly and since the sum relating to that small strip of ground would be very small it would be more sensible if the whole of the net proceeds be retained by the Committee. This provisional agreement was homologated by the Financial Board but it was felt that the fact that part of the ground had belonged to the local Trustees should be borne in mind when proceeding to deal with the future application of the income from the net proceeds of the sale.'[31]

Board members were anxious that Edinburgh might regard the future income of the proceeds as a way of off-setting the annual deficit in the College accounts which was reimbursed by the Committee. It was agreed that this would be unacceptable as it would mean that the College, Aberdeen and the North East would not benefit from the realising of funds which had originally been raised in Aberdeen and the North East. Various subgroups and meetings were set up and the resultant decision was documented.

1. That the capital sum should be invested and that every effort should be made in the future to avoid any encroachment upon the capital of the fund.

---

31 Financial Board Minute Papers, 3 March 1995.

2. That in order to try and maintain the real value of the Capital Fund, one third of the net income accruing each year should be added back to the Capital Fund, reserving always the right to the Department of Education, in consultation with the Financial Board of Christ's College to reduce the said proportion should a) the state of the fund in that year justify such reduction and b) there be a particular requirement in that year for additional income for any of the purposes detailed in Clause 3.

3. That the remaining proportion of the net income each year should be paid each year to Christ's College in order to ensure support for staff appointments in the University of Aberdeen and in Christ's College, necessary to meet the requirements of training for ministry in the Church of Scotland, reserving always the right of the Financial Board of Christ's College to determine in any year that part or all of the remaining proportion of the net income for that year to be used for projects involving (a) expanding Continuing and Distance learning; (b) the provision of text books for the Divinity Library; and (c) the funding of post-graduate opportunities for Ministers and Ordinands.

4. That the sum representing the remaining proportion of the net income, after making provision for a reasonable administrative charge by the Department of Education, be transmitted once yearly in arrears to Christ's College, Aberdeen per its Treasurer.[32]

The above document was agreed by the Committee on Education for the Ministry of the Church of Scotland.

Quincentenary Celebrations

The year 1995 saw the Quincentenary celebrations of the University and a major University-wide fundraising appeal, so it was decided that the annual Divinity Alumni appeal should be made to fund a specific purpose of endowing a Christ's College Lecture

---

32 Ibid., 4 September 1995.

which would be given at the Quincentennial Alumni weekend. The University Appeal had previously asked for the Divinity FAITH Fund contact list but Christ's College felt that they should not provide this under the terms of the Data Protection Act. A volume of essays, to be edited by the Master, was to celebrate the Quincentenary. 'Drafts of all the chapters are now in my hands and the process of harmonising them into an integral whole is the next step when I can find a quiet couple of days amidst the maelstrom of the term. Our target date is the Celebration of the Quincentenary itself at which this hopefully elegant, inexpensive and fascinating collection of essays will burst upon the market!'[33] Sales of this volume turned a profit which was used to buy a computer for the Library. 'It was remitted to the Master and Professor Fergusson to investigate whether or not there was both a need for and space for an additional computer and if appropriate to use the balance in the purchase of an additional computer.'[34]

From March 1996, the Council meetings could revert to just discussing operational matters such as Chapter services, retreats, opening lectures, reunions and missions. The Financial Board, however, was still talking about the use of the sale proceeds and the current dismal state of the Academic Aid Fund.

A meeting was called in early January to discuss the possibility of filling a lecturer's post in Practical Theology. The University had decided to freeze the post after Dr William Storrar had moved to Glasgow. The Faculty of Arts and Divinity was in deficit although Practical Theology was in credit. 'The effect of this [freezing the post] was to have serious impact on Practical Theology both because of the very heavy overburdening of the other members of staff but also because of the inability to provide an adequate number of supervisors for possible postgraduate students with the result that the numbers of postgraduates would inevitably decline. There is a pressing need to have this post filled.'[35] Professor Main explained to the Board that he had started

---

33 Divinity Alumni Association Newsletter, 1994/5. The book in question was *But Where Shall Wisdom Be Found?* (Aberdeen: Aberdeen University Press, 1995).
34 Financial Board Minute Papers, 15 March 1996.
35 Ibid., 9 January 1997.

negotiations with the Department of Education in Edinburgh and the Board wholeheartedly agreed with him that offering financial assistance to the University to fill this post would be an appropriate use of the income from the proceeds of the sale of the building which was now in a fund called the North East Theological Fund. Negotiations were successful and an annual subsidy of £10,000 for three years was agreed. This led to the appointment in July 1997 of the Reverend Dr John Swinton to the post and he was to play an important part in the future of both Christ's College and the Faculty.

Meanwhile Professor Main had been appointed Moderator of the General Assembly and Professor David Fergusson was appointed Acting Master. Chairing his first meeting on 6 July 1998 Professor Fergusson had a long agenda in front of him. The Academic Aid Fund had been amalgamated with others so was no longer in deficit. The FAITH fund annual appeal had only raised £3,000. 'Professor Fergusson felt that the combined effect of the introduction of tuition fees and the gradual expiry of some of the existing Deeds of Covenant suggest that the whole question of fundraising needs to be looked at again.'[36]

He went on to update the Board members on discussions taking place regarding church funding of academic posts and the good news that this would continue at least in the short term. However, he had also had a letter from the Board of Ministry, again suggesting that the management costs for Christ's College were much higher than those of the other colleges. It was suggested the Board consider either moving all the administration to the Church Office at 121 George Street, Edinburgh or asking Aberdeen University to take it on.

The current Secretary of the Council, the Reverend Dr Iain Torrance, was appointed to the Board.

It was a year later before the working party reported back. Aberdeen University were happy to take over the accounts but they would all have to be amalgamated to one fund, which would not be legally possible due to the terms of the various bequests. Professor Fergusson alerted the Board to the fact that the contract

---

36 Ibid., 6 July 1988.

for the eight-hours-a-week secretary expired in May. It was felt that this might be the opportunity to look at the requirements as a whole, especially as the workload of the Master was increasing due to rising numbers of students and all the financial tribulations. The last meeting of the Financial Board in the century took place on 16 December 1999 when it was agreed that it would be appropriate for the Master to have a Personal Assistant. The start of the new millennium saw a tripartite agreement reached between Christ's College, Aberdeen University and what was now called the Board of Ministry regarding the church grant payable to the University for Professors' salaries which was now being supplemented by income from the North East Theological Fund. This would be in place for the next five years.

Mrs Doris Meston in her role as Fieldwork Director had been unofficially acting as a PA to the Master and Professor Main invited her to become his PA for a year, which she accepted. A year later Mrs Gwen Haggart was appointed to the post. This coincided with Graham Hunter retiring from the law practice and hence not able to continue as Secretary and Treasurer. The Board agreed that this role would now be part of the remit of the new PA. The Master was also retiring so it was change all round and the end of another era in the College history. Alan Main and Graham Hunter were invited back to become Board members in their own right and this ensured that their accumulated knowledge and background information about College history and proceedings would not be lost.

The College Survives
2001–18

The first Master in the new millennium was the Reverend Professor Iain Torrance, installed by the Presbytery of Aberdeen in King's College Chapel on 1 October 2001. The Torrances are recognised as a family of leading Scottish theologians. Iain's father was the Very Reverend Professor Tom Torrance and his uncle was the Reverend Professor James Torrance, previously of Aberdeen University. Iain Torrance did his MA at Edinburgh, his BD at St Andrews and his DPhil in Oxford. He was ordained in 1982 by the Presbytery of Shetland as minister in Northmavine Parish Church where he stayed for four years, leaving to join the teaching staff at Queen's College Birmingham and then Birmingham University where he taught New Testament. It was 1993 before he finally made it to Aberdeen University at the age of 44 when he joined the Department of Theology and Church History as a lecturer in Systematic and Practical Theology. He quickly rose to become Dean of the Faculty of Arts and Divinity and in October 2001 was installed as Master of Christ's College following the retirement of the Very Reverend Professor Alan Main.

Chairing his first meeting of the Christ's College Council as Master, Professor Torrance welcomed his new PA, Gwen Haggart, to the Board. He reported on the new arrangements for students to undertake four periods of placement. 'This being so, the church based aspects of their practical theology now takes place in summer schools. This has enabled the academic side of practical theology to develop in new and exciting ways. However despite the positive aspect to the changes, the Master highlighted some significant concerns. For many students their third placement ran in tandem with the final year of their honours degree.'[1] The Master expressed a general concern for the mental and physical health of the candidates placed in this situation, and offered to take this up with the Church of Scotland. Chapter services came under discussion as a number of points had been raised by students who were criticising the traditional style of worship. The Council agreed a worship development group should be put in place.

The Master didn't chair his first meeting of the Financial Board until December 2002. At this meeting he was congratulated on being appointed Moderator Designate of the General Assembly of the Church of Scotland. Mr Hunter thanked the Board for marking his retirement from his period of nearly thirty years as Secretary and Treasurer. He had been taken for dinner and presented with an antique engraving of Aberdeen. The Secretary/Treasurer work was now undertaken by the new PA to the Master, Gwen Haggart. A Board member, Dr Graeme Roberts, asked for clarification of the role of the Christ's College Council and Professor Torrance explained that the Council dealt with the day-to-day academic events, the running of the weekly Chapter services, any extra training provided for the candidates for the ministry and the awarding of prizes. Unlike the Financial Board, members of the Council were not required to be members of the Church of Scotland and this applied to a number of members of staff who served on the Council.

The Church of Scotland Board of Ministry representative then raised the issue of lack of constitutions for the Boards in the Colleges, which was causing concern in headquarters at 121 George Street, Edinburgh. Dr Sefton explained that after considerable research he had come to the conclusion that no specific constitution existed, the layout of the Board being largely in accordance with the guidelines of the Free Church Assembly deliverance under which it was set up in the 1880s. Dr Roberts asked what would happen if there was no longer a Church of Scotland member in the Divinity faculty and Professor Torrance suggested that the position of Master could be given to a local Church of Scotland minister or elder. Was there a sense of premonition here?

---

1 Council Minute Papers, 27 June 2002.

Moderatorial Year

No sooner had Professor Torrance started to make his mark as Master than he had to be absent to carry out his Moderatorial duties. John Swinton was appointed Acting Master and continued the discussion about Chapter services. In view of the fact that the Chapel would not be available for the winter term as a new organ was being installed, it was agreed that this would be a good time to make changes. The School of Divinity and Religious Studies was being enlarged to include Philosophy but it was agreed that the Divinity Library was not big enough to be open for all so access was still to be restricted to undergraduate Divinity and Religious Studies students.

Coming into the twenty-first century the possible advantages of having a website were discussed. It was thought it would cost about £1,500 and didn't happen until much later!

The front page of the Alumnus Newsletter of April 2004 carried a 'Moderator's Reflections' by Iain Torrance. 'Yes I have enjoyed it. It has been an immense privilege. Not only the post itself, but the opportunity it has provided to see things I simply would not have otherwise. It was extraordinary to be received as a sign of hope (in Akobo, Southern Sudan) by a people who had been bombarded only two months before. I have committed myself to do whatever I can in the Church's negotiations to bolster the Sudanese Church's reconstruction and capacity building. Iraq too was memorable and I greatly admired the persistence and sheer courage of the local Reformed Church in Basra, which maintained a Christian community through the sanctions and the war.'[2]

The Moderator ends his reflections with a warning. 'I found utterly determined – and to me inexplicable – resistance to my wish to be a theologian-moderator. The suggestion that we build in planning to read for one day a week was greeted with incredulity. My attendance at the Dialogue with the Orthodox, at the American Academy of Religion and the International Patristics

---

2 Divinity and Religious Studies Alumnus Newsletter, 2004.

Conference all became unexpected minefields. The post should carry a health warning for academic nominees.'[3]

Princeton

Two months after the end of his year as Moderator, Professor Torrance wrote to the Christ's College Financial Board members.

> Dear Colleagues,
> As you know, after I was nominated as Moderator of the General Assembly in October 2002, with your agreement I stood back from the role of Master of Christ's College from April 2003 until the end of May 2004. My expectation then had been that I would resume the role of Master after I returned from my year as Moderator. Professor Swinton very generously agreed to be Acting Master in my place.
>
> Circumstances have changed in ways none of us could have anticipated. I was approached by the Trustees of the Princeton Theological Seminary and was appointed President of the Seminary with effect from 1st July 2004. Professor Swinton is also moving and will leave Aberdeen in January 2005 for a new post at Duke University.
>
> We are faced with a situation which we had anticipated – at least theoretically – but had not expected in the immediate future. In one of the earlier discussions with the Financial Board, I remember suggesting that if an occasion were to arise when there would not be a minister of the Church of Scotland among the staff of the department, a way forward might be to invite a senior member of Presbytery to assume the role. With my own departure and that of John Swinton shortly, it seems to me that this would be a wise and constructive way to act.[4]

The letter continues by outlining suggestions and arrangements and concludes: 'The Mastership of Christ's College is an historic

---

3 Ibid.
4 Iain Torrance, letter to Financial Board, Christ's College.

office in the Church and one which I was honoured to hold. I regret that I held it so briefly, and I am grateful for the friendships and trust which I encountered.'[5] It was in fact the shortest Mastership in the history of the College. Professor Torrance worked at Princeton for the next eight years and continued to be a high-profile, world-respected theologian. In 2005 he represented the Church of Scotland and the World Alliance of Reformed Churches at the installation of Pope Benedict XVI. Professor Torrance retired from Princeton Theological Seminary at the end of 2012 and returned to Scotland where he accepted the role of Pro-Chancellor at Aberdeen University at the invitation of her Royal Highness the Duchess of Rothesay, following her election as University Chancellor. As such he plays a very active role in the life of the University. In 2013 the Queen appointed him Dean of the Chapel Royal and the following year she appointed him Dean of the Order of the Thistle. In her New Year's Honours list of December 2017 Professor Torrance was awarded a knighthood. He said, 'I was astonished by this award but also deeply grateful that causes I have long struggled for – the dissemination of knowledge, electronic access, the dignity of gay people and the inclusion of other faiths – has been recognized.'[6]

Another First

So the College found itself in the situation imagined just a few years before and unimaginable in previous years. As it happened, Professor Swinton did not take up the position at Duke University, but he indicated that he would prefer not to become Master and that the arrangements outlined in Professor Torrance's letter be adhered to. 'He reported that, following discussions between Rev. Nigel Robb, Director of Educational Services, and Rev. Ian MacLean, Clerk of Aberdeen Presbytery, the name of Rev. J. H. A. Dick of Ferryhill Parish Church would be put forward as Master Elect to the General Assembly of 2005 for ratification.'[7]

---

5 Ibid.
6 www.abdn.ac.uk (accessed 04/01/18).
7 Financial Board Minute Papers, 10 September 2004.

At this same meeting the Rev. Nigel Robb, representing the Board of Ministry, explained that the regular contributions made by the Church of Scotland towards the salary of a lecturer in Practical Theology were to cease. Due to the poor financial position of the Church it would no longer be possible for it to fund academic posts. Luckily for Aberdeen University, the money raised from the sale of the main Christ's College building held in the North East Education Fund could be used to continue supporting the Practical Theology post for the next five years.

The Rev. J. H. A. Dick – or Ian, as he is known – had been at Ferryhill since 1982 after graduating from New College. Prior to that he was a senior tutor in Geography in the University of Queensland. He had many candidates and probationers working with him in the parish, was Convener of the Ministries Development Committee, and became a council member of the newly formed Ministries Council at church headquarters.

So the first Master from outwith the College duly took up his post and thus, for a second time in its history, a minister of Ferryhill became head of Christ's College. Exactly 100 years previously Professor James Iverach, the first minister of Ferryhill Free Church, was appointed to be the fourth Principal of the College. Ian Dick was 'introduced' at a service in the Chapel as Master of Christ's College on 2 February 2005. He could not be 'inducted' as previous Masters had been as he was still the inducted minister of a parish. At the service, former Master Reverend Dr Henry Sefton read the charges as Professor Torrance was already in Princeton. Writing his first Master's Notes in the April Newsletter, Ian Dick expressed his pleasure at his appointment. 'I look forward eagerly to sharing with all involved in the life of the College to enable it to play the essential role it has in the formation of ministers. There may no longer be a building of the name Christ's College but Christ's College is still very much in existence.'[8]

8 Divinity and Religious Studies Alumnus Newsletter, 2005.

London Terrorist Bombings

On 7 July 2005 the terrorist bombings in London took the life of a recent Christ's College graduate, Helen Katherine Jones, aged just 28. Her funeral was conducted by her friend and fellow alumnus David Thom. 'Helen was a natural student, yet not afraid to put in the hard work and long hours, she quickly excelled in her degree. Helen was to graduate with a First Class Honours in Systematic Theology. Something she was extremely proud of and no less than her efforts merited. Yet Helen wasn't some bookish academic. She was a weel kent face in the common room, at coffee, an active participant in the Students' Charities campaign. And she still found time for a healthy social life. Indeed the flat we shared for three years was often the scene of Helen's early parties. Something she was to become renowned for in London. All who passed though Christ's College (and indeed life) with Helen will remember her with great fondness and it is fitting that as an alumni [sic], Helen's book collection has now been donated by her family to the Divinity Library to be used by students for many years to come.'9

He was further reported in a newspaper saying 'We're here to celebrate Helen's life and to reflect on the life that gave us all so much. We're here to remember the good times and the memories that we treasure.' The only veiled reference to the bombing of the King's Cross tube train that killed twenty-five people came when Mr Thom told mourners that 'we have anger in our hearts and there are no easy answers'. However, he went on to say: 'But we know that, if life is soured by bitterness, an unforgiving spirit brings no peace.' He then related how Ms Jones had helped him cope as a trainee minister with the unexpected and tragic death of a child. She had told him: 'Any tragedy is never God's will. The first heart to break is God's. The first tear to be shed is always by God.'10

---

9 Ibid.

10 www.scotsman.com/news/uk/family-say-farewell-to-bomb-victim-helen-1-728398 (accessed 05/03/2018).

Highland Theological College

One of the first issues to arise for the new Master was responding to a request from the Highland Theological College to enter into a cooperative arrangement with Christ's College, enabling Church of Scotland candidates to undertake part of their training at the College in Dingwall. This was not a popular suggestion: 'While the benefits to HTC are relatively clear what do they see as the benefits to Christ's College?'[11] Another contentious issue was the possibility that the Divinity Library might have to close due to its inaccessibility.

The General Assembly of 2006 was being asked to recognise the Highland Theological College as an institution for the academic training of candidates for the ministry. Various concerns were raised by the College Board, not least the impact this would have on Christ's College numbers. There was also a huge concern over HTC's views on women in the ministry, but the Ministries Council assured Christ's College that there was no longer a problem over this.

The next meeting of the year confirmed that the Assembly had accepted the proposal regarding HTC and the Master, Ian Dick, said he was awaiting advice from the Ministries Council as to how the students there would participate in the life of Christ's College. At the last meeting of the year there was emotional discussion about disability access to the Divinity Library and whose responsibility this was. A suggestion was put forward that the proposed new University Library might be able to accommodate the Christ's College collection.

At a Financial Board meeting in 2006 it was noted that the Alexander Thomson of Banchory Trust was no longer financially viable and was to be wound up. This had been a great source of finance to the College over the years and the College had inherited many items of historic value. These had been loaned to the University.

The Master had a letter from the legal firm 'trying to track down some of the artefacts previously belonging to the trust and mentioned in documents including a bracelet reputed to have

---

11 Financial Board Minute Papers, 18 February 2005.

belonged to Queen Victoria'.[12] The Board reported no knowledge
of any artefacts and the Master was to reply accordingly. That as
we now know was erroneous.

Reunion

A reunion took place in April 2007 to celebrate fifty years in
ministry for the class who graduated in 1954. There was a celebration Communion service led by the Master, followed by an
open discussion with the Very Reverend Alan Main, former Master, and Ian Dick, entitled 'Christ's College in relation to future
training for the ministry in the Church of Scotland'.

'Reunions are times of looking back, but the day's forward-
looking theme will be continued after the discussion with a tour
of some local churches which are particularly geared up to today's
and tomorrow's ministry (Ferryhill, Gilcomston South and Bridge
of Don Old Machar). There will be time for all to have their
say in a general discussion on "Observations on the State of the
Church Today". The day will finish with dinner together and a
time for sharing memories.'[13]

Twelve men attended the reunion with their wives. There were
no female ministers in training in the 1950s.

The following newsletter contains some thoughts on the day by
one of those who attended. He finishes, 'In current training for
the Ministry there is no need to provide "a collegial structure" for
candidates who are few in number and spread across a number
of institutions. Fifty years ago we were fortunate that Christ's
College provided that structure. We took it for granted. Every
blessing on today's Master as he continues to maintain "a college
without walls".'[14]

As the first 'outside' Master, Ian Dick had been given a three-
year term of office due to end in February 2008. The Ministries
Council and the Board agreed to ask him to stay in post for
another three years and tribute was paid 'to the outstanding

12 Ibid., 16 March 2007.
13 Divinity and Religious Studies Alumnus Newsletter, 2007.
14 Ibid., April 2008.

success of his service as Master over the last three years, his excellent rapport with the Ministry candidates and his work in trying to form closer links between the Divinity Department, Christ's College and the Ministries Council'.[15] Under Dick's leadership the Financial Board was able to consolidate some of the separate funds which at that point were being invested by UBS (United Bank of Switzerland). It was agreed to undertake a review of investment handling on a regular basis.

A New Accountant

There was no meeting of the Financial Board from December 2008 until October 2009 when the Master explained 'that due to the illness of the accountant assigned to Christ's College by the Church of Scotland the accounts had not yet been completed nor sent to the Auditor'.[16] The accounts had been handed over to the Church of Scotland in a money-saving exercise in 2007 as it was still costing the College over £7,000 for the involvement of Ledingham Chalmers. The Master had been in communication with the Office of the Scottish Charities register (OSCR) who had agreed not to penalise the College for the late returns. The Board went on to agree a further five-year agreement to support the lectureship in Practical Theology; from now on it would be known as 'The Christ's College Lectureship in Practical Theology'. In the newsletter of 2009 the Master comments, 'The number of candidates making up Christ's College is the smallest for many years – only seven – yet very diverse in background: two are from the United States, one from Northern Ireland and one from Burundi, with the rest from Scotland. They form a close knit, mutually supportive group who still regard the weekly Chapter Service as the central event of College life.'[17]

The accounts were not actually presented to the Board until May 2010, when 'Mr Dick explained that the Church of Scotland Treasurer's Department had indicated that they were currently

---

15 Financial Board Minute Papers, 23 November 2007.
16 Ibid., 2 October 2009.
17 Divinity and Religious Studies Alumnus Newsletter, 2008.

under great pressure and had called on an outside accountant, Sarah Hollis, to complete the accounts for 2008. He also reported that the department would waive any fee since the long delay had been their responsibility.'[18] Thus Sarah met with the Board and impressed them so much that they appointed her as the College Accountant forthwith – a position she still holds.

Future Considerations

The minutes of 9 September 2011 record: 'At the last meeting the Board had enquired about the possibility of putting some of the money held by the North East Theological Fund to suitable use in courses at the University. John Swinton and the Master had been in discussion about this and John presented a paper on a proposed King's College Centre for Ministry Studies.'[19] There was great enthusiasm for this proposal from the Board and John was able to report that Dr Philip Ziegler, Head of the School of Divinity, History and Philosophy, was also enthused by the idea. This was the birth of the now well-established Aberdeen University Centre for Ministry Studies (CMS). 'As well as courses for Continuing Professional Development for ministers, the Centre would also offer courses on Ministry and Worship for lay people as well as a Doctorate in Practical Theology, with Diploma, Certificate and Masters exit points. It could also offer Summer Schools covering Mission and Evangelism, Emerging and Pioneering Churches, Mental Health in the Parish, Homiletics, Church Leadership and Worship. Professor Swinton suggested that the Centre would eventually become self-sustaining but an initial financial outlay would be necessary.'[20]

A legacy was left to Christ's College by Miss Elspeth McGregor and this was to be invested by UBS and become part of the portfolio. 'Miss McGregor was an elder at Denburn Parish Church in Aberdeen and was also Office Secretary at Beechgrove Parish Church having been a Medical Secretary in Aberdeen Royal

---

18 Financial Board Minute Papers, 7 May 2010.
19 Ibid., 9 September 2011.
20 Ibid.

Infirmary before that. She served for many years as Presbytery Elder and was for some time a redoubtable secretary of the old Unions and Readjustments Committee of Presbytery. Her legacy to the College is much appreciated and reflects the interest she took in the activities of the College in her lifetime.'[21]

The Master then confirmed that he would be retiring from parish and College at the end of the academic year, adding that Gwen Haggart, PA to the Master, had also indicated her wish to step down and thus another era for the College was coming to an end. The retiring Master expressed his thanks to Gwen as follows: 'Not only did Gwen deal with the day to day administration of College business but more importantly she was the first line of contact for candidates and others seeking help and advice. They were always received with a welcoming smile, infinite patience and a sympathetic ear and invariably went away reassured and encouraged. Many have so benefitted from Gwen's kindness and wisdom. Gwen also edited and distributed the annual Divinity and Religious Studies Alumnus Newsletter and so helped maintain contact with former students all over the world. She also acted as the highly capable Secretary and Treasurer of the Financial Board. The Master expressed his own thanks to Gwen for helping him to understand and develop the role of Master and for being so efficient in supporting and enabling him to fulfil that role.'[22] The new era began with the announcement that the Reverend Professor John Swinton would be the new Master and that Clare Davidson would be the new PA.

The Present

So the history of the College is almost up to date. John Swinton's introduction as Master took place in October 2012 and he is still in post. He brought a new approach to the job of Master, recognising that much had changed and with the numbers of Church of Scotland candidates falling rapidly new initiatives were required.

---

21 Divinity and Religious Studies Alumnus Newsletter, 2011.
22 Financial Board Minute Papers, 7 December 2011.

John Swinton is the first black Master in the College history, being born of African descent in Liverpool in 1958. He was adopted by the Rev. Alan Swinton and his wife Mary and brought up in Cumbernauld and Aberdeen with a sister and brother. He trained in nursing and is a registered nurse both in mental health and intellectual disabilities.

He started at Christ's College as a Divinity student in 1990, finishing with a PhD in 1997. He was ordained into the Church of Scotland and was for a short spell a hospital and community chaplain before moving into academia as a lecturer in Practical Theology. In 2003 he was appointed Professor in Practical Theology and Pastoral Care and just a year later he founded the University of Aberdeen's Centre for Spirituality, Health and Disability. His research and teaching is influenced by his background and passion for developing methods of care that are genuinely person-centred and which take seriously the significance of theology, spirituality and religion within the processes of healing.

The plan for developing a Centre for Ministry Studies, which he had envisaged with the previous Master, Ian Dick, was brought before the Financial Board again in November 2012 where it was given a provisional green light. At that meeting it was also agreed to look for a new investment company as the ethics and the returns from UBS were not thought to be the best. 'Following discussion it was decided that the Christ's College staff needed to be on a firmer footing regarding contracts and wage structure ... A sub-group was set up to take a "good hearted" look at the positions of Librarian and Administrator.' [23] Clare Davidson's job title been had changed from 'PA to the Master' to College Administrator to better reflect the nature of the work.

In his first Master's notes John Swinton wrote, 'I am very grateful to Ian [Dick] for building the firm foundation that I now have the honour of inheriting. It does seem a bit odd to be the Master. I have been around the University in one form or another since 1989 and I have seen a number of Masters come and go. I have watched the ways in which they have interacted with and shaped and formed candidates for ministry and I recognise and

---

23 Ibid., 21 November 2012.

appreciate the profound formative influence that my predecessors have had on the formation of the Church of Scotland over time. So it is with a little bit of trepidation that I attempt to tread faithfully and effectively in the footsteps of my "ancestors". But I very much look forward to it.

'In many ways now is a time of great change for the Church as we go through difficult times and are faced with difficult situations that demand difficult decisions. Ours is a time when the Church seems to be losing power. Attendances are falling, the public influence of the Church waning and numbers training for the ministry are becoming fewer and fewer. At one level we might find cause to despair. But at another level if we lift our eyes a little we can see that worldwide the Church is burgeoning. Across the globe with the exception of our own Western context, billions of people continue to worship Jesus. So I guess perhaps the key for us is to keep our eyes upwards and look around at God's world. When we do that I reckon we will be both encouraged and surprised. God hasn't given up on the Church yet and neither should we.' [24]

Since the sale of the main College building in Alford Place, Christ's College office had been based in a room at the Chaplaincy Centre at 25 High Street, Old Aberdeen. That space was needed by the Chaplaincy so in 2013 the office moved to one of the oldest parts of the University where Divinity had been based – the Quadrangle at King's College. Christ's College still exists. It may no longer be a building but a fine office allows space for students and visitors.

No Students

In March 2013 the Master reported to the Financial Board that the Centre for Ministry Studies had been approved by the University so the application for funding was going to the North East Theological Fund. The meeting six months later brought the news that, for the first time in its history, Christ's College, formerly the

---

24 Divinity and Religious Studies Alumnus Newsletter, 2013.

United Free Church College and the Free Church College and founded in 1843, had no students. Former Master Henry Sefton pointed out that the College exists for past students and must remain for future students. In the meantime it was agreed that the work of the CMS was entirely fitting with the mission of the College in providing training for ministers and lay people.

The Rev. Dr Ken Jeffrey, graduate of Aberdeen and minister of Cupar Old and St Michael of Tarvit, was appointed coordinator for the new Centre and Clare Davidson expanded her role to cover its administration alongside that of the College. As intended, the CMS became self-sustaining after three years so the North East Theological Fund money was then channelled into a new position of Christ's College Teaching Fellow. The first person to be appointed to that was Dr Leon van Ommen from Belgium, who after eighteen months in position was given a permanent lectureship in Practical Theology. In December 2017, the Library Assistant, Ina Strachan, retired. Having been employed by the College for nearly thirty-two years she became the longest-serving member of staff, paid or unpaid, in the history of the College since its foundation in 1843. Many students will remember her friendliness and also her strict running of the Library. March 2018 saw the appointment of Dr Katie Cross to be the second teaching Fellow of Christ's College. A PhD student, Alex Mason, is in place in the Library and digitalizing the catalogue.

Following a few lean years Christ's College does have students and staff again and its Library is benefiting from upgrading; but it is unlikely that the College will ever rekindle the heady days of large numbers of candidates for the Church of Scotland ministry and its position as a well-known presence in Aberdeen. However, its history gives it a valid place of importance in university and church life and the influence of its students has spread worldwide.

Bibliography

Alexander, John, *History of the parish of Banchory-Devenick*, Aberdeen: Wyllie, 1890.

Allardyce, Mabel Desborough, ed., Aberdeen University Roll of Honour 1921, www.abdn.ac.uk/library/roll-of-honour.

Blaikie, W. G., *David Brown D.D., LL.D.: Professor and Principal of the Free Church College, Aberdeen: A Memoir*, London: Hodder and Stoughton, 1898.

Brown, Stewart J. et al., *Scottish Christianity in the Modern World*, Edinburgh: T&T Clark, 2000.

Bruce, Alexander Balmain, 'The Rev. Professor Stewart DF Salmond DD Free Church College Aberdeen', *The Biblical World* 8/5 (November 1896), pp. 347–53, www.jstor.org/stable/3139979.

Cairns, David, *An Answer to Bernhardi*, Papers for War Time No. 12, London: Oxford University Press, 1914.

Cairns, David, 'From Union to Union: 1900 to 1929', in *The Church College in Aberdeen*, Aberdeen: Aberdeen University Press, 1936.

Cairns, David, *David Cairns: An autobiography*, London: SCM Press, 1950.

Cameron, N. et al., eds, *Dictionary of Scottish Church History and Theology*, Edinburgh: T&T Clark, 1993, https://en.wikipedia.org.

Ferguson, William, 'Christian Faith and Unbelief in Modern Scotland', in *Scottish Christianity in the Modern World*, ed. Stewart J. Brown et al., Edinburgh: T&T Clark, 2000.

Finlayson, Marlene Elizabeth, *An Intellectual Biography of David Smith Cairns*, Thesis, Edinburgh University, www.era.lib.ed.ac.uk/handle/1842/11739.

Geddes, W. D., *Marcus Sachs: In Memoriam*, Aberdeen: King and Company, 1872.

Henderson, G. D., *A Century Ago ... and Now*, Edinburgh: Church of Scotland, 1955.

Hunter, A. M., *The Work and Words of Jesus*, revised paperback edition, London: SCM Press, 1973.

Iverach, James, *The Other Side of Greatness and Other Sermons*, London: Hodder and Stoughton, 1906.

Lendrum, R. A. 'The Founding', in *The Church College in Aberdeen*, Aberdeen: Aberdeen University Press, 1936.

Life and Work, monthly magazine of the Church of Scotland.

Lochman, Jan Milic, 'Josef Hromádka: Ecumenical Pilgrim', in the Princeton Seminary Bulletin, 1999, http://journals.ptsem.edu/id/PSB1999201/dmd008.

Lumsden, James, *Sweden. Its religious state and prospects: with some notices of persecutions which are taking place in that country*, London, 1855.

Lumsden, James, *The unity of the Church: A lecture delivered in the Free Church College Aberdeen, at the opening of session 1871–72*. Aberdeen: A&R Milne etc., 1871.

Maccraken, Henry Mitchell, *A Propaganda of Philosophy*, New York: F. H. Revell, 1914.

McIntyre, Gary J., in *The Herald*, 3 March 2001, www.britishnewspaperarchive.co.uk.

McMullen, Michael D., *Oxford Dictionary of National Biography*, https://doi.org/10.1093/ref:odnb/33755.

Maier, Bernhard, *William Robertson Smith: His life, his work and his times*, Tübingen: Mohr Siebeck, 2009.

Mearns, Daniel and S. D. F. Salmond, *Testimonial to Sir William Henderson LLD*, Aberdeen, 1898.

Morris, E. D., in *Presbyterian and Reformed Review*, Vol. 7, 1896.

Ogston, David D., *Grey Stone Zion*, St John's Kirk Perth, 2008.

Philip, R. G., 'Chapters From Its History: 1855 to 1900', in *The Church College in Aberdeen*, Aberdeen: Aberdeen University Press, 1936.

Prang, Margaret, *A Heart at Leisure from Itself: Caroline Macdonald of Japan*, Vancouver: UBC Press, 1995.

Rae, John, *Principal Lumsden: A Memorial and Estimate*, Aberdeen: Milne, 1876.

Reith, George M., *Reminiscences of The United Free Church General Assemblies (1900–1929)*, Edinburgh: Moray Press, 1933.

Salmond S. D. F., *The Christian Doctrine of Immortality*, Edinburgh: T&T Clark, 1895.

Salmond, S. D. F., 'Obituary Part 2', *Expository Times*, Vol. 9/4, 1898.

Sanderson Report, Aberdeen University Special Collections, MS3241/9/5.

Sell, Alan P. F., *Defending and Declaring the Faith*, Exeter: Paternoster Press, 1987.

Smeaton, George, *Memoir of Alexander Thomson of Banchory*, Edinburgh: Edmonston and Douglas, 1869.

Stalker, James, 'Principal Stewart Dingwall Fordyce Salmond [Obituary]', *The Biblical World*, 26/3 September 1905, pp. 188–94, www.jstor.org/stable/3141343.

Stalker, James, 'The Advocate's Sermon', in *Sub Corona*, ed. Henry Cowan and James Hastings, Edinburgh, T&T Clark, 1915.

Taylor, Thomas Murray, Collection of Addresses delivered at Graduation Ceremonies in the University of Aberdeen 1946 – 1962, MS 2843/3.

Vaudry, John P., 'A. Caroline Macdonald of Japan', www.renewal-fellowship.ca/93 (accessed 18/07/2018).

Veitch, Thomas, 'As Edinburgh Went, So Might Have Gone the World', *The Living Church*, 138 (14 June 1959).

West, Charles, *Hromádka: Theologian of the Resurrection*, https://worldview.carnegiecouncil.org/archive/worldview/1970/10/1877.html/_res/id=File1/

Wright, David F. and Gary Badcock, eds, *Disruption to Diversity: Edinburgh Divinity 1846–1996*, Edinburgh, T&T Clark, 1996.

University of Aberdeen Special Collections

Financial Board Minute Books:
Volume 3 MS 3241/2/1/3 1869–1916
Volume 4 MS 3241/2/1/4 1916–1981
Senatus/Council Minute Books:
Volume 2 MS 3241/1/2/1 1897–1920
Volume 3 MS 3241/1/2/2 1921–1935
Volume 4 MS 3241/1/2/3 1935–1952
Aberdeen Divinity Bulletins, 1, 2, 3, 5, 6, 7

Christ's College

Council Minutes 1970–2003
Financial Board Minutes 1981–Present
Aberdeen Divinity Bulletins, 11, 12, 13, 15, 20, 21, 22, 24, 25, 26
Faculty of Divinity Alumni Association Newsletters 1990–2001
Divinity and Religious Studies Alumnus Newsletter 2002–2018

Appendix A

Roll of Honour

Extracts from Aberdeen University Roll of Honour, edited by Mabel Desborough Allardyce and published in 1921.

William John Booth
Rank: Private
Regiment: 66th Field Ambulance, Salonika Forces, Royal Army Medical Corps
Biography: Son of Thomas Tait Booth, manager of the Port Elphinstone paper-works, Inverurie; born Kintore, 25 February 1890; educated Inverurie Public School and Gordon's College, Aberdeen; graduated M.A. (III Eng.), 1914; studied at Aberdeen U.F. College, 1914–16, where he had a distinguished career, gaining the Foote Scholarship in Hebrew and the Eadie Prize in New Testament Greek. He enlisted in April 1916, and after training at Aldershot went out in August with his unit to form the 42nd General Hospital at Salonika, being afterwards transferred to the 66th Field Ambulance, Salonika forces. He saw a good deal of service during the two years he spent on the Balkan front, and died of malaria 28 September 1918. Booth had a singularly amiable and attractive disposition, and showed exceptional ability as a student. He was well versed in English literature, and had rare gifts of style and expression, combined with a generosity and bigness of nature which made him wish to share with others the richness of his own wide reading.
Date of Death: 29 [sic] September 1918
Burial Details: Buried at Sarigol Military Cemetery, Greece, Plot D, Grave 693.

Norman Crichton
Rank: 2nd Lieutenant
Regiment: 4th Battalion Seaforth Highlanders
Biography: Son of William Crichton, mason, Stornoway; born Stornoway, 3 February 1888; graduated M.A., 1911; student for three years at Aberdeen U.F. College. In October 1914 he enlisted as a Private in the 4th Gordon Highlanders, and was afterwards commissioned as 2nd Lieutenant in the 4th Seaforths. Before proceeding abroad he was licensed as a probationer by the U.F. Presbytery of Lewis. He rendered distinguished service as a bombing officer in France, and fell in action at Beaumont-Hamel on 15 November 1916. Celtic fervour and eloquence, combined with thorough scholarship, marked Crichton as one who would have proved a highly successful minister. He was a most lovable man, and had gained a warm place in the hearts of those in the Mission where he laboured; the same power of attraction drew his men to him in the army, for they knew he always shared every risk along with them.
Date of Death: 15 November 1916
Burial Details: Name recorded on the Thiepval Memorial, Pier and Face 15 C.

John Forbes
Rank: Sniper-Sergeant
Regiment: 4th Battalion Gordon Highlanders
Biography: Son of Alexander Forbes, teacher, Aberdeen. Born Aberdeen, 12 April 1883; graduated M.A., 1905; taught for seven years in Rathven Public School; in 1912 entered Aberdeen U.F. College, taking the highest place in the examinations open to all the U.F. Colleges; gained Foote Scholarship in Hebrew and Eadie Prize in New Testament Greek. He enlisted in October 1914 as a Private in the 4th Gordon Highlanders; and was sent to Belgium in February 1915. Although he could readily have obtained a commission, he contented himself with the rank of Sergeant, believing that as a N.C.O. he would be able to exercise a greater moral influence on his men. The invaluable services he rendered by organizing a corps of snipers, as well as by the accurate information he was able to gain regarding the German positions, were recognized in a letter addressed to him by the General commanding the Division. He fell at Hooge on 25 September 1915. A more versatile genius than Forbes never passed through Aberdeen U.F. College. A tireless walker, an intrepid mountaineer, a keen sportsman, a humorist, a skilled musician, a linguist, a scholar – no achievement seemed beyond his capacity. Even in the trenches he pursued his studies, and left behind him singularly able notes on the Book of Job, which to the last he studied in the Hebrew original, with the aid of the latest German commentary. Those who had the privilege of knowing him will never forget this distinguished student and Sniper-Sergeant, who was as modest and lovable as he was gifted.
Date of Death: 25 September 1915
Burial Details: Name recorded on the Menin Gate Memorial, Ypres, Panel 38, Column 4.

Andrew Fraser
Rank: Sergeant
Regiment: 4th Battalion Gordon Highlanders
Biography: Son of William Fraser, builder, Tain; born Tain, 18 July 1880; graduated M.A., 1910. He taught in Fraserburgh Academy till 1913 , when he entered the Aberdeen College. At the close of his first session he went to Canada where he took charge of a Mission covering a wide district. In November 1914 Fraser enlisted as a private in the 4th Gordon Highlanders, and was sent to France in December 1915. His conspicuous ability gained for him the rank of Sergeant, and he rendered very efficient service in connection with the Machine Gun Section, till his death in action at High Wood, in the Somme district, on 22 July 1916. Whilst at the University, Fraser was President of the Christian Union, and it would be difficult to find a more popular President or one who more ably filled this difficult post. In the U.F. College no student was more loved and esteemed than Fraser, of whose future career, owing to his sterling character and mental equipment, the highest expectations were cherished.
Date of Death: 22 July 1916
Burial Details: Name recorded on the Thiepval Memorial, Pier and Face 15 B and 15 C.

John Knowles
Rank: Private
Regiment: 4th Battalion Gordon Highlanders
Biography: Son of George Knowles, Aberdeen; born Aberdeen, 26 February 1891; educated at the Grammar School; graduated M.A., 1912; entered the U.F. College in the same year and continued his studies there till the outbreak of War. In October 1914 he rejoined 'U' Company, 4th Gordon Highlanders, in which he had served in his student days. Though his health was not robust, Knowles stuck to soldiering and had just rejoined the Battalion from hospital the day before his death. He was the first of the U.F. College students to enlist and the first to fall, being killed by a sniper's bullet in the neighbourhood of Ypres on 5 May 1915. His genial sunny temperament made Knowles a favourite with his fellow-students. His exceptional gifts as an elocutionist, combined with his scholarship, pointed to a distinguished career as a preacher. He was an active and successful worker in the Mission carried on by the U.F. students in the East end of Aberdeen.
Date of Death: 05 May 1915
Burial Details: Buried at Wytschaete Military Cemetery, Plot 4, Row D, Grave 1.

John Morrison
Rank: Lieutenant
Regiment: 1st Battalion Cameron Highlanders
Biography: Son of Rev. Murdo Morrison, Bernera U.F. Church; born Kenmore, Perthshire, 10 August 1885; graduated M.A. (II Ment.), 1907; B.D., 1911; studied at Aberdeen U.F. College, 1907–11, where he took a very high place in all his classes, gaining the Eadie Prize in New Testament Greek as well as a Lumsden and Sachs Fellowship. He was ordained in 1911 to the U.F. Church at Kincraig. In February 1915 Morrison enlisted as a Private in the 8th Cameron Highlanders, was afterwards commissioned as 2nd Lieutenant in the 1st Battalion, and finally became a full Lieutenant. During part of the years 1915–17, owing to his knowledge of Gaelic, he acted as recruiting officer in Inverness-shire, and was specially commended by the War Office for his services in that capacity. Thereafter he went to France, and was killed by a shell near St. Quentin on 24 September 1918. In the words of one who knew him well, Morrison was 'a brave officer and a good man, faithful to his calling as minister and soldier'.
Date of Death: 24 September 1918
Burial Details: Buried at Vaden Court British Cemetery, Maissemy, Plot 4, Row D, Grave 10.

James Robertson
Rank: Lieutenant
Regiment: 9th Battalion Gordon Highlanders
Biography: Son of James Robert-son, machine man; born Aberdeen, 11 June 1886; student in Arts, 1908–11; studied at Aberdeen U.F. College, 1911–14; licensed as a probationer by the U.F. Presbytery of Aberdeen, 7 June 1915. Robert-son enlisted in November 1914 as a private in the 4th Gordon High-landers; in January 1915 he was commissioned 2nd Lieutenant in the 9th Battalion, and afterwards rose to the rank of Lieutenant. He saw much service in France and Belgium, was several times wounded, once severely, and in April 1917 was awarded the Military Cross for conspicuous gallantry. On 27 August 1917 he died of wounds received in action at Ypres the previous day. Rob-ertson was an earnest and conscientious student, and for several years rendered valuable service in connection with a Mission of which he had charge in the neighbourhood of Huntly. His early death destroyed the promise of a useful ministry.

Honours: Military Cross

Date of Death: 27 August 1917

Burial Details: Buried at Lijssenthoek Military Cemetery, Poper-inghe, Plot 18, Row C, Grave 20.

Simon Ross
Rank: Lieutenant
Regiment: 4th Battalion Gordon Highlanders
Biography: Son of Simon Ross, farmer, Alves; born Alves, 24 September 1887; graduated M.A. with Honours in Classics, 1911; studied at Aberdeen U.F. College, 1911–14; at the outbreak of war was in charge of a mission in Canada. He was licensed as a probationer by the U.F. Presbytery of Elgin in 1915, and had already given promise that he would prove a preacher of no mean order. Ross enlisted in November 1914, retaining the rank of Sergeant which he had held in the Territorial Force. In April 1915 he was commissioned as 2nd Lieutenant, and was made full Lieutenant on the field on 23 July 1916, when he had specially distinguished himself in one of the Somme battles and been severely wounded. He was killed in action near Arras on 23 April 1917. Before going to the Front and also during his period of convalescence Ross rendered valuable service in training recruits. Alike as a soldier and a student he was energetic and enthusiastic, and was held in the highest esteem by all who knew him.
Date of Death: 23 April 1917
Burial Details: Buried at Level Crossing Cemetery, Fampoux, Plot 1, Row 2, Grave 22.

John Thomson
Rank: Sergeant
Regiment: 4th Battalion Gordon Highlanders
Biography: Son of James G. Thomson, cabinetmaker, Fochabers; born Fochabers, 2 September 1889; graduated M.A. in 1911. He was an excellent specimen of what used to be a common type of Scottish student who, faced by serious obstacles, contrived to make their way to a University and professional education. He studied at Aberdeen U.F. College, 1911–14. At the outbreak of war he was in charge of a mission in Canada. Thomson was one of the earliest and the most eager of the band of volunteers who abandoned their studies to take up military service. As a sergeant, he displayed qualities which would, had he been spared, undoubtedly have led to a brilliant military career. He fell a victim to a sniper's bullet in the trenches near Ypres on 22 July 1915. A student of no mean attainments, he was also an athlete and in every sense a 'sportsman' and a 'good fellow'. His enthusiasm found vent equally in mission work in the slums of Aberdeen, on the football field, and in the trenches.
Date of Death: 22 July 1915
Burial Details: Name recorded on the Menin Gate Memorial, Ypres, Panel 38, Column 5.

Ian Duncan Munro no details

Colin Selbie (Professor Selbie's son)
Rank: 2nd Lieutenant
Regiment: 11th Battalion Cameronians (Scottish Rifles)
Biography: Son of Professor Selbie, Aberdeen U.F. College; born Birsay, Orkney, 24 February 1889; educated Maryculter East School and Aberdeen Grammar School; graduated B.Sc., 1910, with distinction in Geology; appointed Assistant Naturalist in National Museum, Dublin, 1911. Specialized in the study of Myriapoda and Crustacea, published 'The Decapoda Reptantia of the Coasts of Ireland, Part I, Palmura, Astacura and Anomura'. Part II, dealing with Paguridea, was nearly ready for publication when, in October 1914, he enlisted as a private in the Royal Scots. Commissioned 2nd Lieutenant in the 11th Scottish Rifles in January 1915, he went to the Front in November, was slightly wounded the following February, but soon returned to duty. On two occasions for considerable periods, he commanded his company in the absence of the Captain. He fell at Longueval on 14 July 1916, when, to quote the Adjutant 'he led his men gallantly throughout the assault, and had the satisfaction of seeing the position won before he was killed by a rifle bullet while heading a bombing attack'. His death cut short a very promising career both as a scientist and a soldier. 'He was a born naturalist, a love of animals being one of his most marked characteristics.' He had also a sense of humour which materially helped him to endure the discomforts of life in the trenches, while his coolness and courage never gave way in the hour of danger.
Date of Death: 14 July 1916
Burial Details: Name recorded on the Thiepval Memorial, Pier and Face 4 D.

Appendix B

The Place of Theological Teaching

From the Senatus Minutes Books, Volume 3, pp. 177–83,
entry for 16 November 1934

While fully recognising the attractions of localizing theological training on the King's College site, we are of the opinion that the advantages of a College in Alford Place outweigh these considerations for the following reasons.

The need for a separate building

It is of primary importance for the purposes of theological training that full accommodation should be provided in a collegiate building for the common life of the students. This is the well-nigh universal practice today in all the English speaking countries. So far as our knowledge goes there is no church in these lands outside of Scotland where it has not been long recognized that for the adequate training of men for the ministry in such an institution as the church, full provision must be made not only for strictly academic training in theological classrooms but for the development of the corporate life of students and the *esprit de corps* which ought to arise out of such intimate fellowship. This is the ultimate purpose of the chapels, common rooms, dining halls, and so on, which are as a rule provided in these colleges. None of these are to be regarded as merely provisions for social fellowship, they are a definite means to a spiritual end. They are meant to help the theological students learn from each other as well as from their teachers. The Church of England has very many such colleges, and we believe that the great majority of their candidates for the ministry pass through them, even those who have had a full university education. All the Nonconformist Churches possess such colleges. This, we understand is also the universal practice in all the Dominions, and also in the United States. Even in Universities like Yale which is a Congregationalist foundation, we believe that there is a separate building for theological students, and the same is true of Chicago University which has a Baptist foundation.

What is perhaps of more immediate interest, all the other Scottish Universities now possess such buildings for theological training and common life. In Glasgow and Edinburgh these buildings are large and very fully equipped, while in St Mary's College, St Andrews possess a building superior to either of these in beauty and historical interest. It is a matter of common knowledge that the students attach great value to this provision for their common life, and if it is not provided for them in Aberdeen, we are convinced that in the long run the University will be at a great disadvantage in attracting theological students. It has sometimes been said that the special common life of such institutions must have a narrowing effect on the outlook of their students and therefore should not be encouraged by a university. This is no doubt the case where, in England, some of the denominational colleges give an approximately complete Arts course as well as a course in Theology and students spend their entire academic life within their walls. In Scotland where every student of Theology passes first through an Arts course at a university and where, further, the residential system is not as a rule followed, the case is entirely different. It would be impossible for anyone to detect any real distinction of that kind between students trained entirely in the University and students trained in part in Theological Colleges. We believe the student body itself would be the first to repudiate any such distinction. It is necessary before leaving the matter of a separate building to emphasise again a point to which passing reference has already been made. It is a vital interest for Aberdeen as well as St. Andrews University that they should both hold their recruiting grounds for candidates for the ministry but it would be closing one's eyes to realities to ignore the fact that these two smaller colleges must carry on their work under a measure of anxiety and strain in comparison with the far larger colleges in Edinburgh and Glasgow. It cannot be said to be unreasonable for a student after he has completed his Arts course at his own University in the North to wish to go South to one or other of the two larger universities which are better equipped both in staffing and in building, and which moreover possess for the abler students scholarships where they may enter a much wider, and in the case of Edinburgh which has many American and Continental students, a much more varied student fellowship and as in the case of both Edinburgh and Glasgow may have a much greater opportunity of procuring a livelihood while they are engaged in study. This disadvantage has always in some measure existed but it is likely to be even more strongly felt in the future as the means of communication and the consequent mobility of the population increase. It is now at least as easy to get to Glasgow from North-western Scotland as to Aberdeen. We have in the last 25 years in the Alford Place College lost comparatively few students who, after studying in Arts at the University went on to Edinburgh or Glasgow. This I think has been very largely due to the *esprit de corps* of the College which has led ministers trained in it to encourage candidates from their congregation to return to the place where they had their own education. But we cannot conceal from ourselves that if the Southern Universities and St Andrews make fuller provision for the corporate life of their students than is made by Aberdeen, the strain of which I have spoken is likely to become greater rather than less.

The University Court has, we believe rightly, strongly supported the College in its claim not to be understaffed in comparison with other university centres and it would seem unfortunate if the University Court made Aberdeen the only centre without an independent and fully equipped building for the Divinity Faculty. It would we believe, put the university into a position of inferiority to all the rest of them. For these reasons we earnestly trust that in whatever quarter of the city theology is taught it will be in a fully equipped College.

Site of the College

But if that is agreed upon the question next arises whether that building should be on the King's College properties or at the Alford Place site. We do not of course propose that the Alford

Place College should remain as it is though we have found it sufficient to meet all the immediate necessities of its students even since the union; it needs through internal reconstruction to bring it up to the standard of modern requirements. We have consulted Mr Bennett Mitchell as our architect and he has prepared plans for such a remodelled college as the circumstances demand. These plans are in the hands of the Secretary to the University. They provide, as will be seen, for seven classrooms, a large hall, a chapel, a senate room, a common room for students, a cloakroom and all other necessary accommodation. In the meantime the plans presuppose that the dining room, library and janitor's house shall remain on the other side of the street. But as will be seen later, should the university and the church agree on the use of the Alford Place site we are prepared to face a more comprehensive scheme which would bring all the buildings under one roof. In the meantime we shall confine ourselves to the more limited project which can be carried out independently of the other. The cost of the complete internal reconstruction Mr Bennett Mitchell estimates at rather less than £5,000. We do not know what the cost of a new building in Old Aberdeen would be but it would certainly be a much larger sum. The immediate problem therefore if the Alford Place project is not approved of would be how is the larger cost to be met. We do not know if the university is prepared to do this or whether it expects the Church of Scotland to meet the financial charges but in the meantime we assume that the latter is the case. We do not think it at all likely that the church as a whole would be willing to bear the costs of building a new college in Aberdeen and to make a gift of the Alford Place building to the Presbytery of Aberdeen. At the present moment the church is doing its utmost in a time of acute commercial depression by local unions and economies to maintain its minimum stipend to avoid the abandonment of stations in the mission field and to raise £180,000 to meet the changes rendered necessary by the tidal movements of population. A case for the expenditure of a large amount of money in Aberdeen would have to be presented to an Assembly representing the whole of Scotland. We believe that the inevitable reply would be that as this is not a matter of providing for theological education in Aberdeen, but a matter of a desirable site in Aberdeen, it is clearly one whose costs should be met in the locality itself. It would be very difficult to meet such an argument. But the College in Alford Place has no funds of its own which could be used for this purpose. Such Trust funds as might possibly be released from their present uses by an order of the Court of Session would be totally inadequate. The only course open would be to sell the properties in Alford Place in the open market and this the General Assembly of the Church of Scotland is not disposed to do.

Appendix C

Shuttle Lane Mission

Extracts from 'Shuttle Lane Mission' by David Cairns in Aberdeen Divinity Bulletin Number 25, Summer 1984

Shuttle Lane Mission has been described by Ronnie Falconer in his admirable autobiography 'The Kilt Beneath My Cassock' as 'The Slum Mission Divinity Students ran in Aberdeen's East end. It was a hangover from the days when comfortable Christians went slumming to save the souls of the wretched men and women existing in poverty and overcrowded, insanitary housing, often escaping their misery via the gin bottle. Shuttle Lane was one such haven for hard pressed mothers, their children, and teenage lads on the dole. On Friday nights we ran a club for the latter.'

The Mission was started sometime I believe in the early 1890's. It certainly existed about 1912. Esslemont Adams, the minister of West St. Andrews, was a lively agent in collecting money for it from his congregation and other friends. One of his rich members, when asked for a contribution, sent him £100. Adams returned the money with a stiff letter, whose message was 'From a man of your wealth nothing less than £500 will be acceptable.' He got his cheque. I think that this money may have been used to purchase the site or to build or improve the hall and the suite of rooms, including a flat for the missionary. The front door of the mission gave onto East North Street, at its eastern end, the back door opened onto Shuttle Lane, one of the worst slums in Aberdeen, an infamous row of wretched houses built in between East North Street and Frederick Street running like them east and west and now long demolished, like the Mission Hall itself. In 1932 I went to be an assistant to George MacLeod in Govan and at once realised that though it too was a place of great poverty, the fundamental structure of even some of its worst houses was much better than that of the buildings of Shuttle Lane.

When I became a Divinity Student just before the union of 1929, the Shuttle Lane Mission, whose purpose had been to give the students pastoral and evangelical experience as well as helping the people of the district, was as an institution, in some decay. Falconer's criticism has some point but we can look at the other side of the picture. Had the churches of the city and the richer suburbs not done anything for the east end things would have been disgracefully worse than they were.

There was a missionary at the Shuttle Lane, usually a Divinity Student who had tenure for a year or two and lived on the premises. There was a good church sister, Miss Smith, and a caretaker, Miss Begg. There were services, I think on Sunday evenings, and on Monday afternoons a meeting where tea was served. The missionary or one of the students took the service, with a local minister from time to time, or a Divinity Professor taking Communion services. The hymn book was the floppy red Sankey and Moody book. I believe that when I began my time as a student there was only one man member, all the rest were elderly women. There was a recognisable congregation of women and a good going branch of the Women's Guild. Divinity Students were asked to parade at the meetings and help with pouring out the tea; this and the occasional taking of a service was all that was asked of them.

[David Cairns and fellow students were invited to start activities among the young male unemployed.]

A first night meeting was fixed and a programme and a plan of action was arranged. There was to be a red folding card of membership given on application, without it people could not enter, and a fee of one penny was exacted for each night. There was to be a programme of table tennis, billiards on a half sized table and touch football and other activities common to clubs of this kind. The students turned up in fear and trembling, the place was packed (over 100). There was one unfortunate incident, at a crucial moment someone switched off the electric light; when it came on a few things had disappeared and there were other regrettable consequences ... but we got the club started and after that we never had any trouble.

Appendix D

List of Masters, Principals and Secretary/Treasurers

Principals	Years of office
James Lumsden	1864–75
David Brown	1876–97
Stewart D. F. Salmond	1898–1905
James Iverach	1905–23
David S. Cairns	1923–37

Masters	Years of office
Adam Fyfe Findlay	1937–47
G. D. Henderson	1947–57
A. M. Hunter	1957–71
James McEwen	1971–77
Robin Barbour	1977–82
Henry Sefton	1982–92
Alan Main	1992–2001
Iain Torrance	2001–05
Ian Dick	2005–12
John Swinton	2012–Present

Secretary/ Treasurer	Years of office	Relationship	Employer
Francis Edmond	1869–74		Edmonds and McQueen
Alexander Edmond	1874–91	Son of Francis	Edmonds and McQueen
John Edmond	1891–95	Brother of Alexander	Edmonds and McQueen
David Edwards	1895–1910		Edmonds and Ledingham from 1890
James Hastings Edward	1919–44	Son of David	Edmonds and Ledingham
Clement Marshall	1944–49		Edmonds and Ledingham
James Gordon Hastings Edward	1949–72	Son of James	Edmonds and Ledingham
Graham Cran Hunter	1972–2001		Ledingham Chalmers from 1991
Gwen Haggart	2001–12		Christ's College
Clare Davidson	2012– Present		Christ's College

Index of Names and Subjects

Hirsh, Raphael (Henry Biesenthal)
34
Hislop, Rev. Stephen 7
Hollis, Sarah (accountant) 195–6
Hromádka, Joseph Luki (alumnus)
1968 visit 148–50
Cairns and 85
notable career of 85
portrait of 149
Hughes, Mitchell (librarian) 130,
145
Hunter, Archibald Macbride
(Master)
appointed Master 140–1
centenary celebration 129
chairs Financial Board meetings
135
church union question 142
handwriting of 123
on Hughes 145
retirement of 153
'rich deep' voice of 143–4
at silver celebration 128
tribute to Henderson 137
The Work and Words of Jesus
140
years of office 221
Hunter, Graham Cran (secretary/
treasurer) 153
on BT income 168
on building sale 174
endowment appeal 171, 172
Northeast and Aberdeen funding
181
retirement of 185, 187
years of office 222
Hunter, Rev. Robert (alumnus) 7
Encyclopaedic Dictionary 7

Innes, Barbara, bequest of 14
Intellectual Biography of David
Smith Cairns (Finlayson) 86
International Patristics Conference
188–9
Iverach, James (Principal) 22, 40

appointment as principal 64
Brown's funeral and 45
death of 78–9
earlier years 64–5
The Ethics of Evolution
Examined 65, 66
Evolution and Christianity 65,
66
'Loyalty: British and German
ideals' 71
Moderator of Assembly 68–9
portrait commissioned 68–9
resignation of 76–7
response to Darwinism 65–6
years of office 221

Jack, George P. (alumnus) 106,
113
Jaffrey, Sir Thomas 75
Japan
Miss Macdonald and 81–2, 84
Jarvis, Right Rev E. D. 132, 133
Jeffrey, Dr Ken 200
Johnstone, William (staff)
appointment of 163
marks Smith centenary 36–7
Salmond's funeral and 61
Wm Robertson Smith Congress
178, 179
Jones, Helen Katherine (alumnus)
192
Judaism, Biesenthal collection and
34–5

Kelly, Dr 107
Kelman, James 163
Kennedy, Prof. 130
Kerr Lectures, Findlay and 119
'The Kilt Beneath my Cassock'
(Falconer) 219
King's College Library
Biesenthal Collection 35
Kingswell Trust 9–10
Knowles, John Forbes (alumnus)
71, 208

Renton, J. P. (alumnus) 155
Rice (Sir Duncan) Library xiii
  see also Aberdeen University
Robb, Nigel 190, 191
Roberts, Dr Graeme 187
Robertson, Alan O. (alumnus)
  129
Robertson, James (alumnus) 70,
  210
Robertson, James A. (staff) 40–1,
  64, 77
Rodin, Scott (alumnus) 172
Rose, W. 14
Ross, John (alumnus) 114–15
Ross, Simon (alumnus) 70, 211

Sachs, Marcus (staff)
  appointment of 1
  becomes Chair in O.T. 7
  life and career of 7–8
  memorial fellowship 31–2
  portrait of 8
  Salmond succeeds 47
  succeeded by Smith 33
Sachs, Mary see Shier, Mary (later
  Sachs, then Edmond)
Salmond, Stewart D. F. (Principal)
  40
  Alford Place house purchase 51
  appointment as teacher 47–8
  Brown's funeral and 45
  character of 48–50
  The Christian Doctrine of
    Immortality 48–9, 63
  death of 60–3
  earlier life 47
  McLean scandal 54–8
  obituary of Brown 37
  other writings of 49
  portrait of 63, 107
  Union of Churches and 59–60
  years of office 221
Sanderson Report 151–2
Scudder, Joseph 30
Sefton, Dr Henry (Master) 69

Academic Aid Fund and 162
Alford Place and 167, 169
appointment as Master 164,
  165–6
Barbour on 160
on constitutions 187
Dick's introduction and 191
earlier career 165
on Henderson 125, 137
launches 150 year celebration
  177
leads McEwen's funeral 159
on McConnachie's ordination
  150
past students 200
portrait of 164
retirement of 175–6
years of office 221
Selbie, Colin 72, 213
Selbie, John A. (secretary/treasurer)
  appointment of 69
  death of 91
  death of son 72, 213
  difficulty in replacing 92–3
  letter to soldier alumni 73–4
Shields, Gordon 105
Shier, Mary (later Sachs, then
  Edmond) 43
  death of son Alexander 43
  later life and death 10
  marriage to Edmond 9
  marriage to Sachs 8, 9
Shuttle Lane Mission 12, 124,
  219–20
Simpson, Colonel, portrait of 106
Slessor, Mary Mitchell 119–20
Smeaton, George (staff)
  appointment of 7
  assists Lumsden 12
  Brown loses post to 29
  on Knox's watch 147
  on Thomson 15
Smith, George Adam 61
Smith, Mrs George Adam 69
Smith, Miss (Shuttle Lane) 220